The Megalithic Imperative

The Megalithic Imperative: A 3rd Stone Anthology

Edited by Neil Mortimer

First published by Strange Attractor Press 2026

Typeset in Ancizar Serif & Rubik

Design and layout by Hiba Shahtoot

Cover design by Louise Mason

 A CIP catalogue record for this book is available from the British Library.

ISBN 9781917674027

A note about image quality: It's not been possible to find the original copies of many of the images used in *3rd Stone*, and where that is the case scans have been made from printed copies of the magazine. Therefore, some of the images included in this volume are by necessity of an imperfect, archival nature.

Strange Attractor Press

BM SAP, London,

WC1N 3XX, UK

www.strangeattractor.co.uk

Distributed by The MIT Press, Cambridge, Massachusetts. And London, England.

Printed and bound in Estonia by Tallinna Raamatutrükikoda.

the MEGALITHIC IMPERATIVE

A 3rd Stone Anthology

The Journal of Archaeology, Folklore, Mythology and Earth Mysteries, 1994-2003

Compiled and edited by Neil Mortimer

Contents

(The numbers in brackets refer to the edition of 3rd Stone *in which the article was published originally.)*

Introduction

In 1994, when the first issue of *3rd Stone* was published, points of contact had already been made between the outer edges of Earth Mysteries and academic theoretical archaeology. Paul Devereux, the editor of *The Ley Hunter* magazine, had in 1991 published a paper on 'Three-dimensional aspects of apparent relationships between selected natural and artificial features within the topography of the Avebury complex' in *Antiquity*, the peer-reviewed journal of archaeological respectability. Meanwhile, attendees of the *Ley Hunter* Moot, ostensibly the magazine's annual get-together of ley enthusiasts, could hear academic speakers such as Ronald Hutton, Julian Thomas and Anne Ross, alongside talks covering the magazine's traditional enquiries into the apparent straight lines of monuments in the British countryside. Leys themselves were now often being referred to as 'alignments', an altogether more acceptable word than either 'ley' and the even more vexed phrase 'earth energy'. Aubrey Burl, the world's foremost archaeological expert on megaliths, was writing articles in regional Earth Mysteries magazines, and theoretical archaeologists such as Jeremy Dronfield, Thomas Dowson and David Lewis-Williams were writing in *Antiquity* and other academic journals on the possible psychedelic-ritual-shamanic properties of prehistoric rock art. Meanwhile, a small but significant number of generally younger archaeologists were occasionally referencing ideas which had originated in Earth Mysteries, for example the relationship of some megaliths to features in the wider landscape. The (ritual) landscape was changing.

Needless to say, not all academics welcomed the attention of the largely-amateur Earth Mysteries scene. During Danny Sullivan's term as editor of *The Ley Hunter* he contacted the senior archaeologist of an excavation of a linear barrow cemetery in Southern Ireland to ask whether a precis of the excavation could be published in the magazine. Danny received a letter back declining the invitation, with the explanation that the excavation report had already fulfilled the needs of the project's 'intended audience'! Equally, not everyone within Earth Mysteries was interested in, or welcomed the crossover with various academic disciplines, and for some the core traditional Earth Mysteries subject matter, including ancient monuments, leys, dowsing, earth energies and UFOs, remained their primary focus.

The selection of articles included in this anthology of past articles from *3rd Stone* has been chosen from a total of around 115 which were considered. The final selection here is intended to be representative of the sort of material *3rd Stone* carried, with a bias towards articles which crossed-over between Earth Mysteries and other related areas, including theoretical archaeology, folklore and neo-paganism. A lot of very good and interesting articles remain in the archives, and some may be considered for a second anthology in the future.

Neil Mortimer
Spring Equinox 2026

GeM
18
BRISTOL LEYS BREDON HILL
ROLLRIGHT STONES
BIG CATS
Folklore and Mysteries of the Cotswolds
A lost stone circle
Crop Circles 94
UFOs, news,views and reviews
£2

Unearthing 3rd Stone

Neil Mortimer

3rd Stone was an Earth Mysteries magazine published between 1994 and 2003. It was created and launched by Danny Sullivan and Jo-Anne Wilder (later Sullivan), a continuation of *Gloucestershire Earth Mysteries* (*GEM*) magazine, which Danny had published since the mid-1980s. Danny and Jo wanted to extend *GEM*'s regional reach, and so issue 18 of *GEM* was the last issue put out under that title, and the next issue was published in the second half of 1994 as *3rd Stone* 19.

The new magazine's name was inspired by the Jimi Hendrix Experience song 'Third Stone from the Sun', a reference to the magazine's intended audience beyond Gloucestershire[1] and of course Earth Mysteries' preoccupation with megaliths – 'The megalithic imperative', as Aubrey Burl's memorable phrase had it. Danny and Jo both came from an Earth Mysteries background, but they were keen to expand the core subject matter – which included leys (or ley lines as they were often referred to by the uninitiated), prehistory, paganism, earth energies, UFOs, legends, folklore, dowsing, hill figures and antiquarianism. These 'traditional' elements of Earth Mysteries, which had been set in the movement's heyday in the 70s and 80s, remained part of the magazine's mix, but were joined by newer approaches to the material.

1 It's worth noting that *GEM*'s transformation into *3rd Stone* involved the loss of 'Earth Mysteries' in the title.

These included a degree of scepticism about aspects of leys, and a growing interest in shamanism, ritual landscapes and, controversially – at least to some of the longer-standing members of the scene – progressive and theoretical forms of academic archaeology and anthropology coming out of university departments. Some of the material in early issues of *3rd Stone* was critical of some of the main strands of Earth Mysteries.

I first learnt of *3rd Stone*'s existence via a classified ad in *Fortean Times* magazine. I was subscribing to various regional Earth Mysteries mags: *Meyn Mamvro*, covering Cornwall and the Scilly Isles; and *Northern Earth*, covering northern England[2]; the fairly short-lived but excellent Devon-based *Wisht Maen*; and the original Earth Mysteries magazine, *The Ley Hunter*. During the early 90s issues of the always-great *Ley Hunter* were coming out fairly infrequently, and to some extent *3rd Stone* filled the void left by *The Ley Hunter*'s non-appearance.

2 All three magazines are still published in 2025.

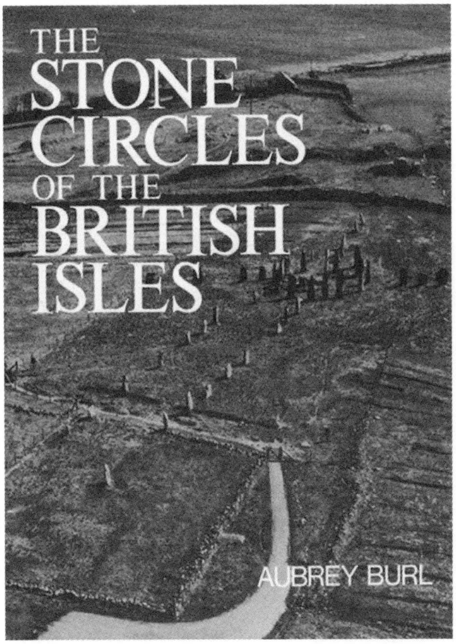

Like a lot of people interested in Earth Mysteries who'd grown up in the 1970s and 80s, I'd become aware of archaeology and folklore not from the profession or the academic study of those areas, but from pop culture references to those subjects[3]. Guided by books such as Janet and Colin Bord's *Mysterious Britain*[4] and some by John Michell, Paul Devereux and others, my partner Hilary and I spent weekends visiting sites in the South and South West, and further afield. Although strictly archaeological, Aubrey Burl's definitive books about megaliths were also the go-to guides for those sites.

In the early 1990s numerous regional Earth Mysteries groups were in existence around the country. We were living in London at the time, so we were enthusiastic members of the London Earth Mysteries Circle, run by Rob Stephenson. Rob's group held seasons of bi-weekly talks and organised occasional weekend minibus trips to sites around London and out towards the West Country. Allen Hunt, an occasional contributor to early issues of *3rd Stone*, was running various evening

3 I grew up in Devon and can remember watching the 'Caveman' episode of the kids TV show *Mr Benn* where he shows prehistoric people how to make hut circles on a fantasy version of Dartmoor. (The character's creator David McKee had attended Plymouth College of Art and Design, located just south of Dartmoor National Park.) The TV shows *Sky*, *Children of the Stones*, *Quatermass Conclusion* and *Arthur C. Clarke's Mysterious World* were all in the mix too.

4 At *3rd Stone*'s peak we regularly used images from Janet and Colin Bord's Fortean Picture Library, and one time when I mentioned to Janet what a huge influence their book had had on me she jokily apologised for introducing me to 'so much weird nonsense'!

THE LEY HUNTER 20th ANNIVERSARY MOOT

DEVIZES, WILTSHIRE 19/20 JULY1997

STAYING OUT FOR THE SUMMER

To Celebrate 20 Years of the Ley Hunter Moot there will be a special summer event at the old market town of Devizes on Saturday 17th July for a day of illustrated talks on ancient sacred sites and their functions, ceremonial landscapes, anomalous aerial phenomena and ancient astronomy.

The guest speakers will be Paul Devereux, Aubrey Burl, Jenny Randles, Michael Dames and Robin Heath.

On Sunday 18th July two of the speakers will be leading guided tours of the Avebury complex and surrounding sites. Free transport to Avebury from Devizes is available if required.

On Saturday evening there will be an informal gathering at the historic Bear Hotel in Devizes.

For full details call 01386 421058. For an information pack send a SAE to TLH Moot '97, PO Box 258, Cheltenham, GL53 0HR.

Please note this is a ticket only event.

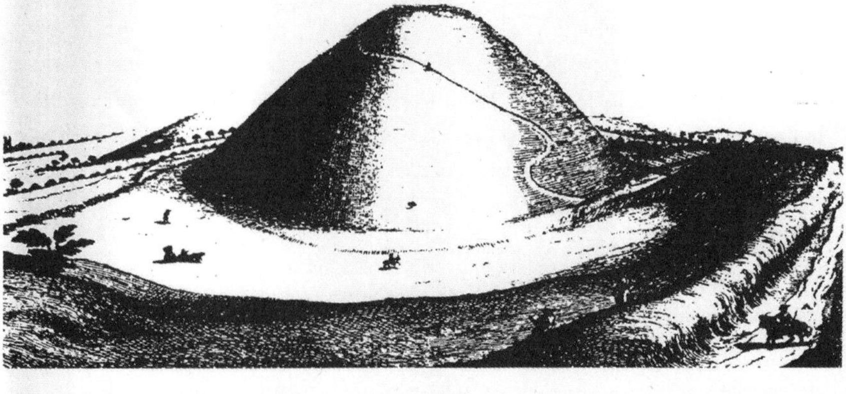

classes on esoteric subjects throughout central London, 'Fringe Religions and Cults of Psycho-Salvation' being one of them. Allen knew many of the key figures in the London pagan/occult scene and introduced us to the legendary esoteric group the Talking Stick, held upstairs at the Wheatsheaf and Black Horse pubs, both on Rathbone Place.

At the *Fortean Times* UnConvention in 1995 I happened to mention to Rob Stephenson how much I was enjoying the new Earth Mysteries magazine *3rd Stone*. Rob knew the editor, Danny Sullivan, who happened to be at the UnConvention that day, and introduced us. Danny was a Londoner but now based in Gloucestershire with Jo, and since we were now living in nearby Wiltshire we became friends.

A few months later Paul Devereux, the editor of *The Ley Hunter*, offered the editorship of the magazine to Danny. Danny accepted, and asked if Hilary and I would like to take on *3rd Stone*, with Jo as consultant editor. I worked at a printing company, so the physical practicalities of producing a magazine wouldn't be a problem, and we decided to give it a go. Danny gave us £100 to fulfil the existing subscriptions. Jo put us in touch with the magazine's current contributors, and passed on various unpublished submissions. Things went smoothly, and *3rd Stone* 23 was the first edition with Hilary and I as co-editors, published in spring 1996.

Three hundred copies of the early issues were printed, 100 going out to subscribers, the rest to local book and head shops and a handful of Tourist Information offices, while some were held in stock to sell as back issues.

3rd Stone's content underwent a subtle change under mine and Hilary's editorship. Jo had an interest in UFOs – or at least the folklore of modern UFO sightings – and saw them as a core part of Earth Mysteries, but under our editorship it moved a bit more towards the mainstream archaeological end of the spectrum, with an all-consuming interest in megaliths and earthworks. After a few years Jo gave up her consultant editor role and from issue 28 I became sole editor, with Hilary continuing to proofread every issue[5].

Over a weekend in July 1997 *3rd Stone* took part in what had become an Earth Mysteries tradition and hosted *The Ley Hunter*'s 20th Anniversary Moot in Devizes, Wiltshire. The first day was held at the town's historic Corn Exchange, with speakers including Paul Devereux, Aubrey Burl, Michael Dames and Jenny Randles. The second day was held at Avebury, in perfect weather conditions. Michael Dames did a talk within the site's earthworks, where he encouraged the audience to take off their shoes and socks in order to better connect with Mother Earth. Later in

5 A task not made easy because the spellchecking facility didn't work on the dodgy copy of Microsoft Word we used for the entire duration of the magazine's existence.

the day Robin Heath did a brilliant audience participatory demonstration of how stone circles may have been laid out.

The early issues more-or-less maintained the high standard Danny and Jo had set for the magazine. However, a significant change came when we booked a flyer to go out with well-regarded and subscription-only magazine *Current Archaeology*. I'd written to Aubrey Burl about the megalithic site of Langdean Bottom, south of Avebury, which had been considered lost but I'd rediscovered. Aubrey had written to *3rd Stone* in 1997 (see the 'Letters' section of this volume) and had described the magazine as 'becoming favourite reading for me'. I asked Aubrey if I could quote that on the flyer, which he kindly agreed to. When the flyer went out with the next issue of *Current Archaeology* we were amazed at the positive response. Within a couple of weeks we had more than 250 new subscribers. Several of the subscription forms returned by new readers contained comments like, 'If it's good enough for Aubrey Burl it's good enough for me', so it was clear what sort of material those new subscribers would enjoy. Within a year we had over 1,000 subscribers and we were selling around 500 copies to shops, and a lot more than that in the summer months. The Henge Shop in Avebury was always our best outlet, usually selling between 250–300 copies of each issue. At the magazine's peak 3,000 copies of each issue were printed, made up of 2,250 subscribers, with 750 going out to shops[6].

To take out a subscription to the magazine prospective subscribers had to send in a cheque and fill out a form with their details. One of these forms came to us with a note written on it: 'What the hell is Earth Mysteries?' Although issues were carrying more 'straight' archaeological material, I still thought of *3rd Stone* as an Earth Mysteries magazine, but some new readers had obviously never even heard the phrase before – presumably people with an interest or background in mainstream archaeology. Meanwhile, the phrase 'Earth Mysteries' itself was starting to fall out of usage, and the phrase 'Earth Mysterian' was starting to be used in a jokey, slightly mocking way. The word 'mysteries', so much part of 70s and 80s pop culture, was sounding a bit outdated, and when the *3rd Stone* masthead tagline was changed to 'Archaeology, Folklore and Myth', I decided to leave 'Earth Mysteries' out.

6 One of the few things I didn't really enjoy much while putting out *3rd Stone* was dealing with shops, particularly some of the nice but out-there people who ran head shops. For example, one didn't sell any copies of issue 24 because the Pantone Green ink used on the cover for an image of the Cerne Giant was giving off 'a lot of negative energy', and the shop owner felt the need to hide that issue in order 'to protect' his customers. Another was the New Age shop in East Anglia whose owner kept on asking me to send them more and more back issues, but hadn't paid a single invoice. I asked them numerous times if they were actually selling any copies, which they assured me they were. Eventually I said I couldn't send them any copies of the new issue until they'd paid for at least some of the several hundred they'd asked me for. A few days later a big parcel arrived, containing the torn off corners of the covers of almost every mag I'd ever sent them, with a cheque for a few pounds and a note saying they'd only ever sold two copies. Doh!

However, I have reinstated the phrase into the title of this retrospective volume as an acknowledgment of the major role Earth Mysteries had throughout the magazine's history and development[7].

The increased number of subscribers meant we had enough funds to start making the issues longer. Issue 30, Spring 1998, had 52 pages and was the first issue to include an article by Aubrey Burl: 'Ever-Increasing Circles' (included in this volume). Jeremy Harte was playing an increasingly important role on the magazine, regularly submitting excellent articles, and also starting to submit news pieces and book reviews. Jeremy was also regularly writing for *At The Edge* magazine, and when its editor Bob Trubshaw decided to concentrate on his Heart of Albion book publishing operation, Bob suggested At *The Edge* and *3rd Stone* merge into a mega-zine. That happened in autumn 1998, and brought in a useful number of new subscribers as well as some of the excellent writers who had been published in At *The Edge*. Bob helped out with various editorial matters on *3rd Stone* too, including his own articles. Jeremy had been putting together an 'Abstracts' section for *At The Edge*, which Bob said his readers enjoyed, and Jeremy agreed to continue that column for *3rd Stone*.

Further changes took place with issue 32, published at the end of 1998, with the first full colour printed cover and a dedicated 'Small Press' section showcasing other like-minded magazines. *3rd Stone* was exchanging magazines with 12 other publications – *The Cauldron, The Dragon Chronicle, The Ley Hunter, Magonia, Meyn Mamvro, Network News, Northern Earth, Pendragon, The Right Times, Source,* the *John Wheelwright Archaeological Society Newsletter* and *White Dragon* – an indication of how healthy the small press scene was at the time.

The magazine was getting lots of enquires about back issues, all of which had sold out, and for a short time we offered a photocopying service where readers could request photocopies of past articles for a small fee. I underestimated how

---

7 Cheryl Straffon's 'Does the Goddess Live Here?' article in this volume touches on some of these issues in more detail. We are looking at these ideas again not to revive any ancient battles, but to examine what members of 'the scene' were thinking about 25-30 years ago. A memorable example of how the phrase 'Earth Mysteries' was evolving took place at one of *The Ley Hunter* Moots (held in Cheltenham, I believe), when at the post-conference evening curry, a veteran of the Earth Mysteries scene casually described *3rd Stone* as being put together by 'archaeologists who know there is money to be made out of Earth Mysteries'. The idea that anyone could make any money out of Earth Mysteries struck me then as pretty unlikely. An alternative phrase to 'Earth Mysteries' which a smaller number of people started using around this time was 'stone bothering', which I first heard Pete Glastonbury use. At the time I said to Pete that the phrase reminded me of 'fox bothering', a phrase used by kids in Devon to describe a 1970s/80s craze of sneaking out of your parent's house at night to hang around with your friends, and which Pete said was called 'badger bothering' in Somerset where he grew up! I recently mentioned this to Pete, who says 'stone bothering' was invented by his friend Graham Johnson, who was from Derbyshire, but had retired to the South West when Pete knew him. Apparently, he'd originally used the phrase 'rock bothering', but had switched to 'stone' when someone complained about standing stones being called rocks. There is a very active Facebook group called 'Ancient Stone Bothering', so perhaps the phrase's time has come... Another alternative phrase people were using was 'Alternative Archaeology', which also seems to have disappeared from general usage.

popular the service would be, and I spent hours copying literally hundreds of articles, so the service was quickly cancelled and as an alternative we put together a 'Best of Issues 23–27' one-off edition, which itself sold out quickly[8].

The following year Pete Gotto of Counter Culture Specialist Book Distributors got in touch suggesting a *3rd Stone* book service, whereby readers could buy copies of books that had been reviewed, as well as getting special offers on back catalogue publications.

8 The cover of this 'Best Of' issue was a pastiche of The Who album *Live At Leeds* which had recently been reissued in an expanded format that Danny and I had been enjoying. That continued the magazine's nerdy tradition of in-jokes referencing pop culture, mainly rock music but also quotes from films and TV shows. Jeremy joined in too, particularly with his funny sub-headings in his Abstracts column. Did readers ever wonder about the source of the sub-heading 'Baby Your Phrasing is Bad' which accompanied a news story about the geological categorization of polished axes?

Issue 36 carried the first 'Site Watch' column by Andy Burnham, which would go on to feature in every subsequent issue. In his first column he described himself as 'accidently becoming a campaigner', but Andy did a great job of highlighting sites which were at risk in various ways, and his column was a key part of the news section of later issues. Andy went on to found www.megalithic.co.uk, one of the earliest, and still ongoing, web resources about ancient sites.

Issue 37 featured Aubrey Burl's 'Myth-Conceptions' article, which argued the case for the transportation of Stonehenge's bluestones from the Preseli Mountains by glaciation rather than people. Aubrey's article prompted a seemingly endless correspondence about bluestones for the next couple of issues. In issue 39 Rodney Castleden wrote an article arguing against glaciation, and so much of the letters pages were being taken up with bluestones that we had to close correspondence on the matter[9].

Issue 38 was the last stapled edition and, briefly at least, the last of the quarterly schedule. That issue also carried a short-lived but very interesting new column, Tome Raider, a 'retrospective review of seminal or heretical works that have influenced modern alternative thinking about past and place'. *The Ley Hunter* had recently ceased publication, allowing Danny to write for *3rd Stone*, and he did the first column looking at John Michell's *The View Over Atlantis*. The following issue John Michell[10] himself looked at Alexander Thom's *Megalithic Sites in Britain*. Jeremy supplied a fascinating article about Theo Brown's *The Fate of the Dead* for the third and final Tome Raider, all of which are included in this volume.

Issue 39 heralded a change of format to a perfect-bound 80-page journal format. We intended to publish just two issues per year because I was finding four issues a year pretty demanding. Also, the mail-out every 12 weeks had turned into a marathon task, with 15 or 20 mail sacks piled in our house. Literally thousands

---

9 The issue still isn't settled – in 2024 the matter came up yet again, and with predictably bad-tempered dialogue online. What is it about bluestones?!

10 Since he died in 2009 John Michell has become a controversial figure in some quarters. Some of his provocative political views, which decades ago may have seemed like bourgeoisie-baiting larks, have more recently been seen by some as having a darker side. So far as I was aware there was hardly any political element to Earth Mysteries – more recent controversies surrounding the George Cross and the right-wing adoption of elements of 'Ancient Albion', for example – were, it seemed to me at least, almost entirely absent from the conversation back then. One evening at the Talking Stick I remember the results of a graduate's research into the political allegiances of members of various pagan groups being discussed, and almost everyone who had responded saw themselves either as apolitical or they'd voted Green or Labour. Bearing in mind the posthumous re-examination of John's reputation, it's ironic that he once said to me that what he saw as the then-recent persecution of 'hippies, mystics and ley liners' was like 'a form of fascism'. That was the only time I ever heard John say anything remotely political. As others have pointed out, in person John was kindly and great fun. An example demonstrating the extent of his eccentric orbit would be once when I bumped into him in Glastonbury. As we chatted John introduced a chap who'd arrived: 'Neil, meet my friend Edward, I was pals with his father years ago'. This friendly, zonked-looking dude was sort-of familiar... Then I recognised him – Eddie Tudor-Pole from the Sex Pistols film *The Great Rock 'n' Roll Swindle* and the new wave band Tenpole Tudor!

of envelopes had to be addressed, stamped and stuffed, the overseas copies including customs forms and other paperwork all had to be organised, and the shop copies had to be packed and despatched. That side of running a small press mag was starting to become a bit of a nightmare.

Meanwhile I was approached by a consortium of people connected with the magazine who suggested putting it on a more professional footing with shareholders and so on. While negotiations were underway, we mutually agreed to return to publishing four issues per year. Unfortunately, the deal didn't come to fruition and the magazine was now committed to publishing four bumper-sized issues per year, the worst of all outcomes[11].

Despite these distractions the issues continued, and still with a lot of really good material. Issue 40 carried Leslie Ellen Jones' fantastic 'Everybody Must Get Stoned – Megaliths and Movies' article, which single-handedly renewed interest in megaliths in TV and film. The same issue carried Aubrey Burl's definitive article 'The Third Stone – The Altar Stone at Stonehenge: prone to doubt' (both articles included in this volume). The magazine was still receiving a ton of correspondence from readers and contributors, and some of the letters were so long that a new section was included, 'Small Stone' for shorter articles of about 750 words. A selection of Letters and Small Stones are included in this volume. Ian Brown joined the magazine as resident illustrator, his 'Mellow Druid' character appearing at least once in most subsequent issues[12].

In spring 2002 *3rd Stone* held a field trip with the-then Wiltshire County Archaeologist Roy Canham, who led a group of readers out onto Salisbury Plain,

11 In the middle of all this slightly unsettling stress, another potential buyer for the magazine came on the scene. Terms were being discussed and things were looking promising until the potential buyer relayed that he had obtained financial backing from a famous conspiracy-minded pseudo-archaeologist who – he'd not mentioned before now – was previously his employer. While I was trying to take all this on board, the buyer told us his accountant had decided the magazine wasn't worth anything, but he'd take it on free of charge as a favour. A lively phone conversation followed and this mysterious fellow was never heard from again.

12 The Mellow Druid lives on in Ian's yearly Christmas card. Here he is, in December 2024.

including some of the Danger Areas on military land which are usually closed to the public. The day finished with a private access visit to Stonehenge in the early evening[13].

Later in the year *3rd Stone* partnered with Strange Attractor (then putting on arts and fringe events) to stage a major event in London – 'Megalithomania: Celebrating 5000 years at the Monuments'[14]. Named after John Michell's seminal book, the conference took place at the Conway Hall in Red Lion Square in Bloomsbury. The speakers included John Michell himself, Paul Devereux, Iain Sinclair, Leslie Ellen Jones, Andy Letcher, Rob Stephenson, Revd. Alan Walker, Robert Wallis and Andy Worthington. A 30-minute collection of clips from TV shows and films with a megalithic theme was shown, and various arts installations took place. In the evening the bands Mount Vernon Arts Lab and Wigwam played, before a pretty out-there performance by the legendary psychedelic occultists, Coil[15]. The following day a smaller group of readers had a private tour around the Museum of London by John Clark, one of the Museum's senior curators, and later that day Rob Stephenson of the London Earth Mysteries Circle guided a group around some of the City's mystical and sacred sites.

Despite all these fun things happening, I was feeling quite frazzled by the four big issues per year schedule. Because of the way the subscriptions ebbed and flowed we were approaching a position where the minimum number of readers were due to re-subscribe with the next issue, and at which point the minimum number of subscribers would have to have money returned for issues they had paid for but would not receive. Therefore with issue 46 we announced that 47 really would be the last issue. Readers were invited to send in photos of themselves at sites to include on the last front cover and plenty were sent in, along with many letters saying how sad readers were to see the magazine close.

Various suggestions came up for how *3rd Stone* might continue[16], but all of them involved me, and I wanted a break from continuous deadlines. I imagined after *3rd*

13 It was great fun meeting *3rd Stone* readers at these events, book launches and so on. The *3rd Stone* editorial number was a regular source of fun too. Memorable calls included the guy who phoned asking if someone would like to join him on a flight in his private plane so he could show how lines of earth energy aren't only on the ground, they could be dowsed up in the sky too. Or the person who insisted they'd discovered the location of an entrance to Hell in Edinburgh, and asked whether someone could come and meet him there tomorrow? Or the lady who called early one Sunday morning: 'Hi, is that *3rd Stone*? Oh great. I don't drive, do you know how I can get from Leytonstone to the Rollright Stones on public transport today?'

14 *3rd Stone*'s 2002 Megalithomania event was shortly followed by an unrelated ancient mysteries conference which took the same name and still operates today.

15 Coil released their set commercially, which comprised a single track, 'The Universe Is a Haunted House', in the live box set *The Key to Joy Is Disobedience*.

16 One suggestion came from a subscriber, the writer Stewart Lee, who suggested a *3rd Stone* radio show on Resonance FM. With so many interesting podcasts out there nowadays, Stewart's suggestion was well ahead of the curve.

Stone closed a new national Earth Mysteries magazine would appear and take its place, but then the internet happened and a lot of the enthusiasm around Earth Mysteries and ancient sites shifted online, with sites such as Andy Burnham's www.megalithic.co.uk and Julian Cope's 'The Modern Antiquarian' website.

Paul Devereux and I founded the peer-reviewed academic journal, *Time and Mind: The Journal of Archaeology, Consciousness and Culture*[17], but a national Earth Mysteries magazine with the sort of in-depth articles *3rd Stone* carried didn't happen, either on paper or in the virtual world. After toying for some years with the idea of a DIY Earth Mysteries 'zine called *Site Hound,* the first issue has now appeared in time for the publication of this volume[18].

17 The March–December 2023 issue of *Time and Mind (Volume 16, 1–4)*, a special issue on 'Continuity and Change in the Cosmological Landscape of Prehistoric Cornwall', contains five papers reviewing the independent research on megalithic cosmology of Bodmin Moor by Roger Farnworth, some of which are expanded versions of material originally published in *Meyn Mamvro* magazine. Readers who would be interested to read a completely fascinating example of how Earth Mysteries-type research has developed in the last 20 or so years are encouraged to seek out this volume.

18 My 2020 self-published booklet/zine *Cosmic Nudge 1 – Stone Circle Scrapbook: A Wally On The Moor* was originally called *Site Hound 1.*

"Tell me the Acts, O historian, and leave me to reason upon them as I please; away with your reasoning and your rubbish ... Tell me the What; I do not want you to tell me the Why, and the How; I can find that out myself, as well as you can, and I will not be fooled by you into opinions, that you please to impose, to disbelieve what you think improbable or impossible".

Rave on William Blake!

Ley Lines: Dead and Buried. A reappraisal of the straight line enigma

Danny Sullivan

This article derives from a presentation Danny Sullivan gave to the *Fortean Times* UnConvention in London in April 1997 and discusses the development of ley hunting from the sedate Sunday outings of the 1920s, through the sub-cultural melting pot of the 1960s, the pseudo-science of the 1980s, and finally to the cross-disciplinary maelstrom of the 1990s.

Seventy years after Alfred Watkins alerted the world to the existence of ley lines, his simple vision of prehistoric traders' trackways has evolved into a confusing and tangled web of delusions, falsehoods and superstition. Today's pendulum swingers, channellers and self-styled pagan mystics perceive leys as lines of power in a global energy matrix, divorced from Watkins' original vision and ignorant of the evidence on the ground. In recent years a radical reassessment of the evidence for archaic landscape lines has resulted in a remarkable paradigm shift. The old straight tracks are the routes of spirits over the land, the trackways of the ancestors and the roads of the dead. Ancient cultures have left traces of such spirit paths all over the world and the belief that the dead choose to travel by the shortest route can be shown to have survived into Medieval Europe.

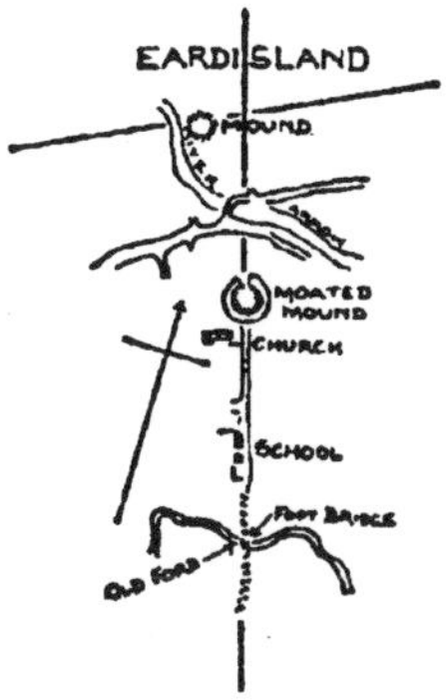

Fig I: Typical Watkins ley (Watkins).

Fig 2: All Saints and Hereford Cathedral align to comer of camp (Watkins).

Ask anyone with a passing interest in 'Earth Mysteries' what they think a ley is and nine times out of ten they will say 'energy line', 'line of force or power' or 'earth energy'. They will all be wrong. In this article I intend to show how the popular 'ley' concept is inadequate to explain the nature of the archaic landscape line and that it is a product of an idealistic, insupportable and ultimately arrogant attitude towards our ancient past.

In 1925 Alfred Watkins brought the idea of leys to the public. Essentially, he 'discovered' that ancient mounds, prehistoric earthworks and standing stones and old moats and churches seemed to fall into dead straight alignments across country. He chose to call these alignments leys because of the frequency with which this Saxon place name occurred along them. In places they overlaid stretches of ancient straight roads and trackways. Watkins' explanation for this seemingly bizarre phenomenon derived almost entirely from his own experience. He was a businessman and trader and spent a great part of his working life travelling around Herefordshire in connection with the family's brewing business. It was therefore inevitable that he should have concluded that his leys were the remnants of prehistoric trader routes. His argument was published as *The Old Straight Track* in 1925.

At a time when diffusionist theory held sway in the archaeological establishment it was to be expected that Watkins' ley idea should be derided and ignored by academe. How could the 'woad painted savage' have been capable of such feats of engineering skill? The ultimate insult was the refusal by the then editor of the establishment organ, *Antiquity*, to accept a paid advertisement for *The Old Straight Track*. Later this drawing of lines in the sand was to form the bedrock of a lasting antagonism between ley hunters and archaeologists which culminated in the 1970s by the refusal of *Antiquity* to take a paid advertisement for *The Ley Hunter*.

Fig 3: An example of orthotenies (Michel).

Undeterred by the orthodox rejection of leys, the Straight Track Club was formed in the wake of Watkins' revelations, and it spent many a delightful Sunday afternoon in the bucolic, pre-war Herefordshire landscape chasing leys and chasing paper, as a postal portfolio made its peripatetic way around Club members. But by 1939 it was all over. The exigencies of war put pay to ley hunting for the next twenty years.

Towards the end of the 1950s the flying saucer craze was to give ley hunting a new lease of life. French UFO enthusiasts (clearly with nothing better to do) had been plotting the locations of sightings on the map and had convinced themselves that they fell into straight lines. These linear phenomena were named orthotenies and formed the basis for the rabid speculation that was Aimé Michel's *Flying Saucers and the Straight Line Mystery* which was published in 1958. In Britain, Tony Wedd, an ex-RAF pilot and flying saucer enthusiast, published a slim booklet entitled *Skyways and Landmarks* in the early 1960s, in which for the first time the ideas of leys and flying saucers were brought together. A melding of French orthotenies, Watkins' leys and a love of countryside had Wedd proclaiming that UFOs used hills and mounds crowned with scots pines as navigation beacons! Two acolytes of Wedd, Philip Heselton and Jimmy Goddard, decided to revive the Straight Track Club, a move which saw the first stirrings of what was to become *The Ley Hunter*. Goddard expressed his enthusiasm for leys and UFOs in *Flying Saucer Review* in 1964:

> *Could it be that the intelligences behind the flying saucers built the ley markers for navigational purposes, or perhaps in order to find readily a form of magnetic current (my italics) that is helpful to them? It is a theory that is extremely difficult for the scientist to swallow...*

The powerful concoction of UFO fever, cultural revolution, drugs and rock 'n' roll in the 1960s stretched the bounds of credulity to the extreme. Anything was possible. The real revolution in attitudes towards the ancient past was, however, not to be found on the fringes but in academe itself. The first body blow to received archaeological wisdom came in the form of *Stonehenge Decoded* in 1965 in which Professor Gerald Hawkins suggested the unthinkable, that the builders of Stonehenge had a working knowledge of astronomy and were able to predict eclipses using their 'Stone Age computer'. Close behind Hawkins came Professor Alexander Thom, whose meticulous surveys of megalithic monuments from Scotland to Brittany attempted to prove the advanced mathematical, astronomical and engineering skills of Neolithic people. Such radical ideas from within the system appealed hugely to an audience stretching themselves both spiritually and intellectually. The fact that the archaeological establishment were as hostile to these incursions as they were to the ley idea made them all the more attractive.

If the revolution was never going to be televised in the 1960s it was certainly going to be published. John Michell, an advocate for the lost Golden Age, made tangible by Thom and Hawkins, had been contributing regularly to the alternative scene's main publication *International Times*, concocting a synthesis of ufology, folklore, leys and archaeology which reached its zenith in *The View Over Atlantis*, published in 1969.

Another long-standing Golden Age myth developed around this time. Michell referred to *The Goat Foot God*, a novel by the occult writer Dion Fortune (written in 1939) which linked the alignment of ancient sites to power centres and lines of force. Thus was born the notion of leys as lines of energy. This idea – fundamentally a purely fanciful and poetic one – has been the bane of serious ley research for years. The mish-mash of ideas about leys, flying saucers and energy lines, now in one big melting pot, was described by an unknown journalist as 'Earth Mysteries'. By 1976 *The Ley Hunter* (*TLH*), which had established itself as the flagship Earth Mysteries magazine, was taken over by Paul Devereux who attempted to fashion the subject into one worthy of serious study. Examples of leys were submitted to *TLH*, examined and put to the statistical test. The archaeological establishment was tackled head on by Devereux and his colleagues in a major confrontation in the early 1980s.

In 1978 the subject of dowsing entered the debate proper. Since the 1930s, French dowsers had claimed that menhirs had been placed over the crossing points of two or more underground streams. In the 1950s Guy Underwood took these ideas a step further by claiming he could detect a complex web of dowsable forces under megalithic monuments, hill figures, earthworks, old roads and paths and ancient churches. Underwood's ideas encouraged a whole new wave of energy

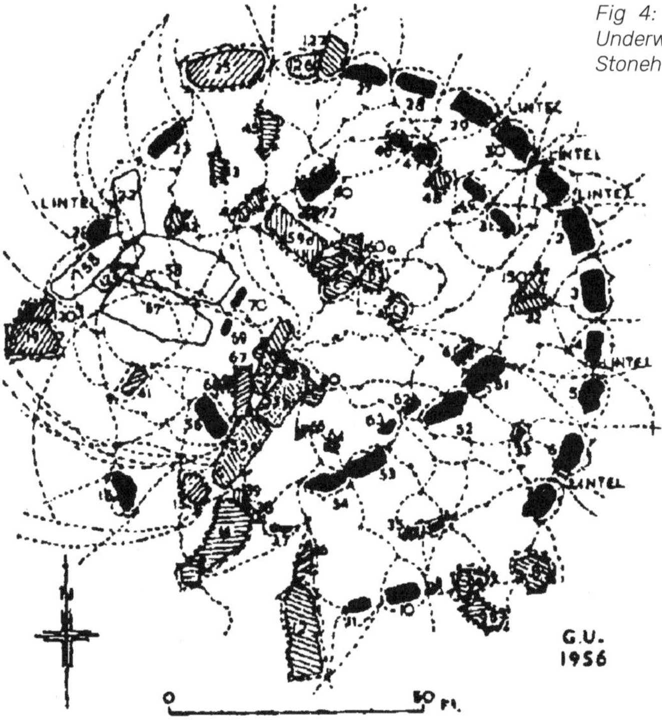

Fig 4: An example of Guy Underwood's 'lines of force' at Stonehenge (Underwood).

dowsers all claiming to be able to detect hitherto undiscovered 'earth forces' at ancient sacred sites.

This idea was taken to its ultimate (and ultimately flawed) conclusion by Tom Graves in 1978 in his book *Needles of Stone*. This was primarily an ideas book in which he attempted to verify the claims of the dowsers by dowsing the sites himself. He claimed he found an overground, *a dowsable line of force above ground* (my italics) at the Rollright Stones in Oxfordshire. Before he knew it leys had become dowsable lines of force linking ancient sites (and some not so ancient). Graves has since retracted his original claims in *The Ley Hunter*, but his protestations have fallen on deaf ears.

Many implausible and unprovable claims have been made for energy lines and leys and for the best part this is how leys are now perceived by most people. This is particularly the case in the USA where Watkins is practically unheard of. Now we have global energy grids and power lines – concepts entirely alien to ancient cultures. Ancient tribal people built their sacred sites within their own distinct cultures and mindsets, not ours. The energy line/global grid concept comes not from some arcane lost wisdom, but straight out of today's modern and mechanised view of the world. These ideas are nothing short of retrospective cultural imperialism.

Devereux, uncomfortable with the energy line ideas and fed up with being shunned by the archaeological and scientific communities (who saw the modern ley concept for the farrago of nonsense that it is), decided to instigate a research programme in which he would apply the scientific method to test whether the earth energy claims held water. This was the Dragon Project (now a charitable trust) which for ten years, at the Rollright Stones and other sites, employed scientific monitoring instruments, dowsers, psychics and even magnetically sensitive shrimps! The conclusion was that apart from variable and rare anomalous features in the earth's geomagnetic field, natural background radioactivity and ultrasound, there was no evidence at all for an unknown 'earth force' and even less for Graves' overgrounds. The whole project was described neatly in Devereux's *Places of Power*, published in 1990.

So where does that leave us now? We know what a ley isn't - so what is it? The key to understanding this enigma is go back to basics; to get back to what is actually on the ground. Straight landscape lines can be found all over the world and if we examine these we may be able to identify a link between them all that might point towards an explanation for them.

At Nazca in Peru, dead straight lines were marked out for miles on the desert plain by ancient tribal people. Some of these lines connect burial places, are associated with ancestor cults and were known as early as 1945, from folk tradition, to have been the routes of spirits. They were also ritually swept by local people, a practice which is still carried out today, though in a Christian context.

Similar straight paths can be found in the Bolivian altiplano, running unchallenged for miles over hostile terrain and undulating topography. These were investigated by Tony Morrison in the 1970s and eagerly seized upon by Watkinsian ley hunters as evidence for leys outside of Britain. Like Watkins' leys the Bolivian tracks ran from prominent hills and mountains to isolated shrines (all now Christianised). Mountains and hills were seen by the local people as being the dwelling places of spirits.

More recently ritual roads have been discovered in New Mexico through the medium of infra-red satellite photography. These roads, barely visible at ground level, run straight out from Chaco Canyon on whose floor lie the ruins of ancient settlements and sacred buildings known as kivas. These roads were made by clearing surface stones and piling them in berms alongside the routes. Some

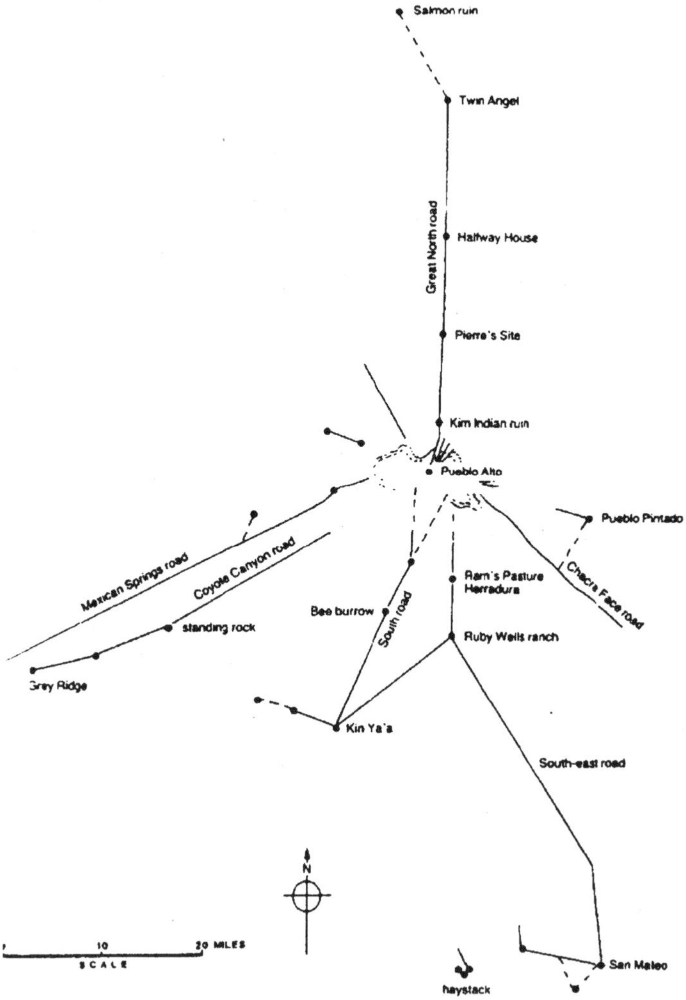

Fig 5: Map of Anasazi roads at Chaco Canyon (from Secrets of Ancient and Sacred Places by Paul Devereux).

roads run parallel to one another, and some go nowhere, petering out in the desert, suggesting that the primary function of these roads was not simple transportation. Further, their function as physical roads must be questioned – the Anasazi did not have the wheel or, indeed, the horse.

The spirit route concept can be found on the other side of the Atlantic, in Ireland, where fairy *passes* run invisibly and straight between fairy forts or raths, circular earthwork enclosures. Folk beliefs hold that otherworld beings or spirits inhabit fairy forts and that they have been seen dancing on the banks as anthropomorphs and as lights. It was considered bad luck to block a fairy pass. A famous story concerns a fellow who built a house on a fairy pass. Thereafter he was plagued with bad luck and ill health. Not until he had sliced off the offending corner of his abode and allowed free passage of the path did his fortunes improve. Most of this spirit geography exists only in the folk mind, although some routes are overlaid by later (straight) roads.

In imperial China straight lines in the landscape were considered unlucky and avoided at all costs, except where the divine influence of the Emperor was concerned. Malign spirits were believed to travel along straight paths, and good luck could be drained from a site along a straight route. The ancient Chinese art of placement, or feng shui, was primarily concerned with the auspicious location of tombs, although this was later adapted to the location of houses for the living too. Again, we have a connection between straightness, spirits and the dead.

What linear features can be found in Britain? An obvious candidate is the cursus monument. These are long parallel banks and ditches enclosing what is believed to have been a sacred or ceremonial space. They run for up to several miles in straightish sections and are often aligned on Neolithic long barrows. Other long barrows are found to have their axes aligned to the ends of cursuses. Later Bronze

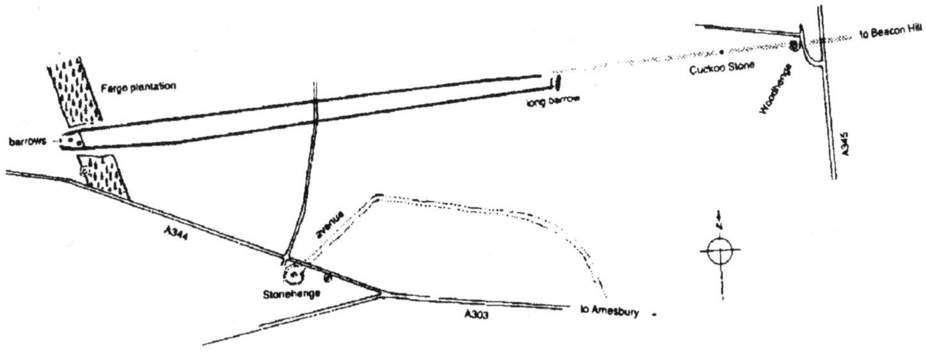

Fig 6: The Greater Stonehenge Cursus alignment (Devereux).

Age round barrows have been found to be connected to cursuses via straight avenues of timber posts. The still visible Greater Stonehenge Cursus has one of its sides aligned to a megalith known as the Cuckoo Stone and beyond to the now lost mortuary house at Woodhenge. No-one knows the purpose and function of cursuses, but again the link with death and ritual is apparent.

Elsewhere in Britain and Europe the prehistoric interest in linearity manifests itself in the stone row and avenue. In Brittany straggling lines of megaliths link together cromlechs; ovoid settings of stones, believed to enclose symbolic sacred spaces which were associated with the dead. In England the Dartmoor stone rows often lead to or from a stone circle or cist. Sometimes a burial cist is incorporated into the row. The function of stone rows is unknown. They may have been ritual processional ways or purely symbolic routes connected with the dead.

Moving forward in time, but still in Europe, Viking cult roads ran straight to burial places, and it was the practice to carry dead chieftains along these straight ceremonial roads to their final resting place. In historical times the link between straightness, death and burial can still be found. In Holland, medieval *doodwegen* or death roads still survive in the landscape, and it was along such dedicated roads that the dead were carried to a burial ground. Documentary evidence shows that in some circumstances it was illegal to carry a corpse on another road. The route had to be straight. Elsewhere rules were laid down as to their width and so

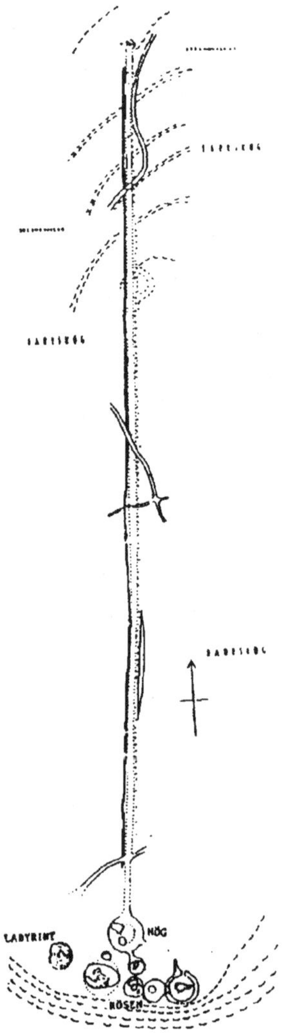

Fig 7: A Viking cult road (Kraft after Lothman and Winberg for Caerdroia *journal).*

on. Such routes were also common in Germany where they were known as *geistewege* or ghost roads. Such funeral paths were often straight, though not always. Also in Germany, some straight roads were deliberately engineered in the medieval period to link churches. These well documented church lines often underlay the plan of a town.

Fig 8: A Cornish church path.

Similar funeral paths survive in England as corpse ways, coffin paths and church roads. Some of Watkins' leys may have been the vestiges of medieval corpse ways. This might explain, more convincingly than site continuity, the occurrence of non-prehistoric features such as medieval churches and burial grounds on his leys.

So, what is the connection? Consistently we find spirit travel, death, sacred space and ritual procession. The Nazca lines were ritually swept – a process for creating scared space, and there may be a parallel with the Northern European tradition of sweeping disused paths to clear spirits away. The ritual sweeping of sacred pathways occurs in the culture of the Kogi Indians of Colombia. These people inhabit a remote mountainous region and have managed to preserve many of their traditional beliefs and way of life, despite the depredations of Spanish invaders and the pervasive spread of Western culture. They were the subject of an evocative film by Alan Ereira in 1990. In the film we were shown the map stone, a megalith criss-crossed with straight grooves which he was told was a map of physical roads in their region. In addition, the map stone showed the location of invisible routes which existed only in the spirit world. These routes were travelled by a class of Kogi adepts known as mamas, who looked after the spiritual well-being

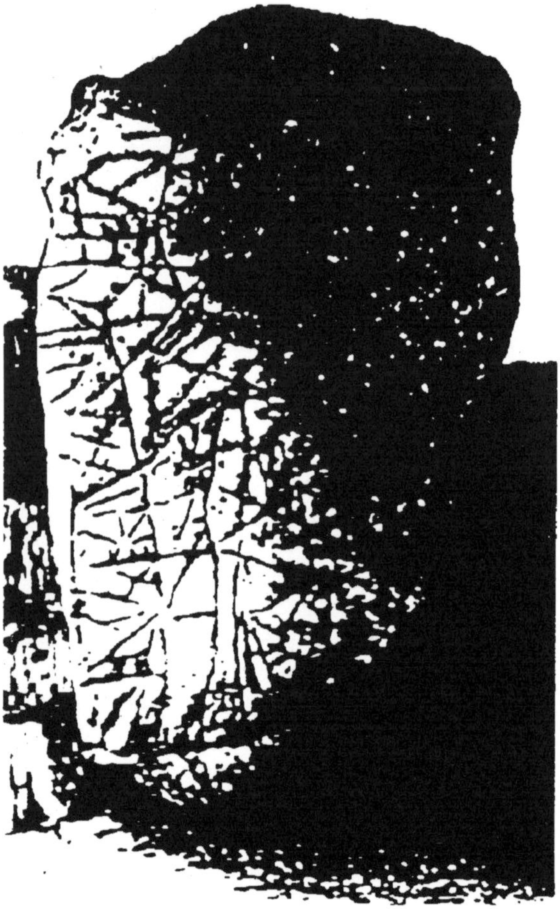

Fig 9: The Kogi Map stone (Devereux, after a photograph by Ereira).

of their people. Part of Kogi cosmology involves the ritual use of coca, shamanic travel and complex traditional practices designed to maintain ecological balance in the environment. This is still a living tradition. The link we have been looking for is spirit travel – most graphically evident in the universal shamanic out-of-body experience.

In traditional tribal societies straight lines were believed to facilitate spirit travel and tangled threads or winding tracks were believed to trap spirits. Hence the medieval use of the witch bottle, and the Scandinavian tradition of fishermen running the stone labyrinth before setting out to sea so that evil spirits would be left behind on shore. Australian aborigines used the thread made from insect filament to draw the spirit of a sick person back to their body. Siberian shamans

Fig 10: Perhaps the out-of-body flight experience has a cultural survival in the belief that witches could fly. Salves and ointments made from alkaloid-containing plants were applied directly to and absorbed into sensitive areas of the skin via the traditional witch's broom or flying stick or wand.

employed red threads in their ceremonies. The Kalahari Kung! climb threads to go out-of-body trance dancing. The cross-cultural occurrence of the concept leads us to the conclusion that the defining link is a human consciousness experience; a core concept that straddles cultural and temporal barriers and manifests itself in similar practices and beliefs all over the world. The obvious place to look for this core concept is shamanism.

The shaman undergoes symbolic death in order to enter the spirit world. Whilst there he or she travels along the same paths as the spirits of the dead ancestors. The shaman enters the spirit world via a trance state of consciousness and undertakes out-of-body flight across the land. This shamanic flight of the soul over the land seems to have been translated onto certain symbolic landscapes in

Fig 11: A flying Eskimo shaman (Jessie Oonark, from TLH 116).

the form of straight alignments and paths. Other lines such as fairy passes and the invisible spirit roads of the Kogi were conceptual rather than physical – existing only in the folk mind.

Neurologically the straightness comes from the entoptic nature of the out-of-body or near-death experience. Spirals, zigzags, lines, lattices or the tunnel motif are commonly 'seen'. Such entoptic or endogenous phenomena have been identified in Neolithic rock carvings in the chambered tombs of Britain, Ireland and Brittany. Newgrange chambered tomb was designed to allow the midwinter rising sun to penetrate the back chamber at the end of a long passage. And on a few days each year, either side of the winter solstice an observer sitting in the central chamber will see a shaft or tunnel of light penetrate the blackness. This is a symbolic and permanent record of altered state consciousness in one of the world's oldest sacred buildings.

Fig 12: Entoptic imagery in Neolithic rock art at Gavrinis, Brittany (Sullivan).

Fig 13: The near-death experience. The bright tunnel image and angelic flight. A medieval depiction by Hieronymus Bosch.

So then, what is a ley? I would say that there is no such thing as a ley. As a defined thing or phenomenon in its own right, it does not exist. Watkins saw the remains of archaic spirit lines, medieval corpse ways and church road alignments and hundreds of chance alignments. He didn't recognise what he saw and chose to weave a theory around the remaining evidence shaped by his own personal experience. The decades of wild speculation that buried his original vision have relegated ley hunting to the academic side-lines, whilst all the time archaeologists, anthropologists, geographers and folklorists have been advancing our knowledge of the archaic landscape line, side-stepping the excesses of the energy line modellers and twig twitchers. It is time that the contribution of genuine ley hunters is more widely recognised. It is time to bury the ley.

Ladye Bay, Clevedon, Somerset

Babyface Cave: A Personal History.

Paul Newman

In the following, I have altered some names and details. Depicting both the living and dead can be a delicate business, particularly when impressions of friends and relatives may differ[1].

It was a dark, frowsty room, entombed with bark-brown cabinets and book shelves, the flat surfaces of which were littered with items like bits of bone, pottery, fossil and Roman coins. On the walls and sideboards were crudely executed paintings of Mendip landscapes – all rendered in blobby greens and cemetery greys – and photographs of standing stones and burial mounds. 'Sit down Paul.'

I obeyed, smiling awkwardly at Guy Wickfrith. He was seated in an armchair next to his stout, haughty-looking wife, Clarice, who had the manner of a grand dame but was a kindly, immensely interesting lady. Guy had a quick, alert face with a hint of suspicious watchfulness, typical of a man who could be easily hurt. Bald save for a few wispy plumes of dark hair, he wore glasses and a flat cloth cap; the latter he did not shed, even when sitting indoors. He had a pipe which he pulled and sucked at in the traditional manner of armchair ruminants.

Besides being a journalist, Guy was a writer of traditional detective puzzles. He had written *Death Goes Fishing*, *Death Goes Caving*, *Death Goes Climbing* and *Death Goes for a Picnic* – dealing with violent extinction in such contexts and the subsequent investigation by his plodding regional sleuth whose name and rank I

1 Paul's original introduction to the article.

have forgotten. Guy's writing was not always on the side of law and order – he also composed gangster titles like *Highsteppin' Jezebel* and *Hot Dames on Cold Slabs*, usually set in New York or Chicago, which slightly amused me as, apart from brief forays to the city, he seldom ventured much beyond Clevedon and Portishead.

Not only was Guy an author, he was also a part-time archaeologist and allowed the terminology of gangster writing to overlap with this more academic interest: Roman officials were 'dudes', Viking warriors 'Canute's mob' and excavated human bodies 'stiffs'.

I knew some of these facts at second-hand, having never before spoken to him at length. Yet our families had often crossed paths in the past twenty years. The Wickfriths lived opposite, in the basement of a massive classical villa called Picton House. My father, who was a politician, had been on conversational terms with Guy whose son, Danny, had played with my brother as a child, later becoming a Bristol journalist and then moving on to become TV critic for the *Mail*. Whenever an election was imminent, Guy tended to pick Father's brains, using the information in his weekly column of country matters and topical observations.

And now he had asked to speak to me. The reason was I had recently authored a book called *The Hill of the Dragon*. It had been widely and, on the whole, sympathetically reviewed. This was pure luck. The work was a tortuous jumble of a study, a narrative that tripped over its self-generating web of suggestions. The subject – dragons – was 'radial' and multi-faceted. It spread and connected with so many other areas that, by the time I had finished, I was in a state of stunned confusion as to what exactly it was all about.

'We have both read your book, Paul, and enjoyed it very much,' Guy began, 'and that's why we've invited you over. You see, there are many people who would reject the stories and folklore that you have paid the compliment of taking seriously. For them, things like ghosts and visions do not exist.' I was glad he thought my opinion valid, but I do tend to get weary and tense if people dollop too much psychic mash on my plate.

Unfortunately, having written a book on a vaguely 'supernatural' subject, the Wickfriths assumed it was the sort of thing I ached for and proceeded to launch a plague of apparitions on my ear, starting with the ghost of a hunch-backed crone seen in the upper reaches of Brockley Combe. It was hard going and twenty blood-curdling, mind-numbing phantoms later, I said to myself – Guy had just finished invoking a misty spectre of a Roman legionary seen on the Backwell-Bristol road – this must be the very last!

Now, surely, I could turn the topic around to something less nebulous. But just as I breathed out in relief, Clarice Wickfrith tapped her husband on the arm, saying,

'I say, Guy, you haven't told him about the ghost of the black pig.'

'Well Paul, do you want to hear about the ghost of the black pig?'

'I'd love to,' I said, 'but perhaps it would be better if you saved it for next time.'

Fortunately the exclusion clause worked. The couple smiled. Talk turned to more concrete matters – in particular, I pointed to a head cast in dark-chocolate resin on the sideboard facing him. It showed a small round, sinister face, smashed on its left side, with a deeply entrenched eye and strong mouth.

'I see you've got a cast of the head.'

'Yes, it was damned difficult getting that, I can tell you.'

'Do you believe it's ancient?'

'I can prove it.'

Guy took a map out of a drawer, opened it and reached for a piece of string with a hazelnut shell on the end. He dangled it over the map, in the vicinity of Ladye Bay, jangling the string a few times and waiting until it became quite still. He frowned hard – steadily it began to move again and he started mumbling and making breath sounds.

'Yes, Celtic,' he said.

'You find a pendulum accurate?' I asked.

'It's never failed Tom, so it's good enough for me.'

Guy told me that he had corresponded with Tom Lethbridge for some years. They were similar types; both had inherited a blunt practical knowledge of sorts. Guy had spent a long time working on the land – in the Channel Islands before becoming an author and journalist; Tom Lethbridge had been on Arctic expeditions as well as being academically inclined. Both were obsessed with archaeology and prehistory, yet also had leanings towards that area where the disciplines touched the threshold region of ghosts and shadows. Eventually Tom had come to visit Guy at Clevedon and the latter had taken him down to examine the cave near Ladye Bay. What was Tom's impression, I asked. 'He was intrigued, thought it unique,' he replied.

Pirates

I was deeply interested in that strange, half mutilated face. In fact, the cave had figured in my youth from about the year 1956, when I was about ten years old. A childhood friend called Tim Davey used to call at my house in Victoria Road, asking me to go out and play with him. We'd explore the beaches and cliffs of Clevedon and often took the path up to Ladye Bay. One summer's afternoon, after we'd been swimming, Tim suggested, 'Let's go to Babyface Cave.'

I had never heard of the place, but I followed Tim along the cliff-path, through the tunnel of foliage to a low, rocky headland overlooking the Channel. We climbed down this and over the rocky shore — into an array of dislodged boulders that had broken away from the cliff-face, many of which, I remember, contained little red quartz bloodstones. We scrambled for several minutes and Tim vanished down a gap between two huge fallen boulders. I went after him, sliding down a wet rock-face and into a damp seaweed-smelling chamber.

It was creepy and cold inside. Rather dramatically, Tim pointed to a carving on the entrance slab - a dark, distorted child's face etched into greenish, slimy rock.

'That's the baby's face,' he said.

'Who carved it?' I asked.

'Pirates,' he replied unhesitatingly.

'Do you think there's treasure buried here?'

'Maybe,' he replied mysteriously.

There seems little point in relating the sophisticated complexities that swirled through my imagination at that point.

Of Unknown Origin

I cannot remember how Tim (who died tragically young, hanging himself in his nineteenth year) first heard of Babyface Cave - from another boy, I imagine. The majority of Clevedon residents were ignorant of the site. It had not been recognised or surveyed by archaeologists, and in lieu of expert guidance, I became a kind of junior cave-guide, showing visitors and friends the place and trying to obtain whatever information about it I could.

I discussed it with Clevedon people. One man suggested that it could have been a prank – someone with a hammer and cold chisel amusing himself – but no solid evidence emerged. Babyface Cave remained a children's hideaway, some of whom called it The Witch's Cave. The approach to it – amid a welter of bruising rocks – deterred the elderly and middle-aged, even if they knew where to look.

Ritual Immersion

But then, some twenty-five years later, hearing first-hand testimony from Guy Wickfrith (who headed the North Somerset Archaeological Research Group) that it was a genuine relic of prehistory, and that Tom Lethbridge had visited it, my interest was re-awakened.

For a start, its setting was odd – a cramped, oppressive sort of place, in a heavily faulted area, geologically speaking. Of course, in earlier times, tide and beach levels had been different; a shrine or roofed enclosure might have been attached to the cliff top.

When sea and weather undercut the cliff-base, the overhang slid forward and broke away; more rocks crashed down, entombing the face in a chamber.

But this could have taken place during the Ice Age. Assuming a prehistoric origin, the head may have been carved *in situ*, for there is the faintest wisp of a track leading to it from the Mariners' Path. Perhaps pilgrims used this way, but it can more credibly be touted as a route beaten out by scrambling children. It is not easy to give a focused impression, but it takes one down to a passage jammed alongside the cliff. There is a steep grassy slope, an immense boulder on the sea-facing side from which a rock-tunnel leads down to the cave. Here the cliff is of sandy, brown-gold stone, quite crumbly – not the hard pennant or limestone of the carving.

If anyone had visited it for religious purposes, the time of the year would be relevant. Topping forty feet, the shore around Clevedon and Portishead has one of the highest tidal ranges in the world, after the Bay of Fundy. During the spring and autumn equinoxes, the incoming swell is forced into the bottleneck of the Severn Estuary causing flood-damage and a dramatic bore upstream – hence the coast is defended by a seawall stretching from Clevedon to Woodspring. If the wind is high, the cave floods dramatically. For anyone into lurid rites of ritual immersion, here, indeed, is scope for a scenario.

Strange Letter

While touching on such material, I will now quote a strange letter that appeared on the desk of the editor of the *South Avon Mercury*, 15 May, 1981:

> *Sir,*
>
> *A colleague of mine from the University of Durham first drew my attention to the so-called Celtic head cut in the face of a cave-mouth in Walton Bay. I happened to have an afternoon off after completing a course of lectures at Bristol and took the opportunity to drive down to Clevedon and examine the carving. The actual engraving is a fairly crude piece of work – far more artistically accomplished stone heads have been unearthed at Priddy – but what particularly intrigued me was the abnormal situation – almost certainly prone to flooding at high tide.*
>
> *To get to the real point of the matter, and it is something I am most anxious to clear up, while inside the cave I heard what sounded like the screams of men under torture or extreme duress. I am of a sane and balanced temperament (at least I hope so), and I have been engaged both as a lecturer and practitioner of archaeology for over 20 years, and I have never until now had an experience which could be remotely termed 'psychic'. But I simply do not know how to account for these groans, wails, screams, and I mentioned the experience to the folklorist Venetia Newell. She reminded me that the Celtic god Esus was frequently honoured by his worshippers submitting themselves to the triple death by burning, stabbing and drowning – but I find such an explanation a bit too fancifully hair-raising. Are there any people from Clevedon or the vicinity who, while exploring in or around the Celtic Cave, have become aware of strange noises or anything unusual? I would be most grateful for an answer; at least then I would not feel alone in the matter. As I am holidaying in Galacia for the next three weeks, I would like any replies to be addressed to the* South Avon Mercury *because I have specially arranged for a colleague of mine to purchase the paper and send it on to my Cambridge department.*
>
> *D. Gleadow, Head of Excavations Cambridge Society of Antiquaries*

Instead of a cavalcade of torrid recollections, there was no response to Mr Gleadow (who, incidentally, seemed to occupy the post once taken up by Lethbridge) only a feebly jesting letter about the screams coming from the cave in response to a recent increase in water rates.

Bran the Blessed

But not quite – for the Bristol papers got wind of the story and a full report appeared, 22 May 81. Investigating the origins of Dr Gleadow, journalists found that he was as impalpable as the apparitions that pursued him. They phoned the Cambridge Society of Antiquaries – he was unknown to them. The Council for British Archaeology was unaware of his existence. He was not in the books of Bristol University either. However, the reporters were told that the study of Celtic gods attracted the 'lunatic fringe' – that minority taken up with distant witcheries, silly spells and so forth. But there was one further piece of information:

> *The cave was authenticated by experts from Taunton and other authorities five years ago (1976). It is possible that it was a carving of the god Bran, the Guardian to protect the coast. South Avon is an area which was thickly covered with Celtic settlement. Estimated to be about 1,500 years old, the head lies among fallen boulders and is the only one of its kind in the South West.*

Bran? The title comes easily to mind. Experts are usually too cautious to ladle out names on the strength of a single visit to a solitary carving. I imagine the reporter took up Bran from a suggestion made by Guy Wickfrith. He wrote a lively column of rustic ramblings (archaeology, farming, local history and gossip) each week for the *Mercury* and may have accompanied the experts from Taunton. Often shrewd in his judgements, Guy suffered from that alluring antiquarian contagion Celtomania (he told me that, in his youth, he had known an elderly lady whose regular expletive was 'Esus!') and I remember him talking of 'Bran the Blessed' whose head, after decapitation, was able to eat, drink and tell the future. What was this exotic personage doing nestling in the cliffs beneath a Victorian garden suburb?

We are told that the Celts believed that the soul resided in the head – hence its healing and talismanic properties. Votive skulls have been fished out of dozens of wells and watery sites in Britain and Ireland. Bran was the son of the sea-god, Lyr, and let us suppose that sector of the Severn Estuary, within dreaming distance of mystic Wales and rich in sprat, herring and conger, was sacred to either deity. Was the head intended to oversee and protect the dwellers on the shore? Or was it clunked out by a wag between the hours of dinner and pub one dull weekend?

The last, desperately droll possibility has to be faced. Quite a few pseudo-Celtic artefacts have received as much – or more – attention down the years as genuine ones, and Babyface Cave, totally unsuited to excavation and lacking supportive deposits, defies contextual analysis. Furthermore, how does one date rock? All stones are literally as old as the hills.

Initially I assumed the erosion of the carved edges had been looked at under a microscope: the wear and tear of centuries as compared with that of fresh-cut rock - a not especially fool-proof method, if one recalls how Anne Ross was deceived by a series of simulated Celtic heads dug up in Yorkshire over a decade ago. Furthermore, the head is fairly deeply gouged - one assumes with a hard metal implement, suggesting a time when such tools were more abundant than, say, in pre-Roman Britain.

Owning Up

Too many questions; too few answers. Furthermore, there is the matter of the professor and the strange noises. Jokers are not inevitably pleasant people. So I feel uneasy about coming clean and admitting, 'Yes folks, I was Dr Gleadow', the shadowy emissary from academia who was better qualified than I ever was or will be - does he stand for some ambitious alter ego, I wonder? Why did I do it? Why did I need to stage my own feeble-witted Piltdown affair? In mitigation, I can only say that I was motivated by a powerful curiosity and wanted to learn more about Babyface Cave. By creating a ripple in the paper, I hoped information of two distinct types might emerge:

1) Genuine first-hand data; early memories of the cave or speculation surrounding it from local people.

2) Fantasies engendered by ghost story or 'fakelore'. On reading a vivid supernatural anecdote, would people start imagining things? Would my experiment create an imaginative impulsion of its own?

It seems that people were not so suggestible and credulous as I had imagined. In Cork or Galway, such a letter might have unleashed a torrent of pure blarney, but it did not make a ripple on the smooth sheen of Clevedonian composure. Dr Gleadow had drawn a blank, but I had learned a little more about the cave[2].

2 The Dark Age date was not scientifically 'authenticated' but may owe something to ideas current in the seventies after Leslie Alcock's excavations at Cadbury (1966-70). The hillfort was found to have been consolidated and reoccupied during the fifth century - inspiring a fountain of speculation about Dark Age warlords, the Celtic prototypes of Arthurian legend and motifs like the severed head found in the *Mabinogion* and the *Matter of Britain*.

For various reasons, I did not stay in Clevedon, leaving my Somerset roots, my Celtic head, my pursuing lynch mob and moving further west to St Columb Major in Cornwall and then on to St Austell. Why are people drawn to places like Cornwall – these cliffs and seaboards, places of junctions and doubts? The sea is markless. It has no TV aerials or compromises. Either you drown in it, cross to America or return to base and reappraise your life.

Exile

Anyway I lived and wrote in Cornwall, producing various books, including *Gods and Graven Images*, a study of hill figures. But I still retained a nostalgia for Somerset, the people and landmarks I had left behind. After some eight years living in the Duchy, Radio 3 invited me to take part in a discussion at Uffington on the origin and meaning of the White Horse, alongside Paul Devereux, Christopher Chippindale and Peter Fowler. The discussion took place on Dragon Hill, and I remember being impressed by Paul Devereux. When the editor of *Antiquity* attacked his ideas head-on, Paul had to halt his reply several times in mid-invective – his voice drowned by a car passing or a plane overhead. It must have been most frustrating, yet each time he began again he was able to summon exactly the same words and exactly the same temperature of rapt indignation. As for me, I twaddled on about the speed, power and pride of the horse as a Celtic symbol while thinking: *why don't you do something useful like shove your head in a bucket.*

A Last Glimpse

Driving home that day from the Vale of the White Horse, through Bristol and down the Gordano alley, I suggested to Pam, my partner, that we take a break at Clevedon, so that I could take a photograph of the carving.

Stopping at a garage, I bought some batteries for my flash. Then we made our way to the point beyond Ladye Bay where the cave was situated. It was a clear summer's evening; there was a brisk wind and rough tide driving in, bubbling and seething between the rocky ledges.

While Pam waited on the headland, I climbed down with camera and flash and prospected around for the cave. Finding it, I dropped the camera into the hatch and lowered myself over the wet slab into the chamber. The head was still there, exactly as I remembered. It looked stranger than ever, with the sun from the west burning over the lip of the entrance, making the eyes seem bulbous, the mouth writhing...

I jammed myself against the far wall, focused the lens, pressed the shutter – but no light came. I tried several times – each time the flash didn't work. Lethbridge wrote of the failure of mechanical devices near sites of ancient sanctity (how on earth did they get all those shots of Stonehenge?) and I had no alternative but to try a hand-held time exposure. The light shining through the cave mouth might draw out the relief pattern. When printed, the result was blurred, yet oddly mobile, with glaring pupils and half-opened mouth and I herewith submit it for the delectation of readers of *3rd Stone*.

Fig 1: Outside Babyface Cave.

Fig 2: Inside Babyface Cave.

ONLY A HOAX?

MERCURY REPORTERS set out this week to establish the claims, in a reader's letter, that supernatural noises were heard in the cave at Ladye Bay where a 1,500-year-old Celtic head is carved . . . and discovered it may have been a hoax.

Fig 3: 'Only A Hoax?' newspaper cutting.

Boscawen-un circle.

Does the Goddess Live Here?

Cheryl Straffon

Cheryl Straffon edits the Cornish Earth Mysteries magazine *Meyn Mamvro* and is the author of *The Earth Goddess: Celtic and pagan Legacy of the Landscape.* This article outlines an approach to ancient sites that is both practical and spiritual.

In the Summer of 1995, a serious attempt was made to steal one of the Merry Maidens circle of standing stones in West Cornwall. A group of people were disturbed by a member of the public as they tried to dig up the stone and make off with it in a waiting van. In the summer of 1997, the centre stone of Boscawen-un stone circle, also in West Penwith, was set alight and badly burned at the top, presumably as part of a ritual to 'honour' the site. I write this, having just returned from the site where a bender, complete with chimney, has now been constructed next to the circle, which is surrounded by gorse that constitutes a fire risk. We live in an age where the ancient sites are, in the words of Cornwall County Archaeologist Nick Johnson, often 'loved to death'.

How can we reconcile this increasing threat to the sites with their growing popularity as places of spiritual connection? This seems to me a crucial question for any of us who relate to the sacredness of the sites, and a central issue for us all to deal with if we have any connection with these places.

Fig 1: Merry Maidens shadows (credit: James Kitto).

Genus Loci

I would like to explore in this article how those of us who go to the sites to specifically connect with the *genus loci*, or spirit of place, deal with some of the complexities and contradictions of these places in late 20th century Britain. So, before we ever get to the sites, we need to be aware that we are not the only people who feel they have a legitimate right to enjoy these places. Leaving to one side the casual visitor who goes to see, scratch their heads, and perhaps take a photo or two of their partner by the stones, who else has needs that might impinge on our own?

Firstly, there are the archaeologists, who, by and large nowadays, are interested in the prehistoric past not solely as a repository of artefacts and bones, but also in the beliefs and social constructs of the people who built them. As long ago as 1978, the excavator of Carn Euny fogou in West Penwith, Patricia Christie, was saying that she thought the site was probably used for ritual purposes, but it has taken some two decades for the archaeological establishment to take this on board.

Nowadays there is much more acceptance that these places were built as 'ritual sites' (even if the archaeologists are not always very clear what this means!) For example, the Sites and Monuments Officer for Cornwall recently wrote to *Meyn Mamvro*[1] with a plea for better understanding of the sites as ritual monuments: 'I am concerned at the increasing evidence of damage to stone circles and other ritual monuments. Most circles have hollowed fire pits at their centres; at others,

1 This quote is from Ann Preston-Jones and comes from a letter in *Meyn Mamvro* Vol 1 no.33 (Spring/ Summer 1997).

Fig 2: Carn Euny.

Fig 3: Goddess at Carn Euny.

turves have been lifted and deposits made beneath the ground. At the least, such actions can make a beautiful monument untidy and thereby spoil it for others. At the worst, they can be highly destructive of valuable archaeological evidence. There may be people who simply do not appreciate that by disturbing the ground within stone circles, they may be destroying the below-ground remains of structures and deposits put there by early worshippers and the people who built these sacred sites. A better understanding of the nature of the sites might help increase the respect paid to them.'

The New Rationalist

So, if archaeologists have learned some of the lessons of their antiquarian and 'dig and destroy' predecessors, who lost so much valuable evidence of the ritual meaning of the sites because they were looking for something else, and are now far more inclined to treat the sites with respect and caution, then who else poses a threat to such places? Well, paradoxically, the 'Earth Mysteries' establishment have sometimes shown as much prejudice when confronted by spirituality as any dyed-in-the-wool archaeologist. 'Earth Mysteries' is of course no longer an acceptable title, replaced by snappy definitions like 'Exploring new interpretations of place in archaeology, folklore and mythology'! No hint of spirituality there: in fact there's no hint of any kind of 'mystery'! With the honourable exception of *3rd Stone*, the 'new rationalists' of the (non) ley-hunting and folklore journals seem to be incredibly threatened by notions of the spirituality of the sites. A couple of examples from recent [1998] small press Earth Mysteries journals should suffice to illustrate the point:

1. 'Perhaps the worst offenders are those involved with the 'Goddess' lobby. In fighting the good fight against Patriarchy... slapping the Goddess label across those phallic stones and claiming the monopoly on spirituality, they endeavour to elevate themselves above all men'. And 2. 'A deeply-rooted popular myth among pagans is that the Neolithic religion was based around worship of a (Mother) Goddess, although there is no evidence to support anything other than local instances'.

The latter statement is a dogmatic belief disguised as an apparent 'fact' (there is in fact plenty of evidence as archaeologists and prehistorians like Marija Gimbutas and Miranda Green have shown), and the former statement is just a diatribe. Leaving aside the total inaccuracy of such comments for the moment, let us ask ourselves the question – what is it about spirituality, particularly Goddess spirituality, that causes such fear and bile amongst certain people, and makes the 'new rationalists' such strange bedfellows with the most reactionary of the old-guard archaeological establishment?

I do have a genuine puzzlement about all this. Where does the fear of ancient sites being places of deep spiritual connection come from? Certainly not from the sites themselves. In case anyone forgets, any megalithic sites built during the Neolithic and Bronze Ages were built by pagans, who worshipped goddesses and gods. To many of us today, they are the places of our direct (spiritual) ancestors. For the Earth Mysteries and 'new rationalists' brigade, such notions are dangerous heresy. The sites have generally been treated as places for imposing pet theories, each one replacing the one that came before – ley lines, grids, shamanic travellers, hot spots, astronomical predictors, electromagnetic anomalies, spirit lines etc) – you name it, there's been a theory about it! Many of us who have been around the Earth Mysteries scene from the beginning are getting very tired of all the in-fighting, and the vicious attacks made by those who adhere to the latest theory against those who refuse to follow the party line. Pagans are often quite contemptuous of those whose approach to the sites is perceived to be very left brain, divorcing themselves from any spiritual connection with the places.

New Age Nonsense

Of course, on the other side there are some pretty weird people out there! Many view the sites as places for going to 'connect with the energies', a kind of later 90s version of spacing out and getting high ('Beam me up, Woden!') One does not have to be a new rationalist to feel nauseated by the thousands of pounds being made out of workshops and New Age courses by those who are proffering some kind of watered-down cultural theft (usually an eclectic mix of so-called Native American wisdom, together with some pseudo-Celtic spirituality, washed down with a seasoning of alien beings and master races from the past). And if I see one more person waving a crystal around at an ancient site in order to 'heal the earth' I think I shall scream and scream and scream! The sites themselves are huge quartz and crystalline structures that need no piece of expensive mineral that has been gouged out of Mother Earth to make them complete. It is humankind that needs to start healing itself – left to her own devices, Mother Earth can look after herself perfectly adequately thank you, without any 'help' from humankind.

So is there any alternative to either the new rationalists or the arm-waving New Age pagans? I believe there is. To me spirituality without research and understanding is as bad as research and analysis without spirit. And both without politics are on fallow ground. It has always astounded me not only how any archaeological or 'alternative' researcher could ignore the spirituality of the sites, but also the ignorance of many, if not most, pagans about the prehistory of them. Many pagans are incredibly lazy about finding out some facts about the places where they celebrate and 'worship', and one has only to look at the pagan Small Press over the years to realise what a small proportion of articles are ever devoted to specific sites or prehistoric research. It is as if people who go to the sites for 'spiritual' purposes leave their brains in a box by the site entrance. Without at least some passing knowledge about the prehistory of the sites, or at least an awareness of ancient and contemporary indigenous peoples, it is not surprising that so much site disrespect and cultural theft takes place. To me, spirituality without research and political awareness is like bread without any butter (or perhaps I should say low-fat vegan spread!)

Sometimes I despair that pagans and new rationalists both seem to have an incredibly selfish and ego-centred approach to the sites, the obverse of each other. To the pagans, as long as you are spiritual (and preferably a member of the pagan Federation!) then you have some kind of spiritual right to worship at the sites. On the other hand, the New Rationalists are so desperately frightened of believing anything that cannot be documented back to the year 2000 BCE, that they have divorced theory from practice and exist in some kind of rarefied state where the sites they write about (but seldom visit) are devoid of all real people and their beliefs. There are some exceptions: those who have one foot in the camp of prehistory and another foot on pagan ground, but they often have their own axe to grind. I find it intriguing that current arguments by some academics (as contentious as they are) that pagan spirituality cannot be traced back into prehistory have been embraced so readily by both new rationalists and some pagans. It is as if it is all a convenient coat peg upon which to hang prejudices. More fear of Goddess spirituality!

The Way Forward

So, what then is the way through this morass of sherd-hunting archaeologists; 'no-spirituality please, we're new rationalists'; arm-waving, white-light healing white witches; and wannabe chief druids and high priestesses, all of them littering the ancient sites with their trowels, their crystals, their dowsing rods and their new paradigms?

Well, I don't have all, or indeed many, of the answers. For at the end of the day, it is not that any one kind of visitor has more right of access to a site than another: archaeologists, Earth Mysteries researchers, new rationalists, pagans, New Age folk, travellers, casual visitors and tourists all need to be accommodated and have space to do what they need to do there, providing they do not harm the site or anyone or anything else. After all, no-one can have the 'right' to own or exclusively control places that were built 4,000 or so years ago for purposes we still do not fully understand. We can only try to be accepting of each other's needs at these special sacred places, oppose any misuse of the sites of whatever kind, and try to avoid a conflict of interests.

Those of us who care enough for the sites in Cornwall at least have come together to form a Protection of Sacred Sites Group. The significant thing about this Group, which may make it a first in this field, is that it consists of representatives not only of groups like the pagan Federation, the Cornish Earth Mysteries Group, the Order of Bards, Ovates and Druids and the editor of *Meyn Mamvro*, but also representatives from the National Trust, English Heritage/Cornwall Archaeological Unit, the Bolitho Estate who own the land that many of the sites stand on, and the Countryside Conservation Officer. It is proving to be a most useful and responsible group that is taking an active and positive role in monitoring and protecting ancient sites and liaising with each other. One of the things we have discussed is an informal 'Sitewatch' group, along the lines of 'Dolphinwatch' and 'Coastwatch', to keep an eye on the use and potential abuse of local sites, particularly apposite in view of the forthcoming total eclipse of the sun in west Cornwall in August 1999, when the world and their partners will descend on west Cornwall.

Developing a Rapport

So far, I have talked about the problems involved for those of us who approach the sites in a spiritual way, and some of the ways we might deal with this. There is no quick fix solution as to how we should approach them and what we should do there: the only things I have are some feelings about what is important for me at these ancient and sacred places. I should therefore like to conclude this article by suggesting some of the things that I feel work for me and allow me to develop a rapport with these places that retains some integrity, and is also spiritually, practically and environmentally satisfying.

The first thing for me is to do my homework properly; to find out what is known about the site, and how it has developed over the ages from when it was built (most sites have been changed and modified, even in prehistory). Sometimes this means searching difficult-to-obtain archaeological reports and obscure antiquarian journals. Often one has to plough through a weight of technical data to find a nugget of research, the significance of which is often overlooked by the site excavator or academic researcher. Armed with this knowledge, one has at least an idea of how the site was built/modified, even if its ultimate purpose still remains a mystery. One then needs to place this knowledge within a context of what is known about, say, Neolithic or Bronze Age societies, not only in Britain but world-wide. For example, if we know that societies all over the area of Old Europe were Goddess-celebrating in the early Neolithic (as it appears they were) then it seems to me a reasonable inference that the people who built the sites in Britain were also part of this culture. To even deny the possibility, as so many archaeologists and new rationalists do, is to allow prejudice to prevent open-mindedness. We can never be certain as to the precise nature of the rituals and rites of our prehistoric ancestors, but we can draw some reasonable inferences based on known data and sociological/anthropological/prehistoric studies.

With this kind of knowledge, I can then approach the site, by myself, with my partner, or with others, with respect and some humility. It seems to me that the greatest lesson any of us can learn about these sites is to listen to what the site has to tell or teach us, and not to go to it with theories to be imposed upon it. Visiting them is like visiting old friends - they change with the seasons of the year, the time of the day and night, and the passage of the sun and moon. They can still be oases of peace in a world of turbulence, places to connect with the inner voice of stillness and contemplation. Even the archaeologists occasionally comment on the 'numinous' or 'spiritual' quality of the sites.

But what do we really mean by 'spiritual' in this context? To me these are places where I can contact my Goddess. They are not the only places: I see and feel and experience her in the land itself, in the sea, on the moors, in my garden, and in many other places.

But the sites are special places, because I can infer or guess that my ancestors also contacted her there. Of course, we all come to these places with our beliefs or non-beliefs. And there are even many aspects of the pagan faiths to which I do not subscribe, in particular its rather superficial acceptance of 'balance' of male and female energies, its focus on 'light' and 'healing' to the detriment of the 'creative inner dark', and its interpretation of the Wheel of the Year in terms of Goddess and God archetypes. None of this is writ in stone, and all is open to alternative interpretations, that for me are focused around Goddess energies in all her 'moonifestations'. But the sites are big enough to assimilate these different belief structures, provided we all bring nothing to them but our peaceful intentions, and take nothing from them but our spiritual fulfilment.

I also feel that we do the sites and the area in which they reside a disservice if we do not bother to learn about the local customs associated with them. How far back in time these customs can be traced is an academic point (sometimes akin to discussing how many angels are on the head of a needle). Personally, I feel that generally they have a much longer continuity than the new rationalists wish to give them credit for, and that they have also encoded within them some keys to unlocking the meanings of the sites, or at least the meanings that have been attributed to them. This is particularly so in the case of the holy wells, and perhaps especially pertinent in the Celtic lands of Ireland, Scotland, Wales, Brittany, Mann and Cornwall.

So much of our ancient spiritual history has been lost, and so many of those who seem fearful of our 'superstitious' past have a rationalistic (sometimes near fundamentalist) and Anglo-centric view of the old customs and ways. But to those of us who live with the sites, often at the Celtic 'fringes' (though they aren't fringes when viewed from that place!), it feels as if they are still 'alive' today in a way that the new rationalists do not seem able to comprehend or experience. Many of these approaches, both pagan and new rationalist, seem to some of us very androcentric, to be more interested in analysis, theory and 'paradigm shifts', rather than in caring, connecting and experiencing. I want a spirituality of the sites that embraces not only knowledge, intelligence and research, but also respect, honour, thanksgiving, and love for Mother Earth and the Goddess. If the sites are to survive into the 21st century, not as Disneyworld theme-park experiences but as places where we can still connect spirit with knowledge, then we have to stop setting fire to them, flinging crystals at them, and turning them into convenient hooks upon which to hang prejudices and 'Grand Unified Theories'. We owe our ancestors and our great-grandchildren nothing less.

Fig 4: CASPN sign.

2024 Endnote

It is fascinating to re-read something that I wrote in 1997 and wonder if I would say the same things nearly 30 years later! I think that the article did raise some important points then, and although I might express them somewhat differently today, nevertheless I still think that they are valid for consideration. Since 1997, some things have changed. Many people have become more aware of the issues surrounding visiting ancient sites, how to respect them and the ground they cover, and how to be careful not to leave behind rubbish and litter (including paraphernalia from ceremonies) for someone else to clear up. Community voluntary groups have flourished, such as the fledgling Protection of Ancient Sites Group, mentioned in the essay, which developed into CASPN (Cornish Ancient Sites Protection Network) and recently celebrated its 25th anniversary. It is now a Charitable Trust and still looks after ancient sites in West Penwith, with monthly clear-ups and events, and guided walks and talks, and its details may be found at www.cornishancientsites.com. The advent of the internet and social media has meant that communications between lovers of megalithic sites can be much more instant and world-wide, and ideas and thoughts spread much quicker and reach more people. All of this can be more positive, and improve how we interact with these ancient sites and how we all communicate our concerns and experiences at them. But we still need to be alert to their use. As the sites have become better known, the number of people visiting them has increased exponentially. A balance has to be found between numbers of visitors and the sacredness of the sites. We still need for them to not be overdeveloped and 'loved to death', and for people to respect what has stood for thousands of years and needs to be preserved for the future. We all have a part to play in this, and we all need to care for these special and numinous places.

Ever-Increasing Circles Exercises in Megalithic Duplicity

Aubrey Burl

As the acknowledged world authority on stone circles, Aubrey Burl needs no introduction to *3rd Stone* readers. In this paper Dr Burl examines a particularly circuitous class of these monuments: multiple stone circles.

Stone circles sometimes present unexpected problems. People going to the Merry Maidens at Land's End can see the splendid ring, the two outlying pillars of the Pipers, other standing stones in the neighbourhood such as Goon Rith, can puzzle over a holed stone opposite the path to the stone circle, can walk down the hill to the decorated entrance tomb of Tregiffian, but the stones, circle and tomb are the scanty vestiges of antiquity, not the complete prehistoric landscape. There has been a transformation. What the visitor will not see is the companion to the Merry Maidens, the vanished stone circle of Boleigh once about 150 m to the south-west.

Until the 1860s four stones stood in a field across the lane. Three others were prostrate, the remnants of a ring about thirty paces or 27 m across, one of the biggest in that part of Cornwall. Early this century an elderly local inhabitant told Hector Bolitho, a colleague of Sir Norman Lockyer, that the circle was 'covered with furze' but 'never shown to antiquarians' by the farmer who was fearful of archaeological interference. Later the field was ploughed and the circle was destroyed.

From Lockyer's account 'Mr Bolitho carefully marked the site thus indicated on a copy of the 25-inch map' (Lockyer, 1906, 268) and it seems that the ring was near SW 431 244. John Barnatt (1982, 158) rightly expressed cautionary words about the accuracy of this reference but, reassuringly, Cheryl Straffon has written that 'Some years ago crop marks of this circle were observed in the right place by someone who was not aware of its location or existence' (Straffon, 1992, 4) and the ring may be regarded as an erstwhile megalithic circle adjacent to the Merry Maidens. The problem is not whether it existed or exactly where but why two imposing stone circles should have stood so close together. There were similar conjunctions elsewhere in Britain and Ireland. They are equally perplexing.

By 1998 some 1,280 rings have been recorded in Britain and Ireland, 214 of them doubtful. Amongst them are a hundred pairs of circles close together, 22 sets of three, 7 of four, there are 3 groups of five, one six, no sevens or eights and 2 huddles of nine, both of them in Northern Ireland.

Of 311 possible rings in England there are 28 pairs including eleven on Dartmoor. There are also 9 threes of which the Hurlers on Bodmin Moor is the best known although Stanton Drew in Somerset is the most remarkable. There are four variegated rings at Broomrigg Plantation in Cumberland and five at Merrivale on Dartmoor, all of them extremely small.

Of Scotland's 506 stone circles 34 are pairs with 6 in Aberdeenshire and 10 in Perthshire. Multiples are rare. Three are known at the quartz-bright hillside of Logie Newton and at Melgum in Aberdeenshire, there is a devastated trio at the Loupin' Stanes in Dumfriesshire; a Christianised set at Fortingall near Aberfeldy and the well-known pair of passage-tombs and a ring-cairn at Balnuaran of Clava just south of Culloden Moor near Inverness. A solitary collection of six rings can be seen on Machrie Moor in Arran, quite typically varied architecturally, two ravaged but stately tall circles, a granite and sandstone oval, an 'Irish' 5-Stone ring, a concentric of loafishly plump boulders and a recently-discovered ring that is neither circular nor elliptical, simply bad.

The 76 circles in Wales contain only six pairs, none visually enticing. Of 185 sites listed for the Republic of Ireland there are 17 pairs, the great majority at the south-west in Co. Cork. There is a trio of rings at Maughanaclea in that county and, miles to the north-west, an intriguing four, all different, one a variant form of recumbent stone circle, at Cong in Co. Mayo.

Fig 1: The Grey Wethers, Dartmoor, from the west.

Northern Ireland is the outstanding country for the juxtaposition of rings and it is notable that it is in the inland regions of the Sperrin Mountains that the custom became almost an obsession. One hundred and fifty-six stone circles are recorded in the north of Ireland, 104 of them, 67 per cent, in pairs, threes, fours, fives, even up to nine, a multiplicity that developed into an obsession in Co. Tyrone. There was a kind of communal insanity in this profusion of paired and multiple rings such as the three pairs straddling tiny cairns at Beaghmore, a fashion that had become almost fanaticism in the central counties. There were no pairs or multiples in the eastern counties of Antrim, Down or Armagh. But there were many in Cos. Londonderry and Tyrone, increasing further south until the custom faded out in Co. Fermanagh to the west of Co. Tyrone where among 16 sites, there was only a single set of three rings at Montiaghroe.

There is a significant increase from north to south in the manner in which ring was added to ring as the coastlands were left behind and the mountains reached. There are only 15 known pairs and 13 of them are in Co. Tyrone miles away from the sea. There are 7 sets of three, 2 fours in Co. Londonderry and 3 in Co. Tyrone. In Co. Tyrone there are also 2 fives and 2 nines.

Co. Londonderry on the north coast has 26 of its thirty-six stone circles associated – 72 per cent; 2 pairs, 3 sets of three, fours at Ballybriest and Corick, five linked at Aughlish. The custom became even stronger in Co. Tyrone. Although only 61 per cent of its 89 rings were side by side the groups were larger in number, fours at Culvacullion, Doorat and Glassmullagh, fives at Broughderg and Tremoge, and, at Copney and Moymore, a bewildering nine, interlinked like discarded scraps of chainmail, shoulder to shoulder as though afraid of the dark.

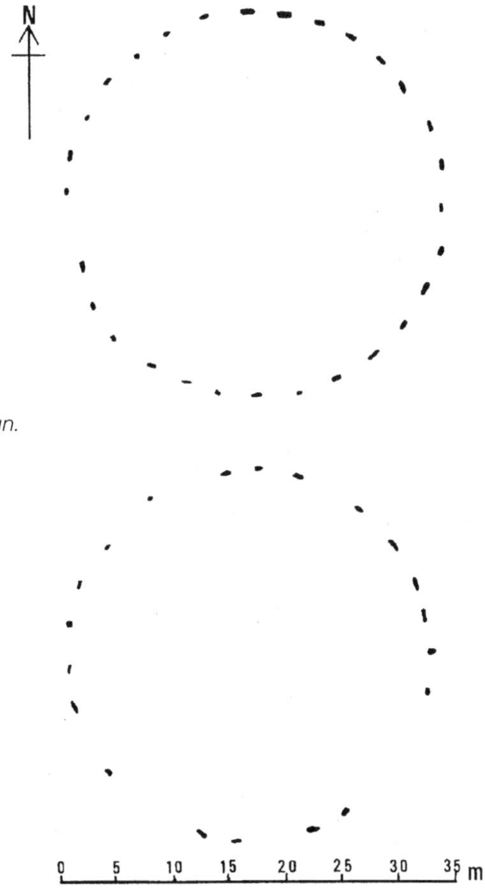

Fig 2: The Grey Wethers, Dartmoor. Plan.

In this statistical bewilderment any attempt to explain the reasons behind such a tradition of joining site to site must begin with an accepted definition of what should be accepted as a pair or a multiple congregation of rings. Rather than embracing haphazard collections, seemingly assembled without pattern or purpose, a pair or a more numerous cluster of rings should demonstrate a congruency implying an intention to form a coherent and well-designed complex. Here it is suggested that the adjacent rings should be approximately of the same size and shape and within about a diameter of each other. The two rings of the reconstructed Grey Wethers on Dartmoor would fit comfortably within this classification, both of them circular, the northern ring 32.7 m in diameter, its southern partner 32.9 m across and its arc only 4.6 m away from its partner (Fig 2).

Conversely, nowhere is a lack of cohesion in size and layout more obvious than at Stanton Drew near Bath where the north-east circle is 29.6 m in diameter, the central 114.6 m and the SSW ring 44.2 m. The spacing is grossly different with 43.3 m separating the north-east from the central circle, 137.7 m from the central to the SSW. The line is grotesquely bent. The orientation from the north-east to the central circle has an azimuth of 234° whereas that from the central to the SSW is 201°. Whatever the reasons for such a complex it cannot be accepted as a congruent site. Nor can Long Meg & Her Daughters near Penrith, the vast ellipse 109.4 m by 93 m some 200 m NNE of a 15 m probable circle seen by Stukeley but now demolished (Crawford, 1934).

The classification would also eliminate the Merry Maidens and Boleigh, 23.8 m and about 27 m across respectively, one circular, the other shape unknown, but probably 150 m apart. Rather than created as a true pair the two rings may more plausibly be interpreted as separate ritual centres erected at the edges of distinct territories.

Multiple sites, pairs, threes, even a projected four at the Priddy henges near Stanton Drew are a feature of south-western England and there has been much debate about the reason for these juxtapositions. Alexander Thom (1967, 94) speculated that the angle formed between the centres of such rings might have been arranged astronomically so that an observer in one circle would have his eyes directed towards another and then to a position of the sun or moon. The results were unimpressive, hardly surprising as virtually every centre was unmarked by anything so that a frustrated observer would have no exact place to stand nor a foresight to look to.

Nothing was found at Wendron, Thom's site no. S1/10. There was one improbable target and two unlikely dates of 1860 BC and 1800 BC at the Hurlers, S1/1, for the rising of the bright star Arcturus, α Boötis, an inaccurate alignment on the setting of the minor southern moon at the Grey Wethers, S2/1 (Fig 1), and a sightline at Avebury, S5/3, to the setting of Deneb, α Cygni, whose proposed declination of 36.5° occurred in the years around 2000 BC, eight centuries too late (Thom, 1967, 97–101; Hawkins, 1966, 41; Whittle, 1993).

Thom's results were equally inconclusive for the five rings on Burn Moor in the Lake District. From the largest, the isolated stone circle of Brats Hill, his site L1/6E, he proposed an alignment to the north-eastern ring of the Low Longrigg pair, L1/6A, 470 m to the NNW, and the setting of Arcturus, in 1900 BC. A similar sightline to Low Longrigg SW, L1 /6B, to the setting of the same star was dated to 1800 BC, implying the paired circles were built a century apart, as they may well have been. There was a possible orientation from Brats Hill to the northern ring of the White Moss pair, L1/6D, about 100 m to the north-west, towards Pollux, β Geminorum, setting in 1600 BC, and, in the opposite direction from White Moss South, L1/6C, to Brats Hill, to the rising of Antares, α Scorpii, in 1700 BC (Thom, 1967, 99). The range of dates from 1550 BC to 1300 BC are not improbable but the multiplicity of targets, which also included alignments to the Sun, the Moon and the meridian, suggest the activity of mistakenly optimistic astronomer-priests rather than the handiwork of pastoral families whose rain-sodden droveway, clearance cairns, field-systems and hut-platformed settlement can still be seen on the exposed plateau near Boar How (Burl, 1976, 93–6; 1995, 42).

If astronomical considerations were not the cause then it might be thought that only guesswork remains, unverifiable hypotheses of whether the rings of these complexes had different functions, one for men, the other for women, or for calendrical assemblies at different times of the year, or for ceremonies associated with birth and death, or for other even more arcane possibilities. Fortunately, a careful inspection of the sites diminishes the problems.

Very often the conjoined rings are of different diameters, 10.5 m and 13.3 m by 12.1 m at Temple Wood in the Kilmartin Valley of Argyll, 21 m and 16 m at Wendron. Their shapes vary, circular and oval both at King Arthur's Down and Tregeseal. Where there are three or more circles their centres do not lie in a straight line as could be expected had they been laid out together. At the Hurlers the centre of the SSW ring at the end of the 125 m long line lies 8 m to the east of the alignment. At the three henges at Thornborough in North Yorkshire, 'almost in a straight line', the middle earthwork is 32 m to the east of the line between the NNW and SSE enclosures (Clark, 1936, 51). At Priddy the centres of the three henges form a 475 m line from which the central henge deviates by 7.3 m to the west. Even more exaggeratedly the unfinished fourth henge is a full 67 m away from the line (Tratman, 1967, Plate 14).

From the accumulated data it may be concluded that rather than being contemporaries the assemblages were composites in which a desecrated or abandoned original had been replaced by a successor to permit more elaborate ceremonies. This sequence becomes obvious at the two Llandegai henges near Bangor in North Wales. A fire-pit near the middle of the north-east henge contained charcoal from which an assay of 2790±150 BC (NPL–220) was obtained. A cremation deposit outside the one entrance gave a determination of 2530±145 BC (NPL-2240), the two radiocarbon 'dates' converting into a bracket of about 3700–3050 BC in real years.

A dedicatory cremation pit outside the south-western of two entrances in the second henge 165 m to the south-west yielded a determination of 1790±145

BC (NPL-222), a range of some 2400–2000 BC in real years. At their very closest, subtracting 145 years from 2530 BC and adding 145 years to 1790 BC, the narrowest range of 2385 BC to 1935 BC being the equivalent of 3050 BC and 2450 BC, the second henge had to be at least six centuries later than the first (Houlder, 1967; 1968).

It seems that most multiple sites are accretions that developed over many years, the original site abandoned or rejected because of blasphemous misuse or a belief that it had lost its power, or sometimes simply added to when more enclosures were needed. Such a development appears likely inside Avebury when a third circle was begun to the north of the existing two, only for two or three of the initial stones to be uprooted when the great defensive ditch and bank were constructed (Burl, 1979, 151, 163–4).

The limited number of excavations are in agreement with this belief that many rings were additions to existing sites, particularly towards the end of the second millennium BC. It is rare for early material to be recovered. Neolithic bowls from Beaghmore, Co. Tyrone are greatly outnumbered by Bronze Age urns at Broomrigg Common and Moor Divock in Cumbria, Gortcorbies, Co. Londonderry, Broomend of Crichie, Aberdeenshire, Machrie Moor, Arran, and Lundin Farm South, Perthshire; by food-vessels at Moor Divock, Gortcorbies and Machrie Moor; and by developed beakers at Broomend of Crichie, Lundin Farm and Ffridd Newydd, Gwynedd.

The impression that many of the paired and multiple sites were aggregates that developed in the later history of stone circles is confirmed by the radiocarbon assays obtained from them. The complex of distorted rings at Beaghmore in Co. Tyrone were excavated between 1945-9. What evidence was there suggested that they had been constructed between 1605±45 BC (UB-23), 1535±55 BC (UB-11), and 775±55 BC (UB-163), a calibrated bracket of about 2000 to 875 BC, with a date later in that period more likely.

Although a seemingly Neolithic determination came from the 1979-80 excavations at the site of Temple Wood North in the Kilmartin Valley of Argyll 3075±190 BC (GU-1296) this related to what may have been a preceding timber structure. Much later assays came from the adjacent and indisputable stone circle of Temple Wood South. Ten C-14 'dates' ranging from 1275±105 BC (GU-1300) to 857±50 BC (SRR-530), averaged 1040±106 BC, the calibrated equivalents of approximately 1400–1150 BC.

Similarly late dates came from the 5-stone circle of Cashelkeelty West in Co. Kerry investigated by Ann Lynch in 1977: 970±60 BC (GrN-9173) and 715±50 BC (GrN-9172), c.1300 to 850 BC; and from Sandy Road West, Scone, Perthshire,

Fig 3: The modern concrete marker where the Obelisk stood. Three low sarsens of the Z Stones can be seen to its right.

excavated by Margaret Stewart in 1961: 1200±150 BC (GaK-787), between 1650 and 1300 BC. Making the crudest statistical average of these corrected dates it would appear that the floruit of many of these multi-phase complexes was around 1322 BC at the very end of the Middle Bronze Age at a time when the stone circle tradition was in decline.

Activities inside them tell us little of their users. Fires and burning inside the Grey Wethers – antlers, animal bones, a human skull, and at the unusual ring of Gortcorbies, flints, charcoal, animal bones, in a 'ceremony of consecration'.

The amassed evidence suggests that there were very few genuinely contemporaneous pairs or multiples in which the adjacent rings were constructed at one time as a unit. Two widely separated regions may contain some. In south-western England there are the Grey Wethers, the pairs on Bodmin Moor at King Arthur's Down, Leaze and Leskernick, and Wendron further south.

There are others, hundreds of miles to the north, such as Tullybeagles in Perthshire. There were similar almost identical pairs in the county, the one survivor at Sandy Road, Scone, dated to about 1500 BC in keeping with the belief that most of these pluralities were raised towards the end of the stone circle tradition. This is certainly feasible for the oddities in Northern Ireland. Also on the hillsides of Perthshire are the coupled rings of Blackfaulds, the two 4-Posters of Blair Atholl, Broad Moss, the strange Fortingall variant 4-Posters, and Shianbank. The rings in these pairings almost duplicate each other in shape and size and nudge together like handcuffs. Sadly, despite prolonged searching, the key remains undiscovered.

Speculatively, Avebury may provide a partial answer. One possibility, and by no means an exclusive one, is that more than one ring was required there for the protracted funerary metaphors of the rites of passage between the death of an individual and its final interment, one circle for its allegorical 'burial', another for ceremonies of purification performed in a symbolic forecourt by the mourners. It is a suggestion that might be appropriate for the transitional 'Dark Age' between the abandonment of chambered tombs in the centuries around 3500 BC and the development of stone circles many generations later.

It has been argued that although the collective sepulchres-cum-temples like West Kennet and the nearby Devil's Den were no longer in use the rituals once enacted outside their entrances continued at the novel representations of their chambers known as coves. At Avebury there were at least two of these unroofed, three-sided settings of colossal slabs, one to the south-west at Beckhampton, later incorporated in an avenue, the other a mile to the north-east, free-standing, inside a Late Neolithic unenclosed settlement. Such coves were sometimes later surrounded by a stone circle like those at Arbor Low, Cairnpapple and Stenness (Burl, 1988).

By 2800 BC the north-eastern cove at Avebury also had standing stones put up around it although whether they formed a circle about 98 m across or a vast megalithic horseshoe of Breton fashion 70 m deep with an open mouth 105 m wide is still unclear. A few metres away was the northern arc of a great stone circle 102 m in diameter. At its centre was a heavy and high pillar, Stukeley's 'Obelisk', now destroyed and replaced by a hideous concrete marker. In its situation the stone was akin to the anthropomorphic menhirs and stelae, female guardians of the dead, armed with axe or dagger, that are common inside many of the dolmens *à couloir* and *allées-couvertes* of Brittany. They are redolent of death.

Around the Obelisk was a probable rectangle of lower sarsens, stones i-xii, that Isobel Smith has felicitously likened to the uncovered kerbs of a chambered tomb (Fig 3). 'The whole plan would resemble that of a long barrow with a forecourt marked out by a symbolic peristalith of small standing stones. The Obelisk, as a symbol of fertility, would have occupied the place of burials in an actual tomb' (Smith, 1965, 250–1; Burl, 1979, 184–5, Z Stones).

Everything was imagistic. These were realities of the prehistoric mind in analogies alien to modern thinking, where the figurative had more significance than the mundane. One might imagine, for it is all beyond proof, funerary processions from the symbolic mortuary house of the Sanctuary stone circle whose timber mortuary house had rotted long before, carrying the dead along the Kennet Avenue, laying the corpse by the Obelisk, symbol of the weapon-bearing protectress, inside the symbol of a stone-built tomb, before the cortège passed to the symbol of the forecourt at the cove in the adjacent stone circle. It was the transit from corruption in one circle to the passage of the spirit in the other. Only after prolonged rites was the body or bones taken to the place of the round barrow whose mound was to be silhouetted against the skyline of the Ridgeway to the east.

It must instantly be stressed that Avebury is a singular exception. Because of its 'anthropomorphic' Obelisk, its kerbed 'long barrow', its 'megalithic chamber' of the cove, it is permissible to theorise about the funerary associations of the two circles – as long as it is understood that it is plausible theory but not certainty.

There are few parallels to Avebury. Most linked rings are plain, unastronomical, unexcavated, so that to ask why there is more than one circle is to listen to silence. Imagination wanders in hope but not expectation. Were the rings for midsummer and midwinter ceremonies, for male and female, for adolescents and puberty, for natives and strangers, for trade and ritual, for matters unconsidered? It is all speculation, perhaps all an illusion. The archaeological past is an illusion in itself but in itself a fascinating link between today and yesterday. Over three hundred years ago Sir Thomas Browne understood:

> *When the Funeral pyre was out, and the last valediction over, men took a lasting adieu of their interred friends, little expecting the curiosity of future ages should comment upon their ashes... Nor were they confused or careless in disposing of the noblest sort, while they placed large stones in circles about the Urnes or bodies which they interred.*

Sir Thomas Browne, *Hydriotaphia,* or *Urn-Burial*, 1658, 92, 110 (London, 1937).

References

Barnatt, J., 1982, *Prehistoric Cornwall. The Ceremonial Monuments*, Wellingborough.

Burl, A., 1976, *The Stone Circles of the British Isles*, London.

Burl, A., 1979, *Prehistoric Avebury*, London.

Burl, A., 1988, 'Coves: structural enigmas of the Neolithic', *WAM* 82, 1–18.

Burl, A., 1995, *A Guide to the Stone Circles of Britain, Ireland and Brittany*, London.

Clark, J.G.D., 1936, 'The timber monument at Arminghall and its affinities', *PPS* 2, 1–51.

Crawford, O.G.S., 1934, 'Long Meg', *Antiquity* 8, 328–9, Fig 1.

Hawkins, G.S., 1966, *Astro-Archaeology. Smithsonian Special Report no. 226*, Cambridge, Massachusetts.

Houlder, C., 1967, 'The henge monuments at Llandegai', *Antiquity* 41, 58–60.

Lockyer, Sir, N, 1906, *Stonehenge and Other British Stone Monuments Astronomically Considered*, London.

Smith, I.F., 1965, *Windmill Hill & Avebury. Excavations by Alexander Keiller, 1925–1939*, Oxford.

Straffon, C., 1992, *The Earth Mysteries Guide to Ancient Sites in West Penwith*, St. Just.

Thom, A., 1967, *Megalithic Sites in Britain*, Oxford.

Tratman, E.K., 1967, 'The Priddy circles, Mendips, Somerset, henge monuments', *PUBSS* 11 (2), 97–125.

Whittle, A.W.R., 1993, 'The Neolithic of the Avebury area: sequence, environment, settlement and monuments', *Oxford J. Archaeology 12 (1)*, 29–53.

Productive excavations of paired and multiple rings

Cornwall Hurlers. Excavated 1936. Flints.

Cumberland Broomrigg Common. Excavated 1950. Urn, jet beads, bronze, cremations.

Devon Grey Wethers. Excavated 1891, 1898. Fires and burning.

Westmorland Iron Hill. Excavated pre-1861. Antler, animal bone.

Westmorland Moor Divock. Excavated c.1860, urn. Excavated 1866. Food-vessel.

Co. Kerry Cashelkeelry W. Excavated 1977. Flint scraper. 970±60 BC (GrN-9173); 715± 50 BC (GrN-9172).

Co. Londonderry Gortcorbies NE. Excavated 1945. Flint, charcoal, animal bones, 'ceremony of consecration'.

Co. Londonderry SW. 1945. Urn, Food-vessel.

Co. Tyrone Beaghmore. Excavated 1945-9. Porcellanite axe, Neolithic bowls, cremations. Complex dated between 1605±45 BC (UB-23), 1535±55 BC (UB-11), 775±55 BC (UB-163).

Co. Tyrone Clogherny Butterlope West. Excavated 1937. Pits.

Aberdeen Broomend of Crichie South. Excavated 1855. Urns, axe-hammer, N2, N3, indeterminate beakers.

Aberdeen Colpy A. Excavated pre-1845. Several urns.

Argyll Temple Wood North. Excavated 1979-80. 3075±190 BC (GU-1296). Timber structure.

Argyll South. Excavated 1928, 1929-30, 1974-80. N3 beaker, barbed-and-tanged flint arrowheads, flint scraper. 10 x C-14 from 1275±105 BC (GU-1300) to 857±50 BC (SRR-530), averaging 1040±106 BC, =c.1400-1150 BC.

Arran Machrie Moor I - V. Excavated 1858, nil. 1861. 3 x food-vessels, flint arrowheads, skull.

Arran XI Excavated 1979-80, 1985-6. 2130±90 BC (GU-2324), 2520±50 BC (GU-2316), 2030±180 BC (GU-2325), timber ring. Stone circle, bipartite urn, flints, cremation.

Perth Carse Farm North. Excavated 1964. Urn, cremation.

Perth Lundin Farm SE. 4-Poster. Excavated 1962. Cremations, urn, AOC beaker.

Perth Sandy Road W. Excavated 1961. Flat-rimmed ware. 1200±150 BC (GaK-787).

Gwynedd Ffridd Newydd. Excavated 1919. 2 x FP beakers.

Margaret Murray and the Rise of Wicca

Dr Juliette Wood

One does not ordinarily associate a learned society with the emergence of a new system of belief. Thus it is all the more astonishing that a book published by an Egyptologist with an interest in folklore at the beginning of the 1920s should be the ultimate source for Wicca, the most influential movement in the revival of modern witchcraft. Dr Juliette Wood, former president of The Folklore Society, reviews the influence of this controversial figure.

Margaret Murray, the Egyptologist in question, is undoubtedly best known for her work on the history of witchcraft. Born in India, she trained as an Egyptologist after her return to Britain and worked at University College London where she was one of Flinders Petrie's most loyal students and supporters. Her work on witchcraft dates from the latter part of her long life. Although she had published articles on the subject in various learned journals, her first book, *The Witch Cult in Western Europe*, only appeared in 1921. It did not have much of an impact until it was reprinted first in 1952 and later appeared in paperback in 1962. Murray claimed that witchcraft was actually 'an old religion' based on the natural cycle of vegetation. The rituals of this religion were dominated by a horned hunting god and his consort, and the religion had been practised in Europe during the Palaeolithic and Neolithic periods. According to Murray's book, the Christian Church persecuted the practitioners of the cult as witches. Nevertheless, the cult survived and could still be found in certain folk practices associated with the changing seasons.

She expanded this idea in subsequent articles and in two further books, namely *The God of the Witches* (1933) and *The Divine King* (1955). Her work was an important, perhaps the most important, influence on the rise of the modern Wicca movement in the 1950s, although many of its practitioners today are at pains to point out that their doctrines are not dependent on Murray.

Fig 1: A 1517 depiction of witches preparing potions by Hans Weiditz.

Murray was president of the Folklore Society just before her death in the 1960s and had been an active member for some years previously. Many members of the Society remembered her fondly, and she was especially keen to encourage younger researchers, even those who disagreed with her ideas. Her ideas, however, have become something of an embarrassment to professional folklorists, embodying as they do the somewhat reductionist assumptions associated with 19th century evolutionary theories which were even by Murray's time outdated in relation to academic folklore studies. Yet even today, this quaint, 19th century approach which sees 'survivals' in every custom and uses 'folk memory' to justify tenuous links between past and current practices, characterises the popular image of what folklore is.

The topic of Murray and her relation to folklore studies was reopened recently by another president of the Society who emphasised Murray's very selective use of material in creating her appealingly romantic, although historically untenable, 'old religion'. Yet even at its first appearance, there was some scholarly dismay at Murray's now famous thesis that witchcraft originated as an ancient fertility cult. Several historians and anthropologists noted that she gave undue weight to this hypothesis and failed to consider that witchcraft might be described within the wider context of sympathetic magic with the fertility elements as a secondary feature.

While the somewhat racy and anti-religious content of *The Witch Cult* caused controversy at the time, it was greeted enthusiastically by the editors of *The Occult Review*. The aspect of Murray's work which appealed particularly to the occult movement was her conviction that the witch cult was a 'secret tradition' which survived despite attempts to suppress it. This kind of thinking was very popular among occultists at the period, and *The Occult Review* carried articles throughout the 1920s and 30s on so-called 'secret traditions'. The journal undoubtedly provided a degree of popularisation for Murray's work, since the original publication sold rather slowly. However, the re-publication of her book in 1952 occurred in an entirely different climate. By that time the witchcraft laws had been repealed and Murray's work had already had an influence on what was to become the modern neo-pagan movement, led by another member of the Folklore Society, Dr Gerald Gardner. In 1954 Murray wrote a preface to his book, and there is even a suggestion that she herself was a witch, a claim she vigorously denied in a letter to a colleague.

However, Murray never made any secret of her antagonism to organised religion. In this and all subsequent books on witchcraft she sympathised with the practitioners of this ancient fertility cult whom she felt were victims of bigotry. It is all too easy to let this kind of controversy get out of proportion. Modern scholars have objected to Murray's ideas on academic, not religious or sexual grounds. A fundamental problem with Murray's work is her exclusive focus on witchcraft as an ancient fertility cult, and her tendency to generalise wildly on the basis of very slender evidence. The consensus today, with the notable exception of a few neo-pagan writers, is that this picture of a benign nature/fertility cult is a construct rather than a record of history. This suggestion that the study of witchcraft might be more fruitfully linked to sympathetic magic rather than to fertility cults has been echoed in recent reassessments of her work. Attitudes range from Norman Cohn's critique which rejected Murray's evidence totally, to the more sympathetic stance of Carlo Ginzburg whose analysis of a local group of 'witch hunters' led him to see some continuity of early religious forms. However, Ginzburg does not propose anything approaching the pan-European cult which Murray advocated.

Murray's autobiography, written as she approached her hundredth birthday, reveals a mind clear and sharp. She rejected utterly the suggestion that she was a witch herself. What then were the elements which constitute her theories about the nature and origins of witchcraft?

Murray's own ideas about the origin of witchcraft were formed in the decades before 1921 when her first book was published. She had lectured on, or published, substantial portions of her first book in *Folklore* and the anthropological journal, *Man*, before then and had covered key themes, such as the number thirteen, child sacrifice, animal transformation, the devil's mark, the witch coven and the familiar, which figure prominently in her subsequent books. The most obvious source for her approach lies in the theories of cultural evolution so important to 19th and early 20th century thinking, especially in the newly developing social sciences.

Cultural evolution is much talked about among scholars who study the history of ideas, and the Folklore Society was an important arena for discussion among leading cultural scholars such as Edward Tylor and Andrew Lang. But 'cultural evolution' was never a monolithic theory, and there were several strands, each with their supporters and detractors. The early issues of the new journal, *Folklore*, and the venerable journal, *The Athenaeum*, played host to several lively debates on whether characteristics of 'primitive culture' were universal, and stemmed from a psychic unity among mankind, or whether diffusion played some role in this model.

Murray's theory incorporated elements from both sides of this argument, and a great deal else besides. Basic to Murray's thinking was the idea of the 'divine king'. Her early studies in Egyptian archaeology indicate that Murray was much influenced by Frazer's concept of the dying god. The theory is centred on Frazer's reading of classical texts in which he identified several metaphors having to do with the death and resurrection of divine and semi-divine figures which seemed linked to the cycle of the seasons. These he interpreted in terms of an all-embracing primitive ritual aimed at ensuring the continuance of fertility which, through the actions of significant individuals such as priests, kings and eventually their substitutes, propitiated certain natural forces. Frazer's rationalist stance saw primitive man as a kind of proto-rationalist who, lacking an understanding of science, attempted to control the forces of nature by means of rituals in which sympathetic magic functioned as a kind of substitute for scientific principles of cause and effect. Murray believed Frazer to be antagonistic to her ideas and thought he was behind a negative review in the *Scotsman* when her book first appeared, but their methods had much in common. Both proceeded from the study of documents, in Frazer's case; classical texts, in Murray's; the records of medieval and early modern witchcraft. Significant elements from these documents were selected out and projected backward in time onto the 'mind' of primitive man. Both shared a mistrust of organised religion. However, Frazer eventually included the Christian resurrection story among his examples of the dying god myth, while Murray maintained a distinction between her witch cult and Christianity.

Another important influence on Murray's thinking was her great friend and colleague in the Folklore Society, the religious historian E.O. James, editor of *Folklore* from 1932-58. His theories about the mother goddess use the same kinds of arguments as Murray's, and his book on *The Cult of the Mother Goddess* is in many ways a companion piece to hers in its use of a Frazerian model moderated by myth-ritual assumptions. James' attitude to the relation between myth and ritual was closer to a group of Cambridge-based classicists usually referred to as the 'Myth-ritual School'. For James, as for Frazer, ritual was concerned with the promotion of social fertility which, in the mind of primitive man, could directly affect the operation of nature. Like Frazer, James' theories developed from reading texts. However, for scholars associated with the myth-ritual school, these texts included not just classical ones, but those from the ancient Near East. In effect, although divine kingship and renewing rituals based on the agricultural cycles still remained central, the myth-ritual approach was essentially a diffusionist position centring on the cultures of the eastern Mediterranean. This was a significant refinement of other cultural evolution theories, notably those of Frazer and Tylor who assumed a psychic unity in mankind and a universal process of culture evolution. Scholars who adopted the myth-ritual approach used terms such as 'adaptation', 'disintegration' and 'degradation'. As a result, the idea of cultural evolution became less one directional and less progressive, while the idea of a primary pattern became stronger. Myth and ritual however remained the product of the needs of an agricultural world, and the 'pattern' involved elements of dying god, divine marriage and the rebirth of vegetation re-enacted in a great annual festival. Murray's theories apparently presented substantive evidence for this. Here was an actual (pre)historical context – Neolithic religion in Europe – whose rituals were dependent on the agricultural seasons and centred around dying and resurrection linked to the vegetative cycle. The supposed survival of these rituals, misunderstood and persecuted as witchcraft, presented a dramatic and profound change to the concept of cultural evolution. The Frazerian myth of the dying god and the myth/ritualist Near Eastern religion were always academic constructs, but Murray's witch cult seemed to make them real and living.

While the idea of cultural evolution provided a theoretical context for Murray's work, there were a number of specific influences as well. The historian Ronald Hutton has recently pointed out similarities between Murray's characterisation of

Fig 2: The Dorset Ooser (replica)
© Raymond Buckland/Fortean Picture Library.

the witch cult and the concept of *la Vecchia religione* in Charles Leland's *Aradia: Gospel of the Witches.*

Leland's somewhat dubious identification of a supposed witch cult in medieval Italy appeared in the 1890s. Theories about the survival of ancient civilisations were becoming increasing popular during the 19th century, and the idea that earlier races survived in later culture under the guise of fairies or witches had been suggested by anthropologists and folklorists (for example Lawrence Gomme, A.R. Wright, and David MacRitchie) working at the end of the 19th century. It is not always possible to say with certainty how much of this was 'in the air' at the time and how much was the direct result of Murray's reading.

Murray gave few hints in her autobiography about the sources of her work. She spent some time in Glastonbury in 1915 recuperating from an illness. Here she became interested in the Holy Grail and probably came across an article on the Dorset Ooser (a mask used in a seasonal celebration, see photograph). She stated that a chance remark from someone, whom she claimed not to recall, that witches had their own religion sparked her interest in witchcraft. She began to work 'only from contemporary records' and 'had the sort of experience that sometimes comes to a researcher', namely that the Devil figure was a disguised man, not a demon. This 'startled, almost alarmed her', and indicated that witches were members of an old and primitive form of religion. Murray believed her witchcraft research, which she characterised as 'the interpretation of beliefs and ceremonies of certain ancient forms of religion', to be her most important work. Her assertion that she forgot who started her on this important endeavour is a little suspect for a woman who paid great attention to detail and had an excellent memory. The whole passage betrays the heightened dramatic tension of autobiographical discourse, and there are in fact several studies which anticipate Murray's ideas very closely indeed.

For example, the great statistician and polymath, Professor Karl Pearson, was Professor of applied mathematics at University College, and a colleague of Murray's. Pearson was interested in eugenics and social reform and this led him to speculate, as did so many fine minds of the day, on the nature of society. His essay 'Woman as Witch: Evidence of Mother-right in the Customs of Mediaeval Witchcraft' appeared in 1897 and drew heavily on Erich Neumann's concept of 'mother-right' (i.e. matriarchy) and on the work of the French historian, Jules Michelet.

Pearson's essay anticipates substantial themes which appear later in Murray. It treated the customs of medieval witchcraft as fossils of the 'old mother age' of prehistoric civilisation. Besides witchcraft, such fossils were to be found in the folklore of agricultural, spring and harvest festivals and peasant dances (all of which were of particular interest to Murray). Both witch gatherings and peasant ceremonies were 'relics' of ancient rites. What Christianity repressed became witchcraft; what it tolerated became associated with seasonal folk festivals. The characteristic features of witch gatherings included a communal feast, a choral dance and a sacrifice under a sacred tree. Since inheritance during the period of 'mother-right' was through the female, it followed that the deities and the presiding spirit of witchcraft were undoubtedly female. Pearson suggested (following Michelet) that originally the male deity had been subservient to the female one. Later however, the male deity became prominent and eventually became the 'devil' of the witch trials. Pearson's attitude to Joan of Arc was also close to Michelet. Both suggested that she was a white witch or folk healer, and

Fig 3: Von den Unholden oder Hexen, 1489, Ulrich Molitor.

the figure of Joan is important in Murray's most extreme book on the witch cult, *The Divine King*.

At the centre of Murray's witch cult was a male deity. The Diana of the historical documents (and of Leland's *Aradia*) becomes a male deity called Dianus (Janus Dionysius) by a philological sleight of hand and, no doubt, also influenced by the literary cult of Pan popular in the Edwardian period. In literature Pan became a symbol of duality, of savage sexual release, of a life of wildness opposed to the strictures of civilisation. Nietzsche defined Pan as primary emotion to challenge Apollonian authority. Here too Murray apparently provided anthropological validation for such a cult and created the possibility for joyous sensual worship sanctioned by ancient religion.

Other scholars also examined this idea of surviving religious cults. Jessie Weston, a noted Arthurian specialist, suggested that coded in the Grail narratives were records of secret societies and rites which had to be kept hidden from prevailing Christian orthodoxy and that these secret rituals were related to mystery religions that involved sacred kingship and sexual initiations of the type described in Frazer's *Golden Bough*. Although Murray never took up the occult angle, she was interested in the same themes and images. In effect, she turned the vegetation myth into a mystery religion which was not merely a fragmentary survival but a living entity. The implications of this were worked out by the modern neo-pagan movement, whose newly revived rituals were given authenticating force via Murray's theories.

The repeal of the witchcraft laws in the 1950s was a significant factor in Murray's popularity. She herself admitted that her second book, *The God of the Witches*, published in 1933, was a failure. However, in 1952 the re-published *Witch cult* sold much better. Gerald Gardner, another figure involved in the witchcraft revival who also had contacts with the Folklore Society and direct contact with Murray, also benefited from the repeal of the Witchcraft Act. Murray's work certainly appealed to the modern Wicca movement. The relationship between the two is somewhat contentious, with academic opinion suggesting Wicca's dependence on Murray as a basis for constructing both their rituals and their history, although Wicca writers, in particular Gardner, claimed their sources antedated Murray.

Vivianne Crowley, an important exponent of modern Wicca, acknowledges Murray's importance, but defends the prior existence of the ancient witch cult. The chapter on the Witch God in her 1989 book *Wicca: The Old Religion in the New Age* follows Murray's argument and use of material, starting with the Palaeolithic cave drawing known as 'the shaman' in the cave of Trois-Frères. Murray wrote an enthusiastic note about this figure and used the illustration in her books. In the first edition of Crowley's account, Murray is mentioned four times; twice in connection with the sacrifice of kings, once in connection with initiation rituals, and once in a discussion of the predecessors of the Wicca movement, in which she is given pride of place. In the revised and updated edition, Murray is less prominent. Crowley still acknowledges her contribution but treats her as one among several early writers on the ancient cult. The revised edition stresses Murray's testimony to Gardner, omits reference to the self-sacrifice of English kings (presumably since this later phase of Murray's ideas on the subject were getting increasingly far-fetched), mentions Frazer only (i.e. omits the earlier reference to Murray) in connection with ritual king murders.

Indeed, Crowley has a point. Murray was not the first to suggest the existence of a vegetation cult and the links to witches, but she did take the elements and forge a new and exciting synthesis on which she wrote several readable books and publicised in her many talks. The fact that Murray was not the first to mention witchcraft as a survival of an earlier cultural practice does not really strengthen the argument that it is in reality an ancient religion.

Many historians of witchcraft suggest that it was Murray's failure to use the newly available records of witchcraft which account for some at least of the problems with her theories. Indeed, although she was insistent that she consulted the original documents, these were mostly already in print, and always mined for the information which she expected to find there. Much the same can be said of the 'fieldwork' which supported her findings. Murray's correspondents were primarily other educated individuals, often connected with local parishes or councils. She asked specific questions to which she received specific answers which she took as further substantiation of her assumptions. This is painfully clear in the papers relating to the Puck Fair. Some of the information actually contradicted her assumptions, but she simply rearranged it to suit her ideas. One must add in her defence that this was typical procedure at the time. Collecting meant finding a 'good' informant who would have access to more popular sources. Murray was one of many educated men and women collecting material from servants, employees and rural workers within a parish context, or encountered on a holiday to some 'exotic' locale within Great Britain.

In theoretical terms Murray's stance was a particular variant of the myth-ritual approach. She historicised the 'dying god' myth as a vegetation cult practised during a particular period of primitive European time. No matter how sympathetically one wishes to look at this charmingly eclectic scholar, folklorists and historians will (quite rightly) continue to point out the mismatch between Murray's construct and what can be read into her sources. However indebted it is to Murray's theory, modern Wicca has certainly gone its own way. Broader-based, more popular, more influenced by feminine principles and increasingly confident as a cult, it is less dependent on arguments about continuity from an ancient period and on the reality or lack thereof in Murray's thinking. Certainly, the movement differs in many respects from the witchcraft cults of the 1960s and its current concerns are linked to ecological thinking and feminism. The latter would certainly have pleased Murray as she was herself involved in the suffragette movement, and her belief in the freedom of expression, especially for women, was a positive force in her own life.

References

Boardman, John, 1997, *The Great God Pan: The Survival of an Image*, London.

Burnett, David, 1991, *Dawning of the Pagan Moon, An investigation into the rise of Western Paganism*, Eastbourne.

Cohn, Norman, 1976, *Europe's Inner Demons*, St Albans.

Crowley, Vivianne, 1989 Revised and updated Thorsens 1996, *Wicca: The Old Religion in the New Age,* Wellingborough.

Frazer, James, Abridged version 1922, new ed. 1993, *The Golden Bough*, Wordsworth.

Gardner, G.B., 1954, *Witchcraft Today*, London.

Ginzburg, Carlo, 1983, *The Night Battles: Witchcraft and the Agrarian Cults in the Sixteenth and Seventeenth Centuries*, London.

Hutton, Ronald, 1991, *Pagan Religions of the Ancient British Isles*, Blackwell.

Hutton, Ronald, 1996, *The Stations of the Sun*, Oxford.

Leland, C.G., 1899, *Aradia or Gospel of the Witches*, London.

Luhrmann, Tanya, 1989, *Persuasions of the Witches' Craft*, Oxford.

Murray, Margaret, 1963, *My First Hundred Years,* William Kimber.

Michelet, Jules, 1958, *Satanism and Witchcraft*, New York.

Pearson, Karl, 1897, *The Chances of Death and Other Studies in Evolution*, 2 vols., Edward Arnold.

Simpson, Jacqueline, 1994, 'Margaret Murray, Who Believed Her and Why' Presidential Address of 1992, *Folklore* 105:89–96.

Fig 4: The Puck Fair at Killorglin (Co. Kerry), water-colour attributed to Margaret Murray, 1952 © The Folklore Society.

2025 Endnote

Since this article appeared, Margaret Murray and her ideas have been the subject of further scholarship and, in the context of the increased interest in neo-pagan movements, her life and her theories have become a popular topic on internet blogs. Her role as an Egyptologist and lecturer at University College London has been recognised in the context of her association with her colleague and mentor, Sir William Flinders Petrie, but her influence as a pioneering woman archaeologist who undertook extensive fieldwork not just in Egypt but at Petra, Malta, Minorca, and several other sites has recently been explored in greater depth, as has her involvement in the suffragist movement (Sheppard, 2013). Murray wrote books on Egyptian grammar and culture, and she published articles on many aspects of these subjects. Nevertheless, the material that has drawn the most interest are her books on the existence of a witch cult which she published as an independent researcher in folklore. Several prominent scholars of the history of witchcraft, notably Ronald Hutton, Ethan Doyle White and Marion Gibson, have explored the influence of her work, both direct and indirect, on contemporary neo-pagan movements.

Murray's first book on witchcraft appeared in 1921, the result of reading and research combined with her experiences during her stay in Glastonbury during the First World War. After its publication, which was not without controversy, she joined the Folklore Society and remained a member for many years. Many of her contemporaries in the Society remembered her fondly, and a collection of notes and correspondence concerning beliefs about witches, fairies and other legendary figures are held in the Folklore Society Archives (Oates and Wood 1996). Although comparatively little of Murray's output was published in *Folklore*, her account of the Puck Fair at Killorglin (Co. Kerry), illustrates her methods of collection and interpretation (Murray, 1953). Local participants denied any pre-Christian element and insisted that the goat was not sacrificed, but in Murray's opinion the 'rustic' festival reflected Pierre de Lancre's description of the Witches Sabbath in the famous Basque witch trials. The idea that early modern witches were the followers of a secret religion became popular during the 1960s, aided in part by the rise of gothic literature and folk horror film. Folklorists and historians reacted to the appearance of Murray's 'witch cult' theory in various ways, and lively discussions about the origins of contemporary pagan witchcraft continue to this day.

Oates, Caroline and Juliette Wood, 1998, *A Coven of Scholars: Margaret Murray and her Working Methods*, London: The Folklore Society.

Sheppard, Kathleen L., 2013, *The Life of Margaret Alice Murray; A Woman's Work in Archaeology,* Rowan and Littlefield.

Hutton, Ronald 'Paganism and Polemic: The Debate over the Origins of Modern Pagan Witchcraft', *Folklore*, Vol. 111, No. 1 (Apr., 2000), 103–117.

White, Ethan Doyle 'Devil's Stones and Midnight Rites: Megaliths, Folklore, and Contemporary Pagan Witchcraft', *Folklore*, Vol. 125, No. 1 (April 2014), 60–79.

Murray, M.A. 'The Puck Fair of Killorglin', *Folklore*, Vol. 64, No. 2 (Jun., 1953), 351–354.

Blót on the Landscape: Re-reading Gregory's Letter on the Heathen Temples

Jeremy Harte

Pope Gregory's letter written to abbot Mellitus in the year 601 is often cited as evidence for the widespread Christianisation of pagan British monuments. Jeremy Harte examines this famous text and looks at its influence on modern notions of site continuity.

People are fascinated by the pagan origins of the English church. I remember a television series on the subject which began, for some reason, among the stones at Castlerigg. Dark, ominous chords – suggestive of heathen goings-on – were succeeded on the soundtrack by melodious chanting as a party of monks climbed up the hill. This was followed by a short period in which the camera waved about violently, presumably to indicate that important historical events were taking place, and when it finally settled down again, the stone circle contained a polystyrene model of the Ruthwell cross.

Clearly site continuity can mean different things to different people. It embraces things as diverse as Egyptian hermits squatting in rock-cut tombs, popes fitting crosses onto the obelisks in Roman plazas, and English country vicars giving churchyard burial to the people whom they had disinterred from barrows (Grinsell

1986). Only recently has attention moved from the general concept of continuity, or re-use, to the different social contexts within which it has occurred. And there is nothing to show what leaders of the Church thought of this process – nothing, that is, apart from Pope Gregory's letter to abbot Mellitus. This celebrated text has been employed many times by writers struggling to clarify their thoughts on Christianity and paganism. It is easy to forget that it represents the views of one man, in a particular historical situation.

Gregory dictated his correspondence. A secretary sat on a folding stool, taking the words down in shorthand; from the rooms beyond there came an echo of scratching pens as the papal clerks wrote the letters out in full. After finishing the fair copy and sealing it for dispatch, they prepared a file copy for the Vatican archives. At the end of the year, these were bound up into a single codex, which is how come the letter with which we are concerned found its way into volume 11 of the Register, covering the year 601. Only a fraction of Gregory's correspondence survives. The letter to Mellitus – or to Augustine, for Mellitus was only acting as a messenger – is the 56th surviving entry for that year, and it will be convenient to refer to it as letter 56.

Most of the letters in the Register are replies to queries from other correspondents. This one is unusual. It represents the pope's own dictation, rather than the standard wording of the papal scrinium. It was initiated by him after he had given long thought to Augustine's mission in England: *diu de causa Anglorum cogitans*. Uniquely, it was forwarded by special messenger (Markus 1997: 183). Whatever Gregory had to say, he clearly thought it was important.

Once the fair copy had been sealed, it was handed to a servant who rode down to the port at Ostia and took ship for southern Gaul. Four weeks earlier, Mellitus had followed the same route with his companions. This party had been laden down with chests containing chalices and patens, vestments, altar frontals and relics – all the equipment needed to re-establish church worship in Britain (Bede I: 29). The original instructions had been to construct new buildings for worship, but letter 56 changes all this to allow the altars and relics to be placed in converted pagan structures – *altaria construantur, reliquiae ponantur.* Together with the precious gospels and lectionaries, Mellitus also carried a sheaf of 24 letters, all dated 22nd June. The clerks of the *scrinium* had been hard at work. He was to hand these over in a dozen towns throughout Gaul, as well as seeking out the Frankish nobility who were underwriting the English project with their political support. It would be a long process, allowing plenty of time for the messenger to catch up with this final letter.

Mellitus' journey retraced the route followed by Augustine four years earlier. The original missionary party had sailed from Rome to the neighbourhood of Marseilles, stopping off for spiritual refreshment at the island monastery of Lérins (Dudden 1905: 2.105). There they would have seen the tomb of Honoratus, who had founded the site two centuries earlier, when it was a wilderness of snakes and brambles. They would have been told how he placed its foundations on the ruins of an old heathen temple; a significant touch. From Lérins Augustine and his company passed northwards, pausing at Tours. Here they could pray at the newly built shrine of Martin, the charismatic figure who had done so much to bring the faith to the illiterate rustics of Gaul. After his death in 395, Martin had become venerated throughout Christendom. The youthful Benedict, later to become the father of western monasticism, had known of him in his isolation at Monte Cassino. Here he cleared a site for the future community by throwing down a temple of Apollo, and on its ruins he built a chapel instead, dedicating it to Martin. Gregory had mentioned this incident in the *Dialogues*, written when he was abbot of his own monastery on the Coelian Hill, where Augustine was prior. So the two men had already shared thoughts on the treatment of pagan temples, many years before the English mission.

At last Augustine reached the Channel ports and took ship for Thanet, where he was to meet Æthelberht of Kent. The queen, Bertha, was herself a daughter of the Frankish royal house and a Christian. On her marriage in 570, she had brought with her a chaplain, Liudhard, who could minister to her and to any other believers at the court. East of the ruined city of Canterbury was an abandoned mausoleum, pointed out by tradition as that of a Christian nobleman in the days before the English came (Wallace-Hadrill 1988: 37). Liudhard fitted it up as a chapel and dedicated it to Martin, the scourge of the pagans. This was as far as he seems to have got in converting the English.

Back in Rome, pagans were not a problem. In 365 the worship of idols had been made punishable by death, with subsequent offences incurring disenfranchisement from public office. Despite these twin threats, pagan priesthoods had continued to officiate, and in 382 they were still rich enough for their assets to be worth confiscating. Successive emperors stepped up the actions against paganism for another fifty years until the old faith was stamped out, at least among the upper classes (Chuvin 1990). Gregory never encountered an educated man who was not a Christian or a Jew.

But the departing pagans had left their cultural heritage behind. There had been some acts of destruction. In the eastern Empire, temples had made easy targets for fanatics from the 340s onwards (Fox 1986: 672). City-dwellers in

Egypt learned to keep out of the way when monks swarmed in from the desert, like Brownshirts in sackcloth, intent on breaking up the altars of the ungodly. The Serapeion of Alexandria was gutted and the church of John the Baptist was built on its ruins. But the governors of cities, themselves often pagan or with pagan connections, were alarmed at the prospect of violence. In 342 Theodosius decreed that urban temples were to be maintained as ancient monuments, a convenient place for works of art. Custodians had to be appointed to throw out visitors who were caught praying to the statuary. In 399 it was re-enacted that 'temples which are situated in cities or towns or outside the towns shall be vindicated to public use'. Justinian repeated the order in 451 (Greenhalgh 1989: 91).

If temples were to survive in the streetscape, their conversion to churches must have seemed a logical step. After all, big public buildings of any kind were in short supply in the sixth century. In letter 56, Gregory says that the temples of the English are to be converted if they are well-built – *si bene constructa sunt* – and this may reflect the situation in Rome. But in practice there was no great rush to convert pagan shrines to the new faith. The most famous of them all, the Parthenon, spent many years lying derelict before it was overhauled and rededicated to the Virgin Mary. Another temple of Athena, at Syracuse, was made into a cathedral, but this did not happen until after 597. In the cities of central Italy there were no site conversions at all until after the time of Gregory. The Forum was still lined with temples, as it had been in the great days of Rome, but they stood empty while churches were fitted into the gaps between them – one accommodated in a disused granary, another in the library of an abandoned palace (Greenhalgh 1989: 95). The unspoken ban on temple conversion was not lifted until 608, when Gregory's successor Boniface IV turned the Pantheon into the church of All Saints.

Things were different in the countryside. City temples had been part of the urban elite's display of wealth and power. The little shrines which clustered around groves and crossroads were for devotion only, with no pretensions to high art, and they had correspondingly few friends. There were still those who opposed their vandalism. 'If anyone with a thought of God wants to burn the wood of these shrines or to tear to pieces and destroy the diabolical altars, they become angry... They even go so far as to dare to strike those who out of love for God are trying to overthrow the wicked idols', as Caesarius of Arles saw it in the 500s (Fletcher 1997: 51).

Under these circumstances, setting fire to temples was the safest and quickest way for religious enthusiasts to make their point. You can see why the owners of neighbouring properties objected, regardless of their religion. Martin of Tours had left a trail of incinerated temples in his campaign against rural paganism, and on one occasion flames from the targeted building were about to engulf the house next door. Being a holy man, Martin simply stood on the roof and ordered the fire to head the other way. Human opponents were less tractable, and in one village near Bourges the bishop was roughly treated when he tried to destroy their temple. Kneeling in prayer, he became aware of two tall figures in shining armour. They stood guard over him while he returned to the work of demolition. Martin assumed that these were angels who had taken on the form of soldiers, but they may equally well have been soldiers who resembled angels. Either possibility could be regarded as a miracle (Fletcher 1997: 43). Martin frequently built churches on the ruins of the temples he had destroyed, and at Mont-Beuvray the shrine of Bibracte, abandoned in about 375, has been found under one of his chapels (Mâle 1950: 32). Today it is the continuity of the site which interests us, but the destruction of the fabric must have made a greater impression at the time.

Letter 56 stands alone in condemning the policies of rural evangelisation to which Martin had devoted such energy (Markus 1970). There is to be no destruction, vandalism or confrontation; instead, the old buildings are to be retained for the new worship, and the change is to be as imperceptible as possible. The festival at which the English sacrificed oxen – presumably the annual *blót* which took place in November – is to be replaced by a feast on the day of the saint whose relics have consecrated the church. Given his background, Augustine may have wanted to initiate his mission by tearing down a few heathen temples, but he would soon have realised that in Saxon Kent there were no soldiers, heavenly or otherwise, to protect him.

Conditions in Britain – and indeed in northern Gaul – must have come as something of a shock to the missionaries. There is nothing to suggest that Gregory had prepared them for the complete breakdown of Roman rule in these parts: probably the pope was unaware of it himself. His ideas on the province were vague in the extreme. In a passage written after the first mission reports, he described the English as Britons, living at 'the extremities of the earth' (Dudden 1905: 2.147) – a literary cliché with a pedigree going back before the Claudian invasion. Gregory assumed that the prefectures of Upper and Lower Britain still existed, with their provincial capitals at York and London, and that Augustine would be able to pass between them, stopping off at two dozen cities where he could found bishoprics. The reality was more disappointing.

Gregory was as unaware of English weather as he was of English politics. He sketches out a picture of the new converts holding outdoor feasts under shelters thatched with the branches of trees. This is not (*pace* Hutton 1991: 272) a detail of existing pagan practices. Gregory was thinking of the picnics which took place around the shrines of saints and martyrs in the Mediterranean countryside, where sunscreens are essential to comfort. They would have offered little protection against an English November.

Gregory's ideas about the temples of the English were influenced by the situation as he knew it in the Italian countryside, but even more so by the language of the Bible. Had not Ezekiel said: 'In all your dwelling places the cities shall be laid waste, and the high places shall be desolate; that your altars may be laid waste and made desolate, and your idols may be broken and cease' (6: 6). Gregory had preached a series of homilies on the prophet, whose messages of devastation struck a responsive chord in abandoned Rome. Of course altars and cult statues did exist in Italy and Gaul as well as in Palestine, and could be smashed up in suitably Biblical fashion. But there is nothing to suggest that they were current among the Anglo-Saxons. When Gregory refers to the English as worshippers of sticks and stones, his thoughts are on Isaiah 40:20 and not on the facts (if any) of tree and megalith cults.

Behind Gregory's ideas about idols is a theology of pride and humility. The things of this world, like Job's prosperity, are given in order to excite thankfulness to the creator (Straw 1988: 238). Christians, who understand the right use of the creation, return thanks to God the giver of all good, just as the converted English will follow their alfresco barbecues with a prayer of thanks – *donatori omnium de satietate sua gratias referant.*

At the same time Gregory had retained an ascetic view of the world from his days as a monk. The body was an untrustworthy vessel, pinning down the spirit with its demands for food and sex. Ezekiel, like the other prophets, repeatedly describes idolatry in terms of sexuality. 'The pollution of idols' was a stock phrase, and significantly it was usually ascetics who were most obsessed with breaking up the white limbs of cult statues. Christian writers developed the literary figure of the virgin martyr, miraculously preserved from seduction either by the pagans themselves or by their idols. What is remarkable about Gregory, given his generally pessimistic view of the flesh, is the latitude which he allowed to the English mission on questions on pollution and purity.

Instead of a purgative destruction by fire, the English temples are to be cleansed with holy water – *aqua benedicta fiat, in eisdem fanis aspergatur.* Then they can be consecrated with altars and relics for the service of the Church. This matches with Gregory's thoughts on purity in the *Responsa*, a series of instructions sent four weeks earlier with the main party. In his missionary duties, Augustine had encountered aspects of life which had never troubled him in the Coelian monastery – pregnant women turning up to be baptised, couples coming to church after having had sex (but before having washed), women receiving communion during their periods or after childbirth. His instincts were to keep all these disturbing reminders of the human condition at bay, but Gregory would have none of it. 'The workings of nature cannot be considered culpable': fault could only lie in the human will, which was redeemed by grace (Bede I: 27). Gregory was making a decisive break with the earlier Christian tradition, which had sought to protect sacred places from ritual impurity (Brown 1981: 434). The body, temple of the Holy Spirit, could be made clean by faith alone. So, presumably, could those other temples which had been polluted by idols. This was a flexible theology, intended to bring converts into the fold. It seems to have worked.

Gregory viewed the growth of the English Church through the lens of Biblical history. The old law, preoccupied by ritual, was to give way to a new dispensation of inward values. Even after their initial rescue from the clutches of the demons, he knew, the English would still be preoccupied with external pleasures in the feasts – *aliqua exterius gaudia* – but they would gradually learn about spiritual joys – *interiora gaudia*. The Christian life was always striving to move from action to contemplation (Markus 1997: 17). When the Jews came out of Egypt, they had been allowed to keep external observances, such as sacrifices, but these were no longer the same – *sacrificia ipsa non essent*. This was not just because they were now being offered to the true God rather than to idols, but because they had acquired symbolic meaning, being types of the real sacrifice, the offering of Christ.

In the same way, Gregory draws on the instructions of Leviticus 23 to sketch out the festive arrangements which will replace the heathen *blót* (Hulse 1998). Like the Israelites, the English have come from an Egypt of diabolical bondage. Now they can gather for an annual feast in which they will kill animals and remember God with thanks. They will construct tabernacula – 'ye shall dwell in booths', 23: 42. These will be thatched with tree branches, *de ramis arborum*, just as their Old Testament counterparts used 'the boughs of goodly trees', 23:40. At one level this is simply a scriptural exegesis of what was common practice around Mediterranean churches. It seems, from the flow of ideas in the letter, that Gregory came up with this England-Israel analogy virtually in the course of dictation. But it fits into a theology of type and antitype. The most familiar *tabernaculum* was that of Moses and Aaron, which was to be translated into the Jerusalem Temple. And the Temple is a type of the Christian community. The pagan English are not just turning their *fana* into churches, they are being encouraged to turn themselves into a Church.

Letter 56 is meant to be practical. Gregory hadn't sent a special messenger hotfoot through Gaul just to offer theological musings, or to share his experiences in town planning. He is aware that he is contradicting his own previous instructions;

on 22nd June, Æthelberht had been instructed, in standard fashion, to suppress the worship of idols and wreck their shrines. Now no attempt whatsoever is to be made to destroy them – *fana destrui minime debeant* is peremptory language. It is not certain how many shrines were in fact converted. The survival of seventh-century placenames with the element *hearg*, often at ecclesiastical sites, suggests that this was the class of buildings being targeted. The *heargs* of the Gumeningas (Harrow) and of the Besingas (unknown: somewhere in Surrey) would have been the places where people assembled for the annual *blót*, and where after the conversion they were to gather for a yearly festival in which they could be catechised and baptised (Morris 1989: 69). In any case, the missionaries had limited resources. The church furnishings brought by Mellitus and his company were too intricate to be replicated by Kentish craftsmen, and they had a limited supply of relics, which were certainly not renewable. Perhaps there were enough in their saddlebags to supply a dozen churches, whether on pagan sites or not.

Æthelberht had been more than accommodating to Augustine. The abbot had arrived with forty men, no small drain on the resources of a small Dark Age kingdom, and had stayed for four years. The king was their friend, but there was a snag – 'he would not compel anyone to accept Christianity'. We have this on the authority of Bede (I: 26), who thought it was an admirable policy, but it may be doubted whether Augustine felt the same way. God had raised up kings to safeguard the Church, not to promote some kind of liberal pluralism. Without the active, coercive power of the state (such as it was) Augustine could end up like Liudhard, a lonely figure ministering to voluntary believers. Gregory had no time for a policy of religious toleration, either. His letter to the king exhorts him to extend the faith among his subjects, whether they like it or not, in imitation of the good emperor Constantine. Admittedly Constantine had governed most of the known world, while Æthelberht was only really secure in his home base of east Kent, but the facts of power were the same in both cases.

Gregory had no compunctions about urging his correspondents to use their authority against rural paganism. Clerics or laymen, it made no difference. The bishop of Terracina had gone soft on tree-worship: Maurus the vice-comes was to lean on him to make sure he inflicted more severe punishments. Landowners in Sardinia should be made responsible for the souls of their tenants, preferably by jacking up the rents of the few remaining pagans until they too came into the fold. 'You have received God's enemies into your power', wrote Gregory indignantly, 'and yet you disdain to subdue and recall them to him'. Spiritual exhortation was the right way to begin, but if that got nowhere they should proceed to whipping for the slaves and imprisonment for the free men (Dudden 1905: 2.148; Markus

1997:81). John the Deacon, Gregory's biographer, described his hero as spreading the faith by sermons and the lash (Vita III: 1). This was not meant to be critical.

There is no doubt that Gregory would have liked Æthelberht to suppress paganism by force, just as he had encouraged Brunhild on the other side of the Channel to restrain her subjects 'by a moderate discipline' from the worship of trees and animal sacrifice (Dudden 1905: 2.62). The flexible policy outlined in letter 56 was a temporary expedient, a response to Æthelberht's obstinately English liberalism. Gregory assumed, correctly enough, that after a transitional stage the kings of Kent would employ coercion rather than persuasion to spread the gospel. In 640 Earconberht ordered the destruction of idols, 'enforcing his decrees by suitable penalties for disobedience' (Bede III: 8). The time for accommodation was at an end.

Gregory's flexibility proved an embarrassment to future generations – not in the matter of the temples, since most missionaries went on following Martin's confrontational attitude, but in the more delicate matter of sexual morals. When Pope Zacharias learned that his predecessor had been prepared to allow the marriage of second cousins, at first he was shocked. Still, *autres temps, autres moeurs*; 'we are prepared to believe that he allowed this because they were as yet uncivilised and were being invited to the faith' (Fletcher 1997: 283). And this just about sums up the context of Gregory's letter on the heathen temples: a document which has received much more attention among historians than it probably ever got among the hard-pressed missionaries of 601 AD.

References

Brown, Peter, 1989, *The Body and Society: Men, Women and Sexual Renunciation in Early Christianity*, Faber & Faber.

Chuvin, Pierre, 1990, *A Chronicle of the Last Pagans* – tr. John Raffan, Harvard University Press.

Dudden, F. Homes, 1905, *Gregory the Great: His Place in History and Thought*, Longmans Green & Co.

Fletcher, Richard, 1997, *The Conversion of Europe: From Paganism to Christianity 371–1386 AD*, Harper Collins.

Fox, Robin Lane, 1986, *Pagans and Christians*, Penguin.

Greenhalgh, Michael, 1989, *The Survival of Roman Antiquities in the Middle Ages*, Duckworth.

Grinsell, Leslie, 1986, 'The Christianisation of prehistoric and other pagan sites', *Landscape History* 8, 27–37.

Hulse, Tristan Gray, 1998, Correspondence, *Source* 5, 41–3.

Hutton, Ronald, 1991, *The Pagan Religions of the British Isles*, Blackwell.

Mâle, Emile, 1950, *La Fin du Paganisme en Gaule*, Paris.

Markus, R.A., 1970, 'Gregory the Great and the origins of a papal mission strategy', *Studies in Church History* 6, 29–38.

Markus, R.A., 1997, *Gregory the Great and His World*, Cambridge University Press.

Morris, Richard, 1989, *Churches in the Landscape*, Dent.

Straw, Carole, 1988, *Gregory the Great: Perfection in Imperfection*, University of California Press.

Wallace-Hadrill, J.M., 1988, *Bede's* Ecclesiastical History of the English People: *A Historical Commentary*, Clarendon.

None of them would believe the horrible stories!! You will, soon...
The Devil himself will be visiting... Is that him knocking at your door?
3rd Stone 44
Strange archaeology and folklore special
Out in October

Millennial Meteors

Alastair McBeath

Did portentous celestial events play a part in the development of early millennial beliefs? Alastair McBeath examines the astronomical signs which it was thought would herald the apocalyptic end-times. Illustrations by Davina Ware.

Millennialism is all Dennis's fault! The 'Dennis' in question is Little Dennis, Dionysius Exiguus (c.500-560 CE), acclaimed as a brilliant scholar, mathematician and astronomer. Tasked by Pope John I in 525 with foretelling the date for Easter, Dennis calculated and later published an Easter date-list which spanned a 95-year period from 532–627 based on known lunar cycles. In his published list he introduced – apparently for the first time – the annotation 'Anno Domini', instead of the then-existing dating system which used 'Anno Diocletiani', after the Roman Emperor noted for his Christian persecutions.

For some reason, Abbot Dennis chose a date 531 years before his own time as his 'Year 1' (zero did not appear in Europe until the Hindu/Arabic numerals achieved wide circulation c.C11–C12), the year of Christ's birth. The dates since proposed for Christ's birth-year span c.7 BCE to c.7 CE. A different year would naturally upset the computations for the end of the current millennium, but our present dating results from Little Dennis and his introduction of the 'AD' concept nearly 1,500 years ago (Duncan 1998: 96–102).

The astronomy-calendar link here is clear enough, as might be expected. Near Eastern religions generally have enjoyed a long history of being rooted in astronomy. For example, the earliest-known deity determinative in the ancient Mesopotamian scripts, c.3300 BCE, is a star, and texts show the Mesopotamians thought of their gods as stars, planets and constellations, amongst other things. This persists in the considerable use of astronomical imagery in Christian biblical and extra-biblical sources, such as eclipses, meteorites, falling stars (meteors), the rising and setting of stars, through to an important star presaging the birth of Christ.

Millennium's end in 2000–2001 can thus be seen as a result of human error, a delightful cause for celebration of our humanity! The origins of millennialism are more obscure. There are increasing signs of it during the second half of the first millennium, as the end of the first thousand Christian years neared. One of the primary Christian sources stressing the importance of the 1,000-year period is *Revelation* (*Rev.*), a book which possesses some of the most striking imagery in all of biblical literature.

After various signs and events heralding the end-times, in *Rev.* 20–21 we find an angel descending from heaven to overpower Satan in the form of a dragon, casting him into the Abyss, there to be chained and sealed-in for 1,000 years. Christ and his risen believers reign on Earth during this millennium, after which the remainder of the dead are revived, and Satan released to lead the nations of Earth astray, prior to the Last Judgement, the end of the present world and the appearance of a new one.

Consequently, it is not unreasonable for Christians to associate the end-times with the millennium's end, as well as looking out for the signs preceding it. The signs include things like wars, famines and diseases, which have been all-too prevalent throughout human history. Clarification of which wars, etc., were to signify Doomsday could be sought in the accompanying astronomical events. One of the most frequently used images new to *Revelation* as virtually unique in the Bible was the falling of stars from heaven.

Generally speaking, the Old Testament (OT) biblical sources are believed to have been written during the last millennium BCE, while the New Testament texts belong unsurprisingly to the opening centuries CE. The OT books show a singular lack of reference to falling stars. The sole unequivocal mention is in *Isaiah* 14:12, where 'Daystar, son of Dawn' (a title of Satan's as Lucifer = 'light-bringer') falls to the ground from the heavens. *Isaiah* 14:15 varies this by having Daystar flung into Sheol, the Abyss, instead, though here 'Daystar' refers to the King of Babylon, not Satan. *Isaiah* is thought to have been written c.C6 BCE.

Numerous OT references are to effects which could be reinterpreted as shooting stars or meteorite strikes, but which are actually stated as being lightning strikes, great hailstones or fire falling from heaven instead. *Job*, which probably dates to the early C5 BCE, has all of these things, in for instance 20:23, or 36:29–33 where Yahweh's tent is specifically described as being a thundercloud. Similar comments recur elsewhere, but perhaps the closest we come to visualized meteors is in the objects like burning coals or torches that dart to and fro between the four winged creatures in the midst of Yahweh's chariot (which themselves vanish and reappear like lightning flashes) in Ezekiel's vision (*Ezekiel* I: 1–28). *Ezekiel*'s dating is uncertain, but the prophet flourished c.593–571 BCE.

Undoubtedly the most famous biblical event of this kind is the destruction of the cities Sodom and Gomorrah, the plain around them and all living things on it by a rain of fire and brimstone from heaven (*Genesis* 19:24–26). This and other rains of fire could well be better visualised as pyroclastic bombs from distant volcanoes or fires started by lightning strikes, as meteoritic impacts. There is a common misconception that meteorites will be hot enough on landing to start fires. Ordinary small meteorites may occasionally have an outer crust too hot to easily handle in the moments after they land, but most are barely warm to the touch on impact.

The popular idea of burning hot meteorites persists, however. On 19 January, 1993 a house in Poreč, Croatia was said to have been struck by a meteorite, and two elderly brothers living there killed. Later, this was changed to a house in the village of Kosinozici near Poreč being set ablaze by a meteorite. Investigation revealed that a house fire had happened in Kosinozici on the same evening that a very bright meteor had shot across northern Italy, ending around 20 km altitude north of the city of Faenza, on the opposite side of the Adriatic Sea (Brown 1993; Korlevič 1993)!

Clear references to falling stars commence with the apocalyptic biblical and extra-biblical material which flourished especially between c.C2 BCE and c.C1 CE. *Revelation* for instance, generally considered a late product of the apocalyptic school, was written around 68–70, possibly as late as c.95 CE. Apocalyptic material continued to reappear reworked in later forms as extra-biblical Christian texts (cf. Sparks 1984; James 1953; Elliott 1993). These survived especially well in early Christian Ireland, where the Church of Rome had no initial influence, most notably in various forms of lists of the signs before Doomsday such as the c.C6/C8 'Saltair Na Rann' and the early medieval 'Evernew Tongue' (cf. Heist 1952; Herbert and McNamara 1989). These helped carry the traditions and beliefs through as common knowledge well into the medieval period, and they continued to appear in both official and unofficial Church teachings until relatively modern times.

At the start of the flowering of apocalyptic literature we find 'The Book of Enoch', sometimes called '1 Enoch' (the most recent translation is Knibb 1984, but Charles 1917 remains a useful text). Much of this probably dates to the late 3rd or early 2nd century BCE. It contains large amounts of preserved Jewish astronomical lore and several fascinating visions. In his second vision (*1 Enoch* 43: 1–44) Enoch talks of seeing the 'other lightnings', which are different to the ordinary thunder and lightning he had seen in an earlier vision. These 'others' are with the stars of heaven, and he sees how the stars' revolution produces them. He goes on to discuss how some stars arise and become lightnings, but then cannot part with their new forms. This is a feasible lay-description of meteors which also invokes Aristotle's doctrine that meteors occurred when vapours rose from the Earth and became ignited by the friction of the rotating celestial spheres, or the change in pressure due to cold higher in the atmosphere (*Meteorologica* Book I, Chapter 4). In a later vision (*1 Enoch* 86:1–3) Enoch sees one star followed by many more fall to Earth to become oxen. These stars are the fallen angels that recur in *Rev.* 12:7–9 where Michael and his angels cast down Satan and his angels from heaven onto the Earth.

The dating of *Revelation* sets it at the other end of mainstream apocalyptic literature, drawing on earlier texts such as *Ezekiel* and *Enoch* for some of its imagery. In Chapter 6, the breaking of five of the seven seals by the Lamb of God brings forth first the four apocalyptic riders and then an altar to the martyred dead, before the sixth seal's breaking causes a variety of astronomical and geological

Dates	Events		
	Comets	**Bright meteors**	**Meteors & meteor showers**
c.250 BCE to c.50 CE	-	Increased flux from c.250 BCE to early decades CE, with peak c.150 BCE	Enhanced activity from c.200 BCE to c.50 CE
c.100 CE	-	-	Possible enhanced activity
200-300	Increased flux	-	-
400-500	-	-	Enhanced activity, with peak in C5 CE
c.600-c.650	-	-	Strongly enhanced activity?
c.750-c.1400	Increased flux C8-C11 and again C13-C14	Increased activity from C9-C13, with huge peak in C11	Enhanced activity c.750-c.1250, with peaks c.850-c.950 and in C11
1400-1600	Increased flux	-	Enhanced activity, becoming greatly enhanced during C17

Table 1. A qualitative timeline showing periods of enhanced meteoric and cometary activity, from c.250 BCE to c.1600 CE, compiled from data in (Bailey et al. 1990; Clube and Napier 1990; Rasmussen 1990).

events (*Rev.* 6:12–14). These include the falling of stars to Earth like figs shaken from their trees in a high wind. In a passage reminiscent of *Ezekiel* 10:1–17, *Rev.* 8:5 sees an angel taking live coals from an incense-altar before God's throne and hurling them to Earth, complete with thunder, lightning and an earthquake.

The sounding of the first trumpet of seven (*Rev.* 8:7) brings a fall of hail, fire and blood to burn the Earth, as frequently found in the OT. Trumpet 2 (*Rev.* 8:8–9) heralds a great blazing mountain being cast into the sea; trumpet 3 (*Rev.* 8:10–11) sees a huge burning star called Wormwood fall on the rivers and springs; and trumpet 5 (*Rev.* 9:1–6) causes a star later described as an angel to fall to Earth, unlock the shaft to the Abyss, and release smoke which rises to darken the sky. From this smoke drop horrific gigantic armoured beasts, part-locust, part-scorpion to attack the people not chosen by God. Here we find a definite link between stars or shooting stars and angels, which persists into much later folklore. The final chief mention of falling stars is in *Rev.* 12: 1–6, where a huge, red, seven-headed dragon sweeps one-third of the stars from the sky with its tail, a prelude to the casting down of Satan's angels in the heavenly war already referred to. Meteors and dragons are also linked together in the popular mind (cf. McBeath 1997).

This is all very interesting, but it gives no clue as to why meteoric activity should suddenly have become so prevalent in apocalyptic literature. Signs and portents were looked-for in the last few centuries BCE, because the Messiah was expected to arrive imminently. This increased astronomical searching may have led the religious authors to discover the genuinely heightened meteor activity attested by other sources, notably in Babylonian and Chinese annals, from c.250 BCE to c.50 CE, with a peak in bright meteors occurring c.150 BCE (see Table 1). Additional similar peaks in meteoric events are known in the C5–C6 CE, the C9–C11 (including the largest peak in bright meteor activity seen in the c.2,000 years represented by Table 1), and especially from the C15 onwards, though this latter is partly due to increasing population levels and greater numbers of active astronomical observers. Other Christian biblical and extra-biblical texts draw on commonly-known images, and because meteor storms or bright meteor showers happened relatively frequently around the C3 BCE to C1 CE period, they seem to have been drafted-in to the repertoire of portents, perhaps helping to fuel the desire to create fresh apocalyptic literature around this same time.

Comets do not obviously feature in early Christian texts at all, which is curious considering how often they were later used in the sign-armoury to bend the will of the church-going masses by the clergy. As Table 1 illustrates, the flux in readily-visible comets showed a significant increase between the C8–C11, latterly coinciding with the great maximum in bright meteor activity. Both were well-timed for the ending of the first millennium after Christ's birth. I discussed this increased celestial activity with particular regard to comets earlier (McBeath 1998).

The level of popular knowledge of the signs before Doomsday being so well-attested by the number of surviving variant texts on the topic, it is scarcely surprising the idea of millennialism should have grown strong in the public mind, and continued to be used as a tool to deter recalcitrance by the Church during much of the second millennium. The power this idea still has over us remains clearly apparent as the third millennium approaches, witness the daily media reports.

It is intriguing that Rasmussen (1990) found a statistically-valid c.1,050-year periodicity in increased meteoric activity seen from Earth, with lesser evidence for a c.325-year periodicity within that longer time. It can be argued that his findings are based on too short an interval (700 BCE to 1850 CE) for certainty, being just under 2.5 times his main periodicity's length. The fact that there is a complete overlap with the c.1,500 years in which millennialism has apparently risen from nowhere may be telling. We should note too that the subsidiary c.325-year period is roughly one-third of a millennium, a short enough interval to perpetuate interest in signs in the sky among humanity in the interval between millennial endings, especially as the c.1,050-year periodicity peaks are neither sharp nor short, often persisting for 1–2 centuries to either side of their most productive times.

We will probably never know when the idea that sky portents reflected earthly events began. The earliest connection between strong meteor shower activity and human disasters I have found concerns the collapse of the important and highly influential Akkadian Dynasty in ancient Mesopotamia, and the utter destruction of its capital city Agade, c.2200 BCE. This date is essentially three c.1050-year periods before the C11 meteoric activity peak, and two such periods before the c.150 BCE meteoric maximum, which may be nothing other than coincidental, but is a curiosity nonetheless. A text compiling prodigies supposedly predicting the end of the Akkadian Dynasty includes the line 'stars fell repeatedly from the sky' (Oppenheim 1956: 283), though the text's dating is not clear. One notable and unique poem 'The Curse of Agade' (discussed and translated in Cooper 1983), probably written within c.150 years of Agade's destruction, makes no mention of falling-star portents, so this may be a later – or merely separate – association. Falling stars were generally viewed as ill-omens in ancient Mesopotamia as Oppenheim's commentary discusses. Another text he quotes with the Agade prodigy runs: 'end of the dynasty, a great star will fall', for instance.

The events at, and for about eighty years after, the end of the Akkadian Dynasty were uniquely catastrophic and chaotic in ancient Mesopotamia certainly. 'The Curse of Agade' condemns the city to perpetual future obscurity, highly apt as archaeological investigations since 1761 have so far failed to locate Agade's ruins, despite the fact that the Akkadian language was the *lingua franca* of the region through until the C8 BCE.

Recent evidence has been found suggesting an abrupt climatic change c.2000 BCE, coupled with distinctive meteoritic impact trace-products in the appropriate archaeological horizons across the Near East (Courty 1999). If this proves correct, perhaps the 'Agade event' was the beginning of meteoric activity being associated with end-times scenarios; the Beginning of the End indeed.

Note: I have preferentially used Wansbrough 1994 as my main source of biblical translations and dating, primarily because of its annotated and recent nature. It also includes most of the accepted so-called OT apocrypha as integral parts of the OT. Other translations of the Bible may vary compared to what I have discussed here however. I have also chosen to refer to what are commonly called 'apocrypha' or 'apocryphal texts' as 'extra-biblical', since 'apocryphal' implies the material was somehow secret or privileged knowledge, which was usually far from the case.

References

Bailey, M.E., S.V.M. Clube and W.M. Napier, 1990, *The Origin of Comets*, Pergamon.

Brown, P., 1993, 'Meteorite fall over Croatia on January 19, 1993', *WGN, the Journal of the International Meteor Organization* 21(1), 47.

Charles, R.H. (translator), 1917, *The Book of Enoch*, SPCK.

Clube, V. and B. Napier, 1990, *The Cosmic Winter*, Basil Blackwell.

Cooper, J.S., 1983, *The Curse of Agade*, Johns Hopkins University.

Courty, M.-A., 1999, 'The 4 kyr BP impact event: the birth of a scientific hypothesis' (in meeting report), *The Observatory* 119 (1151) 168–171.

Duncan, D.E., 1998, *The Calendar*, Fourth Estate.

Elliott, J.K., 1993, *The Apocryphal New Testament: A Collection of Apocryphal Christian Literature in an English Translation*, Clarendon.

Heist, W.W., 1952, *The Fifteen Signs Before Doomsday*, Michigan State University.

Herbert, M. and M. McNamara (eds), 1989, *Irish Biblical Apocrypha: Selected Texts in Translation*, T&T Clark.

James, M.R., 1953, *The Apocryphal New Testament* (Corrected edition), Clarendon.

Knibb, M.A. (translator), 1984, 'I Enoch', in Sparks, 1984.

Korlevič, K., 1993, 'Exploding fireball over the Emilia region, Italy, January 19, 1993, 0h33m20s UT', *WGN, the Journal of the International Meteor Organization*, 21(2), 74–76.

McBeath, A., 1997, 'Meteoric Dragons', *WGN, the Journal of the International Meteor Organization* 25(1), 34–36.

McBeath, A., 1998, 'Comet Myths Ancient & Modern', *3rd Stone* 31, 13–16.

Oppenheim, A.L., 1956, 'The Interpretation of Dreams in the Ancient Near East, with a Translation of an Assyrian Dream-Book', *Transactions of the American Philosophical Society* (New Series) 46(3), 179–373.

Rasmussen, K.L., 1990, 'Historical Accretionary Events from 700 BC to AD 1850 – a 1050-year Periodicity?', *Quarterly Journal of the Royal Astronomical Society* 31(1), 95–108.

Sparks, H.F.D. (ed.), 1984, *The Apocryphal Old Testament*, Clarendon.

Wansbrough, H. (general ed.), 1994, The New Jerusalem Bible (Study Edition), Darton, Longman & Todd.

Fig 1: Doctor Who *'The Stones of Blood'* (1978)

Everybody Must Get Stoned... Megaliths and Movies

Leslie Ellen Jones

Megalithic purists may frown upon inaccuracies in the fictional portrayal of prehistoric monuments in film and television, but most cannot resist the cheesy thrills that these movies offer. Leslie Ellen Jones looks at the iconography of this cinematic sub-genre.

As the availability of films and television series on cable, satellite television, and video increases, the old genre distinctions begin to appear too broad, too crude to adequately categorize this abundance of cinematic narrative. Comedy, drama, science fiction, and horror just don't cut it. We need ever-finer distinctions: period drama, gross-out comedy, splatter flicks; vampire movies versus monster movies versus things-from-outer-space movies. It is even possible to construct a genre of movies that, for reasons ranging from the self-evident to the unfathomable, feature stone circles[1]. But do these films have anything more in common than a bunch of megaliths lurking in the underbrush? Is it possible to construct a consistent iconography of cinematic stones?

1 I have discussed many of these films before in the general context of druidism and Celtic paganism, in Jones 1998 and Jones 2000.

One genre that seems never to have made it to the silver screen is the anthropologically and archaeologically accurate drama of everyday life in Neolithic Britain, and therefore there are no movies in which a stone circle would be as natural and living a part of the scenery as the parish church in a Miss Marple mystery. The long-standing association of druids with Stonehenge and other megaliths, however, means that stone circles frequently appear in movies that feature druids. *Viking Queen* (1967), one of Hammer Studios more ill-advised ventures, is ostensibly a retelling of Boudicca's rebellion against the Romans in 60 C.E., although here the Boudicca figure is named Salina, her Prasutagus-esque father (not husband) is named Priam, her sisters (not daughters) are Beatrice and Talia, and the populace ruled by this British family with such a fondness for nomenclature themselves bear names of randomly Welsh and Irish origin.

Fig 2: The Viking Queen *(1967).*

Their druids worship Zeus and Dis, and have long prophesied that a woman would bear arms against the Romans (who have only just arrived in Britain) and she would be known as... THE VIKING QUEEN! (Thereby anticipating the real Vikings by a good seven centuries.) These druids, as all good druids should, practice their horrid rites of human sacrifice at night in a stone circle, with a pit of fire in the centre that burns the wicker cage full of victims suspended above it[2]. A circle is also the site of royal funerary rites, to be accompanied by the sacrifice of scantily-clad virgins in order to ensure that the dead king will be reborn in a firm, fertile

2 Due to poor lighting, it is hard to be certain, but it looks as though the victims may be Roman prisoners of war, thereby conforming with the Classical ethnographers' statements that the druids preferred such individuals for sacrifice.

body. During the day, when the weather is fine, the druids make observations of astronomic portents from the circle and prophecy doom thereby.

Here the stone circle is very explicitly a temple-cum-astronomical observatory. It functions as a gathering place for the tribe during Priam's funeral, but unless there is a need for a gathering, it is frequented by druids alone. Druidism is presented as a communal religion, in which the lay populace only participates en masse and at prescribed times. The circle does not appear to be numinous in and of itself, furthermore – the power lies in the druids themselves, and the circle is merely where druids hang out. When necessity arises, the chief druid, Maelgan, happily trots off to prophecy doom in Priam's bedchamber or in the royal hall, as need be.

A stone circle is gratuitously planted in front of Tintagel Castle in John Boorman's *Excalibur* (1981), apparently for the sole purpose of providing a magic circle in which the druidic wizard, Merlin, can transform Uther into the likeness of the Duke of Cornwall for the purpose of sleeping with Ygraine and begetting Arthur. There have been myriad cinematic interpretations of the Arthurian myth, ranging from the mystical, as here, to the virtually magicless, as in *The Knights of the Round Table* (1953). The latter film also includes a scene in a stone circle, indeed the Stone Circle, Stonehenge. Arthur and the kings of Britain meet there in parliament, and they talk politics, not magic. Merlin lectures the assembled kings that Stonehenge represents the law of Britain, and the balance of the stones mirrors the balance of an ordered society. Stonehenge as a solar temple reflects the cosmic balance of the universe. Yet Stonehenge does not appear to be an actual temple, at least not at this point in time – Merlin appears to have brought a class of fractious schoolboys on a field trip for an extended civics lecture. This Merlin is simply a sage political advisor with no magic about him at all, a man with his feet firmly planted in the mundane world, leading his Arthur to an equally pragmatic Stonehenge. *Excalibur*'s stone circle is a place of magic in and of itself, a node on a ley line keyed into the body of the mystical dragon that is the numinous life of the Island of Britain. Merlin is a magician and a druid, the last representative of the 'old ways', the pagan world. Magic here is knowledge of the power of the earth, and the stone circle operates almost as an acupuncture needle inserted into the flow of that power. The circle will be powerful whether or not Merlin is there to harness or use its power. The circle also functions, literally, as a magic circle, a circumscribed space in which the magician summons the spirits and carries out his spells.

In *The Knights of the Round Table*, Stonehenge in a sense is Arthur's Round Table, the circular place where no man sits higher than another and all are equals – political or diplomatic equals, for magic has no place at this table. *Excalibur* separates the circles, megalithic and commensal, into the pagan site where all men are so equal as to be interchangeable, and the Christian locus where all men are brothers. The pagan Merlin circles the Round Table, but he does not sit at it. A stone circle, in the iconography of *Excalibur*, is a symbol of the pagan past, but a past that at this point in time is only just slipping away and therefore can be forgotten, for its value is not yet realized in the glamour of the new.

Fig 3: Knights of the Round Table *(1953).*

Movies set in the distant past, such these discussed, may place stone circles in an inaccurate historical context, but nonetheless present the circles as being 'natural' elements of the cultural landscape – they are being used for their intended purpose by the people, or the descendants of the people, who built them. There is no gap in the transmission of the traditions concerning their proper use. (Again, I am talking about the way the use and function of the circle is represented in the film, not in the historical accuracy of the film's representation.) Cinematically, stone circles are part of the living architecture of Iron Age and Arthurian Britain. Then there is a large chronological gap – stone circles are not relevant to the scenery of films that take place from the Arthurian age (which can be placed any time from the sixth century through a vaguely defined High Middle Ages) up to the present[3].

The greater number of megalith movies take place in the present, and while stone circles may be more or less reasonably encountered in movies taking place in ancient

3 Perhaps the sole exception is in various film versions of *Tess of the Durbervilles*, set in the nineteenth century, where the film makers are compelled by Hardy's novel to include the climactic scene at Stonehenge.

times, the appearance of Stonehenge and other circles in contemporary films is often downright arbitrary. Why, for instance, does Stonehenge make an appearance in *Curse of the Demon* (1957; also released as *Night of the Demon*)? The plot of the movie is about a small-time circus magician, Karswell, who has evidently sold his soul to a demon in exchange for wealth and real magical power. The 'Karswell Devil Cult', as they are dubbed by the newspapers, practice a pagan religion that the screen writers seem to have concocted from a suitably sensationalized version of Gerald Gardner's account of his initiation into Wicca: a family-based magical religion that has carried on, unnoticed, in rural England, since the dawn of time. Stonehenge appears twice in *Curse of the Demon*, first under the opening credits, where a newsreel-portentous voice-over informs the audience that 'It has been written since the beginning of time, even onto these ancient stones, that evil, supernatural creatures exist in a world of darkness. And it is also said, Man, using the magic power of the ancient runic symbols, can call forth these powers of darkness: the Demons of Hell.' Later, after Our Hero, Dr.Holden, has encountered the family that appears to be the core community of the Devil Cult, he drives out to Stonehenge and finds the cursing runes that have been planted on him by Karswell, which will call the demon to him on an appointed night to take him as a human sacrifice, carved into the stone of one of the trilithons.

Fig 4: Curse of the Demon *(1957).*

Since there is no explicit reason for Stonehenge to be here (there is no suggestion, for instance, that the cult worships there, and none of the cult members mentions Stonehenge or anything remotely megalithic to Dr.Holden), it must be functioning as an icon, a symbolically-packed image operating as a shorthand for a whole raft of associations. The inscription on the very stones of Stonehenge tells the audience that this is truly a primordial religion and a primeval curse, dating to the earliest stratum of British history. As in the roughly contemporary *Knights of the Round Table*, Stonehenge is an icon of archaism, a physical representation of the depth of British history (contrasted here with the brash American scientist who does not believe in anything he cannot see, touch, and experiment upon). It represents a past that is lost, but perhaps not lost enough. What lingers into the present is evil.

That commodious compendium of paganism, *The Wicker Man* (1973) could not be complete without a stone circle. The circle on Lord Summerisle's estate functions as a classroom in Applied Immaculate Conception, where naked girls jump over a fire in the centre of the circle, calling on the god to impregnate them ('So much more romantic than a spotty teenager,' as Lord Summerisle notes). Later, the circle is the site of the beheading game at the culmination of the Morris dance procession, where the sacrificial victim is identified. The circle is therefore central to both the death and (re)birth aspects of Summerisle's paganism. However, in contrast to Merlin's paganism in *Excalibur*, which is a continuous religion, albeit on its last legs, the paganism of Summerisle, for all its lusty vitality, is a reconstruction, built from the ground up by a Victorian plant scientist with an anthropological bent.

Contemporary megalith narratives invariably have roots not just in folklore, but in modern folklore scholarship and its analysis of what have been perceived to be 'survivals' from ancient times, fragmented and no longer entirely understood – until, of course, the light of scholarship has beamed its illuminating rays upon them. Innumerable legends connect stone circles to the Devil in some way. Common motifs in origin legends attached to megaliths are that the Devil tossed the stones into their current location, sometimes aiming at a nearby church, or that he was transporting them somewhere and dropped one. The stones are often said to be petrified humans who were struck into stone while dancing on the Sabbath, or to the tune of the Devil's fiddle. Stones are said to stroll periodically down to nearby rivers for a drink, and they cannot be accurately measured or counted – the numbers come out different at every attempt. Also, attempts to move megaliths invariably fail, for the stones stubbornly return to their former location in the night (Simpson and Roud, 2000, s.v. 'Standing stones'). All of these motifs appear in megalith movies. At the same time, the rise of archaeoastronomy, beginning with Gerald Hawkins' *Stonehenge Decoded* (1965) , has contributed its own motifs to the mix. It is taken for granted that megaliths are observatories aligned to the sun, moon, and stars, and indicate an astonishing technical and intellectual sophistication on the part of the 'savages' who erected them. Just as the size and immovability of the stones themselves inspired fantastic etiological tales requiring supernatural, divine, or satanic intervention, the astronomical orientations of the stones require

Fig 5: Psychomania *(1973).*

etiological tales that often call upon those modern bogies, space aliens and mad scientists, to explain their enduring fascination. The stories are now told, not around the hearth, but in the cinema or on the television. All too often, apparently archaic pagan cults turn out to be manipulated behind the scenes, and the puppetmaster is extraterrestrial in origin or orientation. Or in the case of the classically B-grade *Psychomania* (1973), the butler did it. The premise of *Psychomania* is that it is possible to achieve immortality: the trick is to commit suicide while really, really believing that you will come back to life. That, at least, is what Our Antihero, Tom Latham, has been led to believe by Shadwell, his mediumistic mother's ever-so-sinister butler. It appears that it is not that we are each given only one life that ends in death, but that we each get only one death, and if you manage to transcend that death, life will just keep going on forever and ever. Essentially, in order to live forever, you have to be the kind of sociopath who truly does not care whether you live or die, for if, at the last moment, your intention wavers and you realize that you actually do want to live, you are just dead. It sounds suspiciously like hell, and so it should be no surprise that the man behind it all, Shadwell, is the Devil in disguise. It also appears that this trick only works if you are part of a biker gang whose leader is the son of a woman who sold her soul to Satan, dedicating her baby son to the Devil on the altar stone of a stone circle where you now all hang out, revving your engines and singing surprisingly lousy folk rock songs about being sociopathic bikers[4]. There is a certain amount of cognitive dissonance

4 This must represent some deep cultural divide between Britain and the United States. In American movies, there is a law that bikers can only be represented with soundtrack backing of 'Born to be Wild', although bikers in *Pee-Wee's Big Adventure* (1985) seem to have made a one-time exception for 'Tequila'.

in the idea of nihilists who want to live forever, although the real appeal seems to be not so much the eternity as the impossibility of punishment. While Tom is quick to take advantage of his new immortality to kill whoever crosses his path, the first act of the reunited gang (aptly named The Living Dead) is to blow into town and trash a supermarket. Now that's nihilism! The stone circle is once again a point of community gathering, the burial place of their 'king' and the site of his rebirth (bursting out of his grave, where he was conveniently buried upright on his motorcycle), and, inevitably, the place where the wicked are turned to stone, when Tom's mother renounces her deal and the Devil claims his own. In a nice touch, Tom turns into one stone, and the gang, who have functioned all along as a unit rather than as individuals, turn into another.

A stone circle is the location for a battle between good druids and the Son of Satan in *Warlock: The Armageddon* (1993), one of the more peculiar druid movies in the genre. These druids have been driven very far into the west – all the way to Northern California, where, like all good druids, they have erected a stone circle and practice their art in secrecy. It appears that once every millennium, an astronomical alignment allows Satan's son to be reborn, and if he can gather six runestones[5] and beat the ordained druidic champion, his father will reign again on Earth. The motifs of druidic astronomical knowledge, the association of both druids and Satan with megaliths, and the somewhat attenuated theme of human sacrifice – this is, after all, a battle to the death – occur, but as one might expect in a movie where a millennium lasts all of six hundred years, the execution is muddled, to put it lightly[6].

Three of the best examples of the mad scientist/space alien subgenre of megalith movies were made in the late 1970s for British television: *Children of the Stones* (1977)[7], the 'Stones of Blood' episodes of the Key of Time series of *Doctor Who* (1978), and the final instalment of the Quatermass series, *The Quatermass Conclusion* (1979), emphasizing the astronomical alignment, moving/uncountable stones, and gathering place motifs, respectively. While most megalith movies call on the instantly-recognizable icon of Stonehenge, or else make use of anonymous small-scale local circles that can carry the generalized legend motifs required by the plot, *Children of the Stones* is unusual in that

5 Given that the actual druids had their own cryptic alphabet, ogham, and that ogham has its own influential, historically and anthropologically inaccurate cult following as a result of Robert Graves' *The White Goddess* (1948), why do so many Bad Druid Movies insist on dragging in Germanic runes? Indeed, the shot-gun marriage of runes and druids dates back to Iolo Morganwg's writings in the 18th century (see Jones 1998: 173-188), and he passed it on to the Welsh National Eisteddfod in the early 19th century, but again, why did Iolo, who surely must have come across ogham in his vast reading in Celtic folklore, abandon ogham for Germanic runes?

6 This is, however, one of the very few movies in which the druids are the good guys.

7 I am indebted to Neil Mortimer for obtaining a video of this series for me, and to Don Klipstein for translating it into a format that my VCR would play.

Fig 6: Children of the Stones *(1977).*

was filmed in, and effectively utilizes, the village and circle of Avebury under the *nom-de-pierre* of Milbury.

The stone circle of Milbury is, like Merlin's circle in *Excalibur*, a magic circle, but this one is large enough to encompass an entire village. Once people enter, they cannot leave. There are fifty-five stones in the circle, and fifty-five inhabitants of the village, once the latest residents arrive: Adam Brake, an astrophysicist with a grant to study the magnetism of the stones, and his teenaged son, Matthew. There are some other recent arrivals as well, the farmer Tom Browning and his son, Jimmo; Dr.Lyall and his son, Kevin; and Margaret Smythe, archaeologist and curator of the museum, and her daughter, Sandra. (A rather statistically unusual accumulation of single, widowed parents, if nothing else.) All the older inhabitants of Milbury are disturbingly cheerful and greet each other with, 'Happy day!' Their children are all strangely well-behaved and have remarkable mathematical abilities. The local squire is Hendrick, a retired astronomer who discovered a black hole in the constellation of Ursa Major. He has come to live in Milbury because an ancient manuscript, 'older than Bede,' contains what appears to be an oral tradition of an actual eyewitness account of his star turning into a black hole, some four thousand years ago, at the time the stone circle was erected. The circle, you see, is not aligned to any of the common astronomical events that stone circles mark – the rising of the sun and moon on solstices or equinoxes, or even the movements of the larger planets – it is, in fact, aligned straight upwards, at the black hole in the heart of the Bear.

One by one, the newcomers fall victim to Happy-day-itis, a psychological disorder that seems to replace emotion with a facility for solving complex mathematical problems and discordant chanting. Not only are their emotions turned to stone, but the townspeople themselves, particularly the Brake's housekeeper, Mrs.Crabtree, have a tendency to show up in the middle of the road looking like megaliths. Can this be a survival of a pagan cult, preserved in this rural backwater for four millennia? No, for Hendrick is revealed to be a Mad Scientist in the grand tradition, using his highly advanced technology – a digital clock – to time the beams from the black hole into his dining room, where they suck up the evil from his dinner guests, leaving them brainwashed and oh, so very, very happy. Hendrick sees himself as a magus, a scientist/priest, leading his people under his benevolent rule to a state of bliss and higher maths. Adam and Matt manage to break the spell by adjusting the time on the digital clock so that Hendrick opens his skylight five minutes too early, but while this is a blow for free will and non-mad science everywhere, it has the unfortunate side effect of turning Hendrick into an ancient man in a white robe, and all the happy villagers into megaliths. Yet in the morning, it seems that everything is back to normal, albeit a slightly parallel-universe normality. Adam and Matt can leave the circle, but as they do, a new prospective squire, who looks exactly like Hendrick, drives up to take possession. Is it possible that time, as well as stone, is circular?

Children of the Stones turns on the astronomical angle, but it manages to hit virtually all of the other stone motifs: the archaic religion that is actually a modern reconstruction, the stone circle as magic circle, the stones that move, that are in fact petrified people, that sing and dance, plus ley lines, druidic associations, Morris dancing, apotropaic serpents, psychometry and remote viewing, the crushed barber-surgeon from the real Avebury, a nearby hill that bears a strong resemblance to Silbury Hill, and an incoherent Welshman who knows more than he is letting on.

'Stones of Blood' (1978) goes straight for the angle of stone circle as (historically inaccurate) druidic temple. Doctor Who and Romana, searching for the third segment of the Key to Time, land the Tardis near a Cornish circle known as the Nine Travelers. There they encounter a rather batty old female archaeologist, Dr.Rumbold; a sinister feminist named Vivien Fay; and the members of the British Institute of Druidic Studies (BIDS), who naturally are performing sacrifices in the circle and worshiping the Cailleach, crow-goddess of the stones. And since this is, after all, *Doctor Who*, Miss Fay turns out to be an intergalactic criminal on the lam for the last four thousand years, and the reason the stones are uncountable and surveys of their location unreliable is that two of them are Ogri, a globulin deficient silicon-based life form from the planet Ogros, who, if they are not fed the blood of sacrifice, will lumber off to fetch it themselves.

Much of *Doctor Who* is based on the Frazerian premise that magic is misunderstood science, and since the Doctor is an intergalactic Time Lord, humans of all eras misunderstand extraterrestrial science in the way that Victorian anthropologists believed that 'primitives' misunderstood the laws of nature. Throughout *Doctor Who*, demons, spirits, and monsters are invariably space aliens stranded or experimenting on Earth, and folklore and mythology are the feeble attempts of Earthlings to explain the 'magical' effects that extraterrestrial science can achieve. Although the Doctor always gets his digs in about these inexplicable events being quite simple science, really, his function is to serve as an intermediary between humans and aliens and to exorcize the 'demons' and send them on their merry way. In 'Stones of Blood,' sacrifice – human and animal – is quite literally a means of feeding the stones, which are alive. The folklore about stones moving and drinking is actually evidence of this life, and therefore, for all the Doctor's 'scientific' attitude, the series suggests that the world is animated, folklore is true, and it would be well to take it seriously and at face value.

The Quatermass Conclusion (1979) contrasts the antiquity of stone circles, artefacts of the dawn of human endeavour, with an apocalyptic extraterrestrial threat to human existence. Society has broken down and the cities, at least the cities of Britain, are in ruins. (If *Children of the Stones* is *Invasion of the Body Snatchers* set in a stone circle, then *The Quatermass Conclusion* is *Mad Max* with megaliths.) As society disintegrates, masses of young people are forming nomadic cult-like caravans, calling themselves 'Planet People', preaching that an extraterrestrial intelligence is going to take them away from this wasteland and transport them to a new planet, soon, soon. They follow ley lines by dowsing, which leads them to stone circles and other ancient places of gathering around the world. But when a critical mass of young bodies accumulates at these sites, a beam of energy shoots down from outer space and disintegrates them, leaving only a fine ash behind. Quatermass gradually realizes that humans are being harvested, as we in the past have harvested musk deer, taking only a small portion of the whole for our luxurious purposes and discarding the rest. Furthermore, it is only young humans that the extraterrestrials are harvesting – old age pensioners are immune from the siren beacon that lures the Planet People to the ancient gathering sites.

Stone circles, it turns out, are not sites where humans practiced human sacrifice, but the sites of extraterrestrial harvest that humans have marked with stone in order to warn people to stay away, to resist the lure activated by buried extraterrestrial bait. The circle does not form a magic circle of protection, keeping

Fig 7: The Quatermass Conclusion *(1979).*

external forces from damaging the magician, but rather is an attempt to contain the dangerous force[8]. Folklore – in this case, a nursery rhyme, 'Huffety Puffety, Ringstone Round' – is, again, an accurate guide and warning to the real danger marked by the stones. The story ends with Quatermass's own self-sacrifice at a latter-day temple of science in the act of delivering a nuclear 'sting' to the harvesters, warning them to back off and leave humanity alone.

There are a number of points of similarity between *Children of the Stones* and *The Quatermass Conclusion*. Each feature blinding beams of light descending from the skies to suck up some human essence in 'sacrifice' to an extraterrestrial entity. Each also, while located in England, feature an outsider – another kind of alien – who is driven mad by the terror of what happens in the circle: the Welsh poacher, Dai, in *Children of the Stones* and the Jewish scientist, Joe Kapp, in *The Quatermass Conclusion*. Each serve as a subtle reminder of alternate origin myths of the circles, the eighteenth century etiologies that not only ascribed stone circles to the Celtic druids, but also derived the druids from wandering Jews, the Lost Tribes of Israel, and the post-Babel diaspora (Piggott 1989).

8 It has been proposed that this is, in fact, the orientation of stone circles where the ditch is inside the bank, as at Avebury. For defensive purposes, the ditch should be the first thing the hostile force encounters, with the bank towering above it. The 'defences' of Avebury therefore face into the circle rather than away from it.

Nineteenth century anthropology congratulated Western culture with its scientific triumph over nature, and compared itself favourably with the savage and primitive peoples with which expanding colonialism had brought it in contact. The monsters that grew out of this tradition, such as the vampire, Count Dracula (Stoker 1897/1981), were survivals of past European savagery that threatened the enlightened present and were overcome by modern scientists, such as Dr.van Helsing, a specialist in diseases of the blood. Cautionary tales, such as *Frankenstein* (Shelley 1816/1965), warned that man's fascination with science might outstrip his ability to control its results, producing monsters rather than marvels. (This trend evolved into the type of 1950s horror movie in which nuclear radiation creates mutant bugs that terrorize cities.)

Megalith movies seem to operate in another mythic context, however. The realization, beginning in the mid-1960s, that stone circles revealed not just remarkable engineering skills in simply obtaining and erecting the huge stones, but also a sophisticated astronomical knowledge in their alignments, made it impossible to regard them as primitive in any way. The people who built them must be seen as modern man's intellectual equals. Modern knowledge of the stars is thus not a new discovery, but rather a rediscovery of something that was lost. The motif of the stone circle, then, illustrates not only the magic circle of circumscription, but also the circular nature of human knowledge.

Claude Lévi-Strauss based his theory of structuralism on the premise that myths attempt to mediate binary oppositions such as man and woman, raw and cooked, wet and dry. The most basic and unmediable opposition is the opposition between nature and culture, wild and civilized, feral and domestic (Lévi-Strauss 1969). In most traditional myths, humankind belongs on the same side of the equation as culture, civilization, and domestication, and the purpose of the myth is to demonstrate how humankind became differentiated from nature, wildness, and the feral.

The iconographic message of the megalith, however, tends to erase the opposition between primitive and technologically advanced – it does not so much mediate the opposition as call it into question. And by calling this opposition into question, it also calls into question humankind's place at the top of the traditional oppositions. We are not on the side of culture, civilization, and control after all. Perhaps we are just animals to be harvested, and the extraterrestrials are the ones who actually hold the place that we thought we held in the grand scheme of oppositions. Perhaps our intellectual achievements are no more advanced than those of children. Perhaps what makes us adult is our evil. Perhaps the primordial past is exactly the same as the present.

Rock and Roll Megaliths

There is a strange subgenre of megalith movie that takes the rock in rock and roll very literally indeed. It starts with the Beatle movie, *Help!* (1965). Scotland Yard's idea of a safe place to guard the Beatles while they cut a record is out in the middle of Salisbury Plain, surrounded by the army, with Stonehenge looming in the background. At the time of the filming, the Beatles were at a peak of popularity and societal approval (not yet having claimed to be bigger than Jesus or made public comments about drug use), having weathered the first wave of outrage at their long hair and anti-authoritarian ways. The plot of *Help!*, in which a cult of Kali-worshipers attempts to sacrifice Ringo, presents the Beatles as the crown jewels of Britain, precious and in need of protection from an alien threat (pre-Christian cult, human sacrifice, alien threat, does any of this sound familiar?). They are sequestered first in the heart of the English Establishment, Buckingham Palace. Then they are sent to Stonehenge, where the juxtaposition of rocks and rock plays on the accusations of rock and roll's 'primitive' excitement, its primal punch, and at the same time places megaliths and megastars in the same category of English National Heritage monument.

Probably the most notorious Stonehenge musical appearance is in *This is Spinal Tap* (1984), the satirical 'rockumentary' about a fictitious British band making an American come-back tour. Midway through the disastrous tour, the band decides to inject some energy into the show by reviving their Stonehenge number, complete with life-size megalithic set. Unfortunately, Nigel Tufnel sketches out the trilithons with indications of height in inches rather than feet, and the band's grandiose chords and dramatic lighting effects reveal an eighteen-inch high styrofoam minilith complete with midgets in druid costume dancing a whimsical jig. Not only does the number fall flat, the trilithons do as well.

The episode is claimed to have been inspired by Hawkwind's summer solstice concert at Stonehenge and by a Stonehenge set used by Black Sabbath on a Canadian tour, but both took place in the same year as the filming of *Spinal Tap* and it seems more likely that all were part of the same *Zeitgeist*. What is being mocked, however, is the pompousness and general grandiosity of a certain strain of British rock which tried to capitalize on the very associations already outlined in the juxtaposition of the Beatles and Stonehenge in *Help!*. The puns and metaphors are really almost too much to resist – rock, getting stoned, the notion of rock and roll as a return to primordial emotion and energy, the rejection of conventional mores and a return to primeval purity and innocence.

One of the most recent rock megalith moments is in *Still Crazy*, another story of a British band reunion tour. Four members of the band Strange Fruit meet at a pub in Avebury to decide whether to reunite, when they discover that the fifth member is dead. Their first reaction is to scrap the whole idea of a reunion, but then they take a stroll through the stones, recalling (in flashback) the time that they had come to Avebury, tripping on LSD, for an album cover shoot. In mid-reminiscence, the sound of their own music comes blasting through the air, seeming to emanate from the stones themselves. In truth, it turns out to be emanating from a shepherd's boombox as the sheep come streaming over the bank, but the band take it as a sign from 'the gods of rock and roll' that the tour shall go on. It is a pivotal scene in the movie's plot, and it works precisely because of the symbolism of the stone circle: the place of death and rebirth, the place of contact between worlds, the place where the gods of rock speak.

Fig 8: This is Spinal Tap's *'Stone 'enge'.*

Fig 9: The Beatles' Help!

Megaliths and Movies: Looking Back from 2024

I wrote this essay, as well as papers on what I call 'The Bad Anthropology Film Festival' (presented at the American Folklore Society conference in Milwaukee, Wisconsin in 1994 and the UC Celtic Colloquium/Celtic Studies Association of North America joint meeting in Los Angeles in 1996), well before the emergence of the field of Folk Horror studies in both academic and popular discourse. I suppose I have passed the torch (licking at the straw wisps hanging off the Wicker Man) to the younger generation of scholars of Dangerous Things That Happen in the Woods. I do still have dreams of putting on my film festival in real life, or even wilder dreams of getting Turner Classic Movies to allow me to host a series for them, if only for the thrill of forcing perfect strangers to watch *Psychomania* while I laugh fiendishly in the background and point out Sgt. Benton from Jon Pertwee-era *Who* apparently moonlighting in his UNIT uniform at the local police station.

The problem with this this topic is that the damned movies and TV shows keep coming out faster than I can watch and critique them. And serious ideas about what stone circles were for, who made them, how they dragged the stones around and from where, what's the druids' secret agenda, etc., etc., etc., keep evolving. Good lord, pot is legal in California now – you can't even giggle at 'stoned' jokes in the same way anymore. There's so much more to say, if only I had time to say it...

Maybe it's due to the Marvelization of Hollywood, but I'm finding more interesting uses of mythology in print than on celluloid these days. Female-centered retellings of Greek myth are practically a genre in themselves, as are tales of Middle Eastern djinns and East Asian fox spirits, sometimes even in the same story. In my Bad Anthropology wish list, I devoutly hope that Ben Aaronovich's *Rivers of London* books finally get turned into a TV series, because I adore his melding of modern multiculturalism with mythology – and also his sneaky references to obscure volumes published by the Folklore Society in the late nineteenth-early twentieth centuries that haunted my graduate studies. I want to see those Nigerian Thames River goddesses on the screen, dammit! I want to see the dream of a *Knights of the Round Table* revived Arthurianism firmly put to rest in favour of the spirits of the trees and the rivers, the fairies and the foxes. All this stuff remains, as Claude Lévi-Strauss put it, 'good to think with.'

But that's what it really comes down to: myths are good to think with. And Bad Anthropology movies, by their very badness, their ridiculousness, their insistence on narrating mythically rather than logically, startle us into thinking differently, creatively, about the past, about our relationships to nature and spirits and the weirdnesses that don't fit into the dominant social narratives of what's allowed to constitute reality. Myths tell us that they're going to explain how it was In The Beginning, but actually, they're telling us how things are now. And as these movies so insistently remind us, we would do well to pay attention to what they say. Or else.

References

Graves, Robert, 1948, *The White Goddess*, Amended and enlarged ed. New York: Farrar, Straus and Giroux.

Hawkins, Gerald, 1965, *Stonehenge Decoded*, New York: Doubleday.

Jones, Leslie Ellen, 1998, *Druid Shaman Priest: Metaphors of Celtic Paganism*, London: Hisarlik Press.

Jones, Leslie Ellen, 2000, 'Stone Circles and Tables Round: Representing Early Celts in Film and Television.' In Amy Hale and Philip Payton, eds., *New Directions in Celtic Studies*, 30-51. Exeter: University of Exeter Press.

Levi-Strauss, Claude, 1969, 'Overture.' In Claude Levi-Strauss, *The Raw and the Cooked*, translated by John and Doreen Weightman, 1-32. Chicago: University of Chicago Press.

Piggott, Stuart, 1989, *Ancient Britons and the Antiquarian Imagination*, New York: Thames and Hudson.

Shelley, Mary Wollstonecraft, 18 I 6/1965, *Frankenstein, or the Modern Prometheus*, Reprint. New York: New American Library.

Simpson, Jacqueline, and Steve Roud, 2000, *The Dictionary of English Folklore*, Oxford: Oxford University Press.

Stoker, Bram, 1897/1981, *Dracula*, Reprint. New York: Bantam Classic.

Filmography

Children of the Stones, 1977, Peter Graham Scott, director. Jeremy Burnham and Trevor Ray, screenwriters. HTV West.

Curse of the Demon, I957, Jacques Tourneur, director. Charles Bennett and Hal E. Chester, screenwriters. Based on *Casting the Runes*, by M.R. James. Columbia.

Excalibur, I981, John Boorman. director. John Boorman and Rospo Pallenberg, screenwriters. Based on *Le Morte d'Arthur* by Thomas Malory. Orion.

Help! 1965, Richard Lester, director. Charles Wood and Marc Behm, screenwriters.

Knights of the Round Table, 1953, Richard Thorpe, director. Talbot Jennings, Jan Lustig, and Noel Langley, screenwriters. MGM.

Psychomania, I973, Don Sharp, director. Arnaud d'Usseau and Julian Zimet, screenwriters. Benmar Productions.

Quatermass Conclusion, The, 1979, Piers Haggard, director. Nigel Kneale, screenwriter. Thames Television.

Still Crazy, 1998, Brian Gibson, director. Dick Clement and Ian La Frenais, screenwriters. Columbia Pictures.

'Stones of Blood.' *Doctor Who*, 1978, Darrol Blake, director. David Fisher, screenwriter. BBC.

This is Spinal Tap, 1984, Rob Reiner, director. Christopher Guest, Michael McKean, Harry Shearer and Rob Reiner, screenwriters. Embassy Pictures.

Viking Queen, 1967, Don Chaffey, director. Clarke Reynolds, screenwriter. Hammer Films.

Warlock: The Armageddon, 1993, Anthony Hickox, director. Kevin Rock and Sam Bernard, screenwriters. Trimark Pictures.

Wicker Man, The, 1973, Robin Hardy, director. Anthony Shaffer, screenwriter. Republic Pictures.

Note: 3rd Stone *would like to thank Phil Roberts, Pete Glastonbury and Roy Stilling for helping us obtain copies of several films mentioned in this article.*

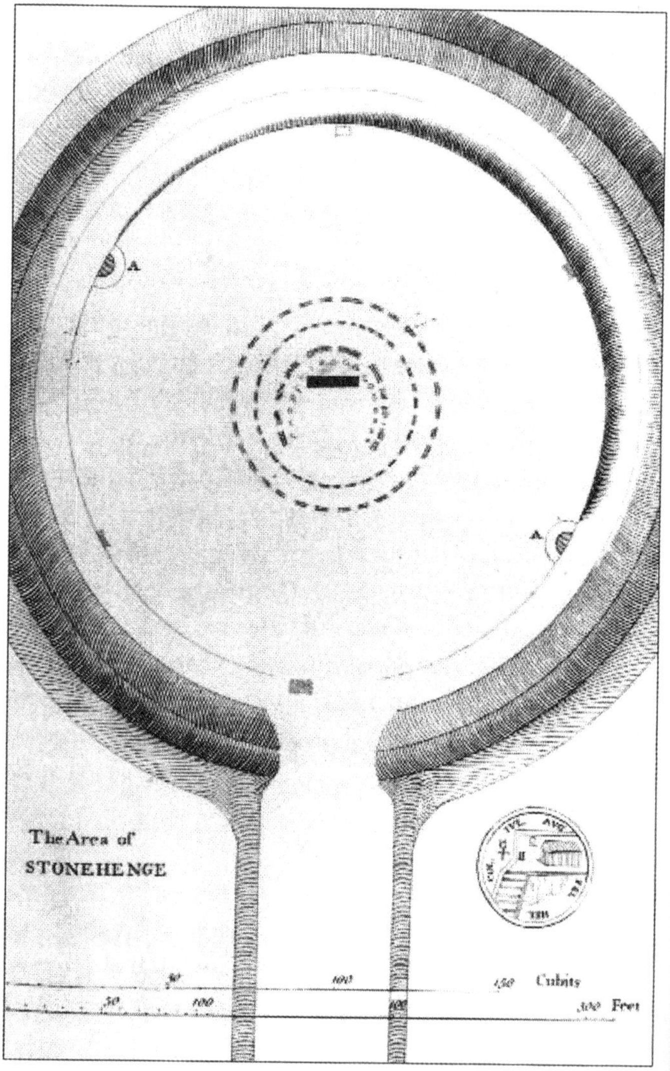

A
A
The Area of
STONEHENGE
50
100
150 Cubits
50
100
200
300 Feet

The Third Stone
The Altar Stone at Stonehenge: Prone to Doubt

Aubrey Burl

Until now Stonehenge aficionados have been in general agreement that the so-called Altar Stone originally stood upright. But Aubrey Burl has changed his mind.

'Heresy. A belief contrary to orthodox doctrine and what is normally accepted'.

Mea culpa. The writer is already guilty of two heresies about Stonehenge, the first that its bluestones reached Salisbury Plain by glaciation and not by human transportation (Burl, 1987, 130–5, ibid., *3rd Stone* 37, 2000, 6–9). The second heresy was that the architecture and art of Stonehenge's sarsens were greatly affected by influences from Brittany (*WAM* 90, 1997, 1–12; Burl, 1999, 151–69). The present paper offers a third heresy, that Stonehenge's 'phallic' Altar Stone was never erect.

> *'They that approve a private opinion, call it opinion; but they that mislike it, heresy; and yet heresy signifies no more than private opinion'.*
>
> T. Hobbes, *Leviathan*, 1651, I, 11.

Introduction

Until 1901 the south-west arc of Stonehenge was confusion (Fig. 1). A long stone lay half-buried there. Crushing it down was the bulk of a massive but broken top of a huge slab. Against it, also over the long stone, was another whose far corner covered the side of a fourth tumbled pillar whose end was hidden by the bottom half of the broken slab. Alongside it a sarsen column, once the longest of all the stones, leant sharply forward, propped heavily on a low standing stone. It was as though giants had been playing pitch-and-toss with sarsens, dolerites and sandstones. The first stone of this disarray, part-buried under the two stones and pressed into the ground, was the Altar Stone.

> *'Other buildings fall by piece-meal, but here a single stone is a ruin, and lies like the haughty carcase of Goliath'.*
>
> William Stukeley, *Stonehenge...*, 1740, 12.

At Stonehenge there are three isolated stones. They are all controversial and they are all misnamed. The Heel Stone stands outside the ring on the far side from the true Friar's Heel (Burl, 1991). The Slaughter Stone, now prostrate at the entrance, was once erect and never did act as a sacrificial slab for the disembowelling of human offerings by soothsaying druids (Burl, 1991). The Altar Stone near the heart of the circle was neither an altar nor a flat-topped block for human offering to the gods.

Despite the suggestion in 1655 by Inigo Jones that there had been an altar at the centre of Stonehenge, a few years later John Aubrey was sceptical. 'He [Jones] supposes an Altar stone: here are fall'n down, this supposed Altar being one of them. Perhaps they used no altar, for I find the middle of those monuments voyed' (1980, 75).

The disposition of the Altar Stone is a series of contradictions. Away from the middle of Stonehenge the prostrate 5 m long sarsen, Petrie's Stone 80, is weighed down by the top of trilithon 55 and its adjacent lintel, 156. Everything is odd. Although the stone lies across the north-east/south-west axis of the circle it nearly 3 m south of the ring's centre. Nor is it's at right-angles to the axis but skewed 6 1/2° away from 90°. It is not even equidistantly placed across the axis, 2.6 m of its length lying to the west but only 2.4 m to the east. Neither is it level.

In his punctilious survey of 1877 Petrie noted that it was tilted, higher to the east by more than 18 cm. It is a study in idiosyncrasy.

Like a popular film-star it has been given many different roles. It was: used for executions; the pillar of an astronomical sun-dial to indicate the midsummer solstice; meticulously laid over a seven-coiled geo-spiral marking a powerful blind spring; the personification of a female guardian of the dead from Brittany; the top of a low table in a temple designed by Egyptian astronomer-priests; the centrepiece of a Holy of Holies; an erect symbol of the male sexual organ; the lintel of a missing sixth trilithon; and the Womb or Goddess Stone that annually was inseminated by the shadow of the phallic Heel Stone in a cosmic mating. No wonder it lies flat!

Everything is argumentative about it. Why was it brought to Stonehenge? Did it ever stand upright? Is it in its original position? Why is it not central to the circle? What was its function? Only its fictitious name has remained constant.

The Name

It was first called the Altar Stone in 1620 by James I's architect, Inigo Jones. He died in 1652 but his posthumous 'indigested notes' of 1655 stated that inside the ring 'there is a stone appearing not much above the surface of the earth (and lying towards the East) four foot broad, and sixteen foot in length. Which, whether it might be an *Altar* or no, I leave to the judgement of others, because so overwhelmed with the ruines of the Work, that I could make no search after it, even with much difficulty, took the aforesaid proportion thereof'. (Jones, 1655, 57). His uncertainty has lasted for almost four hundred years. He added that he believed sacrifices had been offered at the centre of the ring 'wherein the Victims for oblations were slain' (ibid., 75).

The Stone

It rests on rising land 1.5 m above the bench-mark on the Heel Stone 82 m down the slope to the north-east. Stonehenge's early 18th century researcher William Stukeley, described it. 'Our altar here is laid toward the upper end of the *adytum* [the inner sanctum of a temple], at present flat upon the ground, ... 'Tis a kind of blue coarse marble, such as comes from *Derbyshire*, and laid upon tombs in our churches and church-yards... This altar is plac'd a little above the *focus* of the upper end of the ellipsis'. (Stukeley, 1740, 30)

The Altar Stone is not a local sarsen from the Marlborough Downs in Wiltshire but a pale greenish-grey sandstone flecked with fragments of mica and garnet grains. It is the largest of the 'foreign' stones, some 5 m long, 1.1 m wide and about 0.53 m thick, weighing over 6 tons. The two fallen sarsens lie on it 'and their weight has probably pressed it down to its present position' (Atkinson, 1979, 56). It had been carefully dressed to shape.

Despite the widespread belief that it had come from the Cosheston Beds near Milford Haven it contains mineralogical differences from those sandstones. Being highly micaceous its source was most feasibly from the expanse of the Senni Beds from Kidwelly in the west to Abergavenny in the east (Kellaway, 1971, 245, ibid., 1991, 267; Thorpe et al, 119). If so, the nearest source would have been at least thirty miles from Milford Haven and the farthest almost ninety.

Aubrey Hole 1

An explanation for the Altar Stone being at Stonehenge is that it had been found by a bluestone party returning from the Preselis towards Milford Haven and selected because of its 'myriads of mica platelets' that glittered in the sunshine.

What has been overlooked in the glaciation/human transportation debate is that a glitterless sandstone was found at Stonehenge in an earlier context than the bluestones. It came neither from Wessex nor the Cosheston Beds. Known as OU9, in Cleal et al (1995) it mutates. On page 99 it is a bluestone. On page 377 it becomes a Cosheston Beds sandstone. It ends as a silicified rock on page 394. It is sandstone.

It was found by Hawley on 29 April, 1920 deep in Aubrey Hole I. Deposited alongside the north-eastern entrance it was geologically dissimilar from the Cosheston sandstones, lacking garnet and 'definitely did not derive from the Cosheston Group or the Senni Beds'. The most likely source was the 'Silurian or old Lower Palaeolithic sandstone in the Caledonian fold-belt of south-west Wales' (Thorpe et al, 152–3). How it arrived at Stonehenge is unknown but its pre-bluestone date and its origins far from Milford Haven supports the case for glaciation.

Despite geological optimism the Altar Stone is not proven to be from the neighbourhood of Milford Haven. The provenance of OU9 is completely different. It makes the popular belief that the Altar Stone and the bluestones were brought to Salisbury Plain by human transportation extremely far-fetched (Burl, 1987, 130–5, 1999, 107–23).

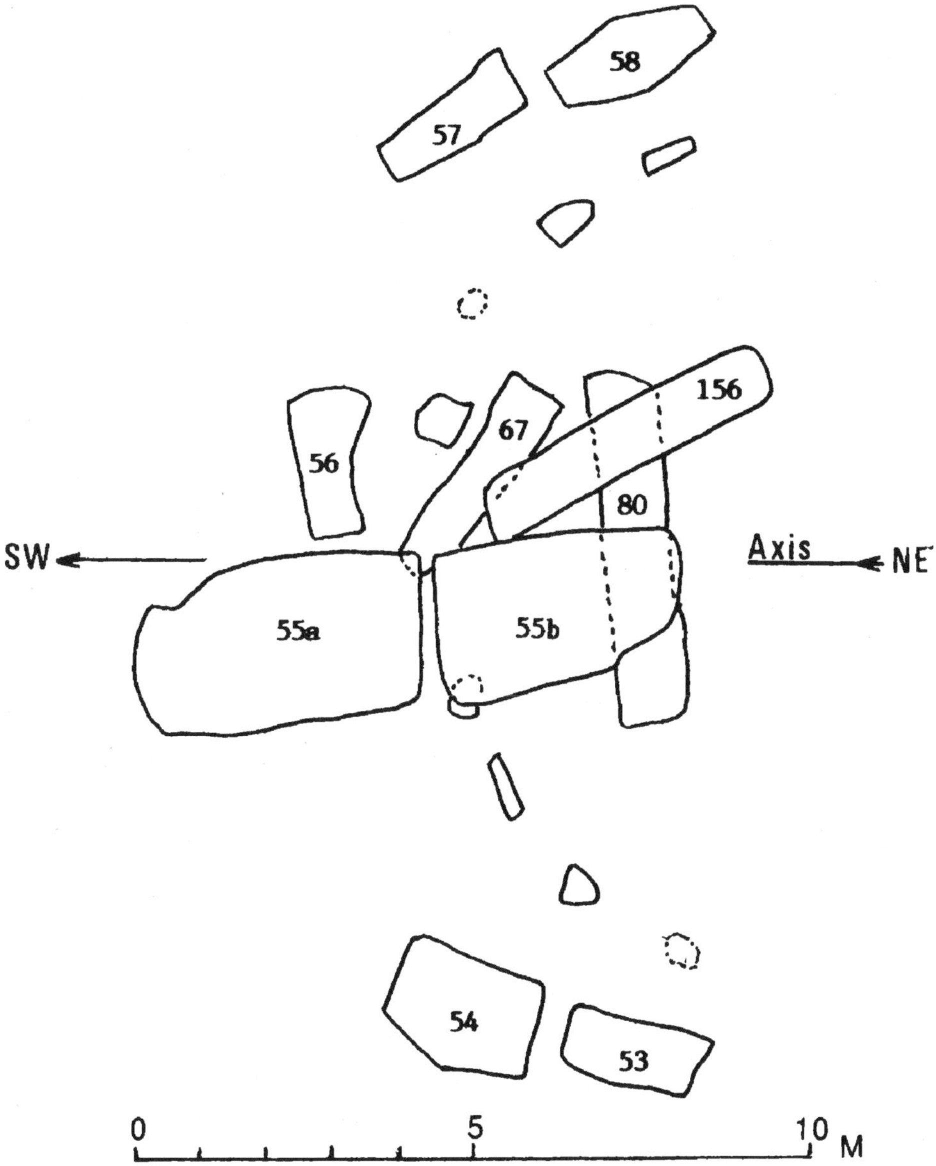

Fig 1: The south-west arc of Stonehenge prior to the 1901 excavations.

Supposedly dragged, hauled and rafted from the Preselis of south-west Wales with the 'magical' doleritic bluestones, that idea derived from the misunderstood fable of the early 12th century chronicler and myth-maker, Geoffrey of Monmouth (1136, 196–8; Burl, 1984). The Altar Stone is not from the Preselis and it is not dolerite but sandstone. There was no reason for it to have been taken by superstitious men searching for health-giving bluestones. More probably it arrived on Salisbury Plain by glaciation, just one of an indiscriminate collection of plain and spotted dolerites, rhyolites, volcanic and calcareous ashes and tuffs (Burl, 2000, 6–9).

Excavations

> *Holes have been dug at many times under and near this stone from the Middle Ages onwards looking for treasure. Needless to say none has been found.*
>
> (Newall, 1953, 7).

Men had been plundering Stonehenge since mediaeval times, usually close to its tempting centre, and the looting continued well into the reign of Queen Victoria. It was only at the beginning of the 20th century that the term 'excavation' can properly be applied to the depredations.

In 1620 James I visited Wilton House, the home of the Earl of Pembroke, accompanied by a troupe of courtiers including the Duke of Buckingham and Inigo Jones. While there Buckingham 'did cause the middle of Stonehenge to be digged; and there remaines a kind of pitt or cavity still, it is about the bigness of two sawepitts; and this under digging was the cause of the falling downe or recumbency of the great stone there [55], twenty one foot long' (Aubrey, 1980, 93). The duke was justifiably assassinated at Portsmouth in 1628.

Aubrey was mistaken about the fall. Stone 55 was already broken half a century earlier. Lucas de Heere made a copy in 1575 of an earlier sketch by an acronymic 'R.F.' that showed the sarsen lying on the ground (Bakker, 107). The trilithon could have collapsed centuries, even millennia earlier. Roman coins, including sestertii of Commodus and Antonia, were found in Gowland's 1901 excavation 'only in the superficial layers' near the trilithon but not beneath the fallen and broken sarsen (Gowland, 1903, 27–8).

There has been a succession of unsuccessful diggers for treasure. The first to be recorded was Inigo Jones. Probably in 1621 the king ordered him to make a report on Stonehenge. Through William, Earl of Pembroke, Jones 'received there his Majesty's commands to produce out of my practice in *Architecture* and experience in *Antiquities* abroad, what possibly I could discover concerning this of Stonehenge', 'I caused the foundations of the stones to be searched' (Jones, 1655, 1). Buckingham had delved into the middle of the monument the year before.

Stukeley himself made an investigation right against the Altar Stone. '5. July 1723 by Ld Pembrokes direction I caus'd a pit to be sunk on the inside of the altar at the middle of the stone. it was 4 f. long upon the edg of the stone & 6 f. forwards or towards the grand entrance. at a foot we came to the solid chalk mixt with f[l]ints into which had never been dug we went 2 f. & 1/2 perpendicular under the stone & found it perfectly solid chalk that had never been stird. I found the altar 20 inches thick, but broke into two or 3 pieces by the upright and architrave falling upon it... the altar is 3 1/2 f. broad. nicely squared. 29 inches thick cub[it] & 1/2. tis very plain all the stones have been squared' (Stukeley, 1723, 45).

Almost a century later on 28 September, 1802 William Cunnington also dug there. In a letter of November to John Britton he wrote, 'I have this summer dug in several places in the area (taking care not to go too near the Stones) ...and particularly at the front of the altar where I dug to a depth of 5 feet or more, and found charred wood, animal bones, and pottery; of the latter there were several pieces similar to the rude urns found in the barrows, also some pieces of Roman pottery. In several places I found stags horns...' (Cunnington, R.H., 1975, 39).

In a second letter of April 12, 1803 he added, 'I have dug two or three times before the altar stone, once to the depth of 6 feet. At about *three feet deep* I found some Roman and other pottery; at the depth of *six feet* some pieces of sarsen stone, and three pieces of coarse half-burnt British pottery with charred wood'. (Cunnington, W., 1884, 147).

As if the area had not already been mutilated beyond optimism about forty years later a Captain Beamish had a huge cavity dug, reputedly 2.4 m square by 1.8 m deep working backwards from the Altar Stone towards the centre of Stonehenge unearthing nothing but charcoal and lots of rabbit bones. 'Before the hole was filled up', Joseph Browne informed William Long, 'I buried a bottle containing a record of the excavation' (Long, 86–7; Burl. 1987, 57–9). If Browne was correct Beamish must have shifted almost twenty tons of sterile chalk already disturbed by Buckingham, Stukeley, Cunnington and a skulduggery of anonymous scavengers.

The Altar Stone Was Shaped

As usual the curious Stukeley was perceptive about the sandstone. 'Tis 20 inches thick, a just cubit, and has been squar'd. It lies between the centers that of the compasses and that of the string: leaving a convenient space quite round it, no doubt, as much as was necessary for their ministration' (1740, 30–1).

William Cunnington in his first letter to John Britton remarked that the sides of the stone 'still retain marks of the tools with which it was originally wrought', and in his second, 'Now to return to Stonehenge, I will pledge myself to prove that the altar stone was worked with tools of some kind, also that Mr. King's 'Slaughtering Stone' stood erect'. (Cunnington, R.H., 1975, 41).

In 1958 when trilithon 57-58 was being restored a small excavation was made around the Altar Stone to determine by examining its shape whether it had ever been intended to stand upright. The northwestern end had been battered by treasure-seekers but originally had been squared off. The other end was more informative. It had been dressed to an 'oblique, bevelled outline, [pointed] very much like the bases of some of the sarsens' to facilitate the erection of the stone (Atkinson, 1979, 211–12). It is unlikely that having done this its masons did not bother to erect the pillar.

Stoneholes

Decades or centuries before the construction of the sarsen circle and during the introduction of the 'bluestones' to Stonehenge, Atkinson's Phase 2, a big but unaccompanied stone was set up. On the south-west end of the henge's axis the wide gap in the indeterminate setting of Q and R, 'Quaere', Holes was broken by a large circular stonehole which had largely been destroyed by post-mediaeval interference. In the disturbed pit there was a ritual deposit of a broken Group I Cornish greenstone axe indicating the importance of the hole to the people who were to erect the stone (Cleal, et al, 181; Souden, 1997, 109).

The pit probably held a single 'bluestone of exceptional size' standing opposite the widened north-eastern entrance. The pit was 2.6 m behind where the Great Trilithon 55-56 would stand. (Cleal et al, 171, Fig. 80, Hole no. WA3639). With the heavy stone still standing the ramp for Stone 56 had to be dug from the north-western side to avoid it (Cleal et al, 181). The pit was too big for an average bluestone and it is tempting to believe that the Altar Stone had stood there.

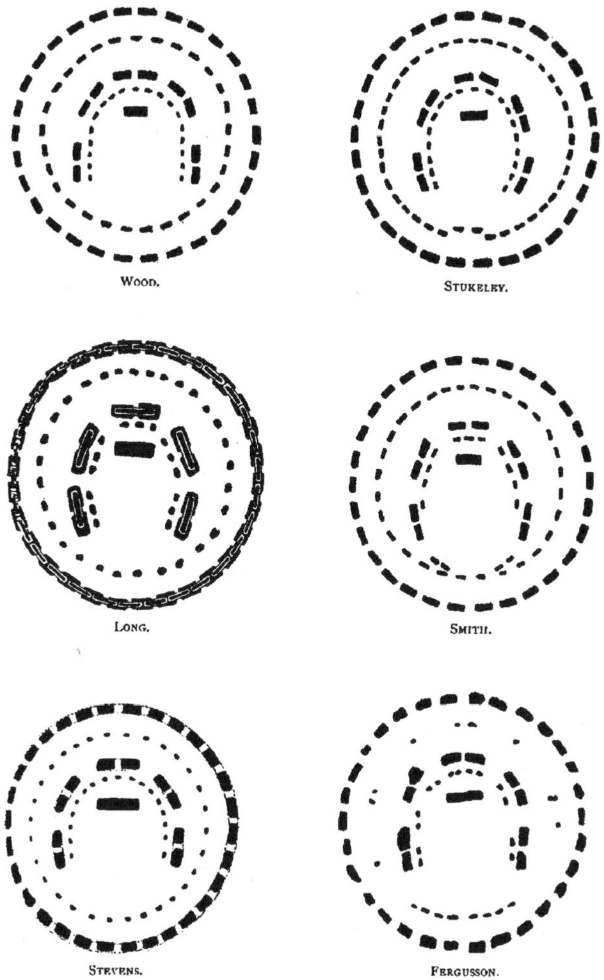

Fig 2: Early views of Stonehenge with a supine Altar Stone.

If the Q & R Holes had formed a concentric horseshoe-shaped setting 12.5 m deep and 22.5 m wide at its south-west mouth then the stone would have stood by itself exactly at the south-west, perhaps acting as a backsight for observations of the midsummer sunrise. It was much larger than its companions, a dominant pillar.

With the subsequent completion of the sarsen circle the stone was removed. Eventually the Altar Stone was placed in front of the tallest of the pairs of lintelled sarsens, the Great Trilithon, 55-56. Whether it stood or lay flat is the most debatable of all the questions about it.

The Fall

John Aubrey did not even believe in the stone. He noticed where Buckingham had dug in the middle of Stonehenge and where, over forty years later, there was 'a kind of pitt or cavity still, it is about the bigness of two sawe-pitts... but there is no signe of an Altar Stone... It is true near to the pitt doe lie three rude roundish stones, which are frustrums [littered broken sarsens]' but nothing more (Aubrey, 1980, 92–3).

Stukeley did believe in it and that it had always lain flat. 'The trilithon of the upper end of the adytum, was an extraordinary beauty. But alas through the indiscretion probably, of some body digging there, between them and the altar, the noble impost is dislodg'd from its airy seat, and fallen upon the altar, where its huge bulk lies unfractur'd' (Stukeley, 1740, 28).

Others disagreed. Theoretically an erect Altar Stone had been pushed to the ground by the fall of Trilithon 55 and its lintel, 156, tumbling it askew of the axis. Trilithon 55, now broken in two halfway along its length, had always been unstable. Faulty construction caused the collapse. Stone 56, fifty tons of sarsen, was 9 m long with 2.5 m of its length buried in its stonehole. Its partner, Stone 55, ten tons lighter, was only 7.3 m long with a mere 1.2 m in the ground (Atkinson, 1979, 41). To counteract the instability its base was club-footed, 'a large projecting foot left in working, to go under ground' (Petrie, 1880, 11). When 55 fell its partner, 56, was pulled out of true and leaned more and more precariously until straightened by Gowland in 1901. The collapse of the trilithon is unquestioned. Whether it knocked over an upright Altar Stone or simply collapsed onto a supine stone has been debated since the time of Inigo Jones.

Erect or Supine?

Amongst the serious students of Stonehenge those in favour of a standing Altar Stone are numerous: Charleton, 1663, 32; Hawkins, 1966, 56; Atkinson, 1979, 57; Richards, 1991, 61; Castleden, 1993, 135; Chippindale, 1994, 271, Cleal et al, 1995, 268; Souden, 1997, 39; Ruggles, 1997, 218; even Burl, 1999, 195–7.

It is an honourable list. So is that of its opponents (Barclay, 1895, 57). It is interesting to see how widespread the belief in a supine Altar Stone was amongst early antiquaries (Fig. 2): Jones, 1655, 56; Stukeley, 1740, 28; Petrie, 1880, 18; Stevens, 1882, 95; Stone, 1924, 19; Cunnington, 1935, 16–18; to which must be added Stevens, 1936, 14; Niel, 1975, 50; Freeman, 1998, 7. Recent opinion has favoured an erect stone. Popularity, however, may not equate with reality.

E. H. Stone was sure that the stone had never stood. 'Some persons have supposed that this stone once stood upright. There is, however, nothing to support such a theory, and all the evidence which can be gained from an examination of the stone itself and from a consideration of its position indicates that it was placed where it now lies as forming part of the original design of the structure [and] would have an obvious use as a dais or platform' (Stone, 1924, 19).

There were practical experiments. Fernand Niel believed the block had always lain flat and 'Wishing to determine this more precisely, I reproduced the fall of the Great Trilithon by means of a scale model. The Altar Stone in the model was displaced in the way described above [slightly shifted from the horizontal by Stone 55's collapse]. It is therefore quite likely that it originally had a symmetrical position in relation to the axis. It would be rather surprising if it had not' (Niel, 1975, 50).

Others agreed. 'The present orientation of the Altar Stone relative to those of sarsens 55 and 56 makes it mechanically improbable that the falling 55 and 156 knocked over a vertical Altar Stone. This combined with the fact that the Winter sunrise and Winter sunset intersect above the *centre* of the Altar Stone make it virtually certain that the Altar Stone is still in its original orientation. Stone 80 was probably pushed downward [into the ground] by 55' (Freeman, 1998, 10).

Archaeological features lying across the axis of a monument are not unknown. Robert Henry Cunnington, great-great-grandson of William Cunnington who excavated at the Altar Stone in 1802, remarked that at Woodhenge the shallow grave of a child had been dug 'in precisely the same relative position as the Altar Stone at Stonehenge. It lies across the axis and at right-angles to it and halfway between the centre and the circumference of the inner ring' (Cunnington, R.H., 1935, 96–7).

It should be added that from the centre of Stonehenge an upright Altar Stone 3.7 m high would have hidden the 2.3 m tall bluestone 67 behind it, utterly spoiling the visual effect of the carefully graded heights of the bluestone horseshoe of which 67 was the apex.

Rather perplexingly, despite Petrie's 1877 survey and Stone's 1924 report on the stones any reader seeking details of lengths and breadths has to refer to John Wood's September, 1740 plan (Wood, 1747, 33, 34).

For the truth about the Altar Stone the choices are simple. Originally it had either been upright or it had been supine. For the first alternative there are three possibilities: that it had fallen of its own accord; that it had been pushed over in Roman or in mediaeval times before 1575; or it was flung down by Stone 55.

If the Altar Stone had simply fallen then it probably would have been in the direction of its ramp where the disturbed chalk was weakest. This remains unprovable because the hypothetical ramp and pit would be concealed beneath the stone itself and the bulk of Stone 55b on top of it. But (a) if it had fallen then of its 4.88 m length about 1.2 m would have been in its hole meaning that the pillar would have had to 'kick' back a further 1.2 m to account for 2.4m of the stone to be east of the axis. It is possible but unlikely because no force except gravity had been applied. The likelihood is that the pillar would have tumbled with its base over or just a little to the east of its damaged pit. It should also be recalled that although far from conclusive Stukeley burrowed under the Altar Stone in search of its hole but found only 'perfect solid chalk, that had never been stir'd' (Stukeley, 1723, 45).

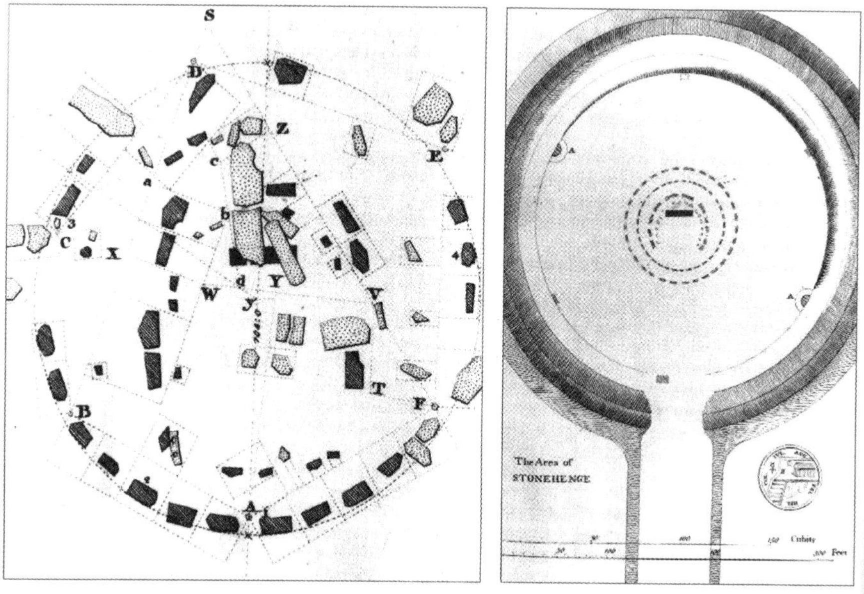

Fig 3: Two plans of Stonehenge in 1740, by Wood (left) and Stukeley (right).

There is a second objection (b). The chances of the stone being so neatly disposed at nearly 90° from the axis are statistically highly improbable, the odds being in the region of 165:1 against when allowing for its 6 1/2° diversion from the right-angle. If its position had not mattered it could have lain anywhere between l° -181° and 179° - 359°.

For Roman or mediaeval interference objection (b) applies as cogently. To this must be added the observation that had Romans been intent on despoiling a centre of druidical resistance they were likely to have battered and ruined the sandstone. Equally, had mediaeval thieves disturbed it then once the stone was out of its hole there was nothing to prevent it being dragged away just as so many bluestones and lintels were stolen before 1575.

For the third theory that an upright Altar Stone had been slammed down by Stone 55 then Niel's and Freemans' claims that the stone could never have been thrust into its present position by the fall of the trilithon are probably correct. Mechanically it would have been almost impossible for that to have occurred. Three stones, 55, lintel 156 and bluestone 67 are the keys.

A likely sequence for the calamity of Trilithon 55-56 would begin with Stone 55, already precariously balanced in its insecure pit and standing on the south-western weather side of Stonehenge, exposed to gusts and gales beating in across the unprotected Plain. The stone began to shift. At a critical angle its lintel would be detached from 55's peg but, still held temporarily by 56, would swing anti-clockwise and downwards, tugging 56 out of the vertical, smashing into 67 which was hurled to the west where it lies at an angle with the now free-falling lintel dropping onto its end and across the western edge of the Altar Stone.

The broad and heavy 55 had fallen almost directly forward, breaking and hitting the Altar Stone which, if standing, would have been forced forward with its top thrust towards the centre of the circle. It could never have been edged so far to its left that it fell neatly athwart the axis, nearly at right-angles, as it does today. Nor could it have been shifted after the catastrophe. Logic demands that it was prone, lying flat as a symbolic 'doorway' or 'entrance' with bluestone 67 rising in front of it, its top forming the bottom of a 'window' through the gap between the trilithon where the midwinter setting sun would shine across the circle between the sarsens at the entrance and up to the Heel Stone and its companion.

Speculation becomes near-reality by the knowledge that there were supine stones in similar cross-axial situations in two other ritual monuments in Wessex, the Sanctuary near Avebury and Woodhenge near Stonehenge. By coincidence both were excavated by Maud Cunnington.

At the Sanctuary a 1.8 m long but only 60 cm deep stonehole was found at the SSW between the two outer rings of postholes, B and C (M. Cunnington, 1931, 308, Hole 3). Pairs of postholes which were not part of the rings were discovered on either side of the hole. Each was only a metre wide 'suggesting entrances or passages into the ring at this point analogous to the southern entrance at Stonehenge' (Pitts, 2000, 284–5).

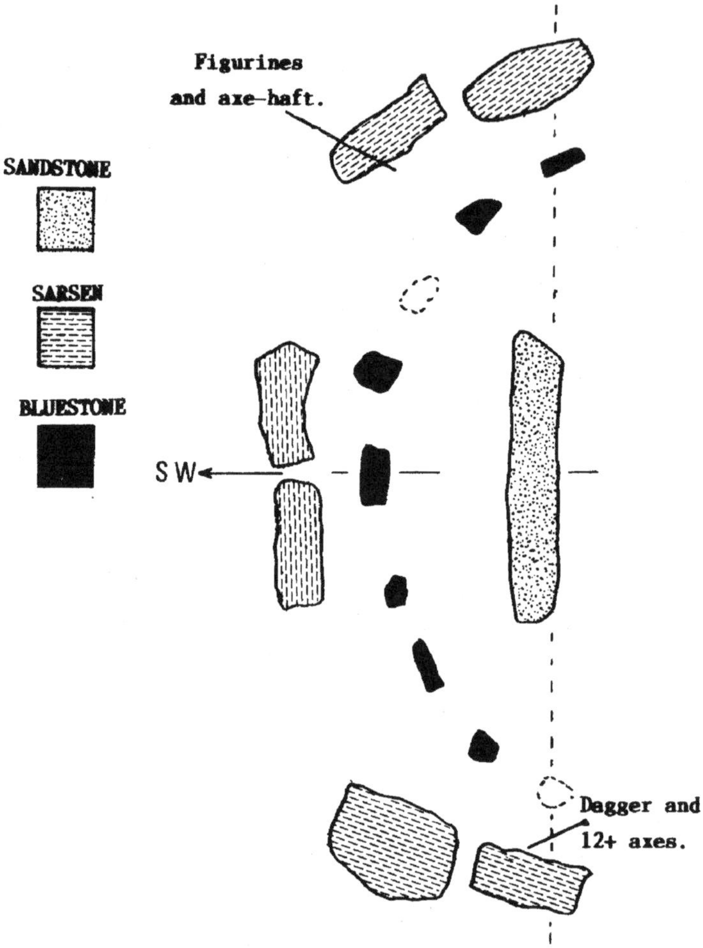

Fig 4: Stonehenge today. It is still possible to identify relationships between a supine Altar Stone and other aspects of the monument.

It is an insight made even more relevant to the Altar Stone by the presence of a comparable stonehole, Hole i, at Woodhenge less than two miles ENE of Stonehenge. Like its counterpart at the Sanctuary it lay between the two outer rings of postholes, A and B. The shallow 2 m long hollow, lying east-west, also rested between two posts, B8 and B9, cutting into and destroying the ramp of B9. The sarsen that had occupied the hole was later broken up.

The combination of a prostrate stone between two uprights intrigued Maud Cunnington. She envisaged an affinity with the architecture of stone circles in Scotland. 'The position of this hole, especially if it did actually contain a stone, is of great interest, for it recalls that of the recumbent stone found in so many circles in the north-east of Scotland'. She cited references to Fred Coles' reports in *PSAS* 34 of 1900 and 37 of 1902 (M. Cunnington, 1929, 14, 15, 38). There are similar but later rings known as multiple-stone circles in south-western Ireland.

The Scottish and Irish sites are both four hundred miles from Salisbury Plain but a belief in a connection at such a distance is unnecessary. The Boyne cemetery in Co. Meath is half the distance, half of it an easy sea-crossing. The prototypes of the Aberdonian recumbent stone and its tall flankers were almost certainly the large prostrate slabs outside the entrance of Boyne passage-tombs such as Newgrange and Knowth (Burl, 2000, 218–19). Those blocks with their intricate, abstract carvings have been interpreted as spiritual barriers between the outside world of the profane and the sacred areas inside the tomb.

With Irish/Wessex trade in copper, bronze and gold well established in the formative years of the Early Bronze Age an interchange not just of objects but also of concepts can be accepted, albeit with native adaptations. With the Boyne entrance blocks in mind the Altar Stone can be visualised as performing a related function, an arcane symbolic 'entrance-sill' to the most secret part of Stonehenge.

It explains why it was that although the stone had been set down symmetrically across the axis of Stonehenge it was some 3 m south of the centre. This was not true of other rings with so-called 'centre-stones'. Such pillars, which were always erect, were seldom at the precise middle of a ring but they were never raised far from it (Thom, 1967, 62; Burl, 2000, 252). The Altar Stone, lying flat and displaced from the centre by a tenth of the ring's diameter, was obviously different.

The probable reason was that it separated a third of the circle from the rest of Stonehenge. To reach that area was akin to passing through a cathedral to reach the Lady Chapel and its mysteries. It was a 'cell' made special by the grandeur of its high bluestones and towering trilithons, by its chosen association with the midwinter sunset, and by the presence of the only art inside Stonehenge (Cleal et al, 30–3).

Even in ruin and with stones removed it is still possible to see how carefully the area had been designed (Fig. 3). Directly in front of the Altar stood the tallest bluestone, 67, and behind it rose the Great Trilithon. These were gigantic but plain stones. To their left and right were subtleties.

To the left, south of the Altar Stone was Trilithon 53-4. There were carvings on Stone 53 but a bluestone, now missing, would have obscured any decoration on the lefthand side of the sarsen's inner face. There was none. The famous dagger and a dozen or more axes were ground and pecked out on the far side

Fig 5: A detail of Stukeley's view of Stonehenge's interior, from Stonehenge... *(1740).*

of 53 to the right of the bluestone leaving them in full view of anyone standing at the Altar Stone.

To the right, west, of the Altar Stone there were carvings of a figurine and the haft of an axe on Stone 57, the lefthand sarsen of Trilithon 57-8. Bluestone 69 and a lost one between it and 68 concealed the righthand side of 57. The carvings can be seen head-high to the left, like Stone 53 placed where they would be visible from the Altar Stone.

'Grey ruined choirs' wrote Shakespeare, and it is true of Stonehenge, its meaning as nearly erased as mediaeval wall-paintings whose bright colours and sermons of the sickle-bearing skeleton of Death have been obliterated by puritanical iconoclasts and 19th century plaster. They were unnecessary at Stonehenge. Time and weather were the destroyers.

But fragments of glory remain for the present to wonder and worry over. The Altar Stone is still there, lying close to where it was placed before the collapse of Stone 55 disturbed it. Bluestone 67 can be seen under the lintel that once rested high on the top of the Great Trilithon. Those sarsens exist, 56 made vertical and concreted solidly in 1901. Its companion, 55, is down, broken.

It demands imagination to recreate the scene, re-erecting the trilithon and the bluestone and having the Altar Stone lying across the axis in front of them. The wreckage has been so harsh that imagination is demanded.

As so often, William Stukeley half-anticipated this by several centuries (Fig. 4). His drawing of 6 June, 1724, 'A peep into the Sanctum Sanctorum' depicts that powerful scene perfectly (Stukeley, 1740, 12, Tab. VII).

References

Atkinson, R.J.C., 1979, *Stonehenge*, Harmondsworth.

Aubrey, J., 1980, *Monumenta Britannica*, 1665-93, I, Milborne Port.

Bakker, J.A, 1979, 'Lucas de Heere's Stonehenge', *Antiquity* 53, 107-11.

Barclay, E, 1895, *Stonehenge and its Earthworks*, London.

Burl, A., 1984, 'Geoffrey of Monmouth and the Stonehenge bluestones', *WAM* 79, 178–83.

Burl, A., 1987, *The Stonehenge People*, London.

Burl, A., 1991, 'The Heel Stone, Stonehenge: a study in misfortunes', *WAM* 84, 1–10.

Burl, A., 1994, 'Stonehenge: slaughter, sacrifice and sunshine', *WAM* 87, 85–95.

Burl, A., 1999, *Great Stone Circles*. London.

Burl, A., 2000, *The Stone Circles of Britain, Ireland and Brittany*, London.

Castleden, R., 1994, *The Making of Stonehenge*, London.

Charleton, W., 1663, *Chorea Gigantum, or the Most Famous antiquity of Great-Britan, vulgarly called Stone-Heng, standing on Salisbury Plain, Restored to the Danes*, London.

Chippindale, C., 1994, *Stonehenge Complete*, 2nd ed., London.

Cleal R.M.J., Walker, K.E and Montague, R., eds., 1995, *Stonehenge in its Landscape. Twentieth Century Excavations*, London.

Cunliffe, B. & Renfrew, C. eds., 1997, *Science and Stonehenge*, London.

Cunnington, M.E., 1929, *Woodhenge*, Devizes.

Cunnington, M.E., 1931, 'The "Sanctuary" on Overton Hill, near Avebury', *WAM* 45, 300–35.

Cunnington, R.H., 1935, *Stonehenge and its Date*, London.

Cunnington, R.H., 1975, *From Antiquary to Archaeologist. A Biography of William Cunnington, 1754-1810*, Princes Risborough.

Fergusson, J., 1872, *Rude Stone Monuments...*, London.

Freeman, G.R. & P.J., 1998, 'Stonehenge: winter solstice sunrise and set lines accurate to 0.2' in 4000 B. P. Unpublished paper, Edmonton, Canada.

Geoffrey of Monmouth., c.1136, *The History of the Kings of Britain*, Harmondsworth, 1966.

Gowland, W., 1903, 'Recent excavations at Stonehenge', *WAM* 33, 1–62.

Hawley, W., 1921, 'Stonehenge: interim report on the exploration', *Ant J* 1, 17–41.

Hawkins, G.S., 1966, *Stonehenge Decoded*, London.

Hoare, Sir R., 1812, *Ancient Wiltshire*, London.

Jones, I., 1655, *The Most Notable Antiquity of Great Britain, vulgarly called Stone-Heng*, London.

Kellaway, G., 1971, 'Glaciation and the stones of Stonehenge', *Nature* 232, 30–5.

Kellaway, G., 1991, ed. *Hot Springs of Bath*, Bath.

Long, W., 1867, *Stonehenge and its Barrows*, Devizes.

Niel, F., 1975, *The Mysteries of Stonehenge*, New York.

Newall, R.S., 1953, *Stonehenge*, Wiltshire, London.

Petrie, W.M.F., 1880, *Stonehenge: Plans, Description, and Theories*, London.

Pitts, M., 2000, *Hengeworld*, London.

Richards, J., 1991, *English Heritage Book of Stonehenge*, London.

Ruggles, C.L.N., 1997, 'Astronomy and Stonehenge', In. eds. Cunliffe, B & Renfrew, C., 203–230.

Souden, D., 1997, *Stonehenge. Mysteries of the Stones and Landscape*, London.

Stevens, E.T., 1882, *Jotting on some of the Objects of interest in the Stonehenge Excursion*, Salisbury.

Stevens, F., 1936, *Stonehenge Today and Yesterday*, London.

Stone, E.H., 1924, *The Stones of Stonehenge*, London.

Stukeley, W., 1723, 'The history of the temples and religion of the antient Celts', MS. 4,253, Cardiff Public Library.

Stukeley, W., 1740, *Stonehenge a Temple Restor'd to the British Druids*, London.

Thorpe, R.S., Williams-Thorpe, O., Jenkins, D.G. & Watson, J.S., 1991, 'The geological sources and transportation of the bluestones of Stonehenge, Wiltshire, U.K., *PPS* 57 (2), 103–57.

Wood, J., 1747, *Choir Gaure, vulgarly called Stonehenge, on Salisbury Plain...*, Oxford.

The Secret History of Corpse Ways

Paul Devereux

Paul Devereux looks at hidden dimensions of medieval corpse ways.

There are two kinds of history. The standard one is what most scholars concern themselves with, dealing with rulers, governments, and social upheavals like wars, invasions, changes in religious practice, and major technological developments. The other involves the beliefs and practices of rural people that are much less documented and thus out of sight of the more mainstream, overall cultural phenomenon of a society. As the Italian scholar Carlo Ginzburg has observed, historians are poor at studying 'invisible mental structures' of this kind[1]. No archaeological feature is a greater victim of this historical double vision than the medieval corpse way.

Vision One

The standard historical view of the corpse way is straightforward enough. Such features (also referred to as church paths, coffin lines, burial roads, lyke ways – from Old English *liches*, corpse – and various other appellations) provided a

1 Ginzburg, Carlo, 1989, *Ecstasies – Deciphering the Witches' Sabbath*, Penguin Books, 1992.

functional means of allowing corpses to be transported to cemeteries that had burial rights, as Jeremy Harte has previously explained in the pages of this journal[2]. In England in the tenth century, for instance, when there was a proliferation of village churches being built within the territories of existing mother churches or minsters, burial rights became an issue. There was a demand for autonomy from outlying settlements that minster officials felt could erode their authority, so they decided to ritually bind their parishes together by instituting corpse ways that led from outlying locations to the heart of the parish, the mother church, which held the parish's rights of burial. For some parishioners, this meant corpses had to be transferred quite long distances, sometimes over difficult terrain. Most of the funerals conducted along these corpse ways were walking ones. At points along such routes there would be wayside crosses or rough-hewn, often lozenge-shaped coffin stones where bearers could rest their burden, and where prayers would be said or hymns sung.

Nevertheless, these uncontested facts about medieval corpse ways in Britain and elsewhere in Europe provide only a surface history. It is not the whole story.

Vision Two

Corpse ways disclosed spirit lore already long extant in isolated rural populations, attracting it to them like magnets, for they ran not only through the physical countryside but also through the invisible country, the mental terrain, of pre-industrial country-folk. What was this spirit lore? It is revealed by a variety of 'virtual' and physical features across Old Europe.

The virtual features were folk beliefs that were geographically located. An example existed in Nemen, Russia (in a region that was formerly eastern Prussia), where there was the tradition of a *Leichenflugbahn*, literally 'corpse flightpath'. The town had two cemeteries, one German, the other Lithuanian. The spirits of the dead in one cemetery would visit those in the other on stormy nights. A straight line connecting the two places was kept clear of trees, shrubs, fences, hedges, houses, and walls, because the ghosts were said to fly very close to the ground, and so should not be hindered. On one occasion, a newcomer built a house on this line, despite the warnings from locals. Sure enough, the house was destroyed. In another incident, a local man wanted to erect a shed between the two cemeteries. However, this fellow had 'second sight' and could see spirits, so he marked the passage of the flitting cemetery ghosts by placing a stick in the

2 Harte, Jeremy, 1998, 'Show Me the Way to Go Home', *3rd Stone*, April–June.

Fig 1: A corpse-way track cuts across summer fields to Streat Church, West Sussex (P. Devereux).

ground and erecting the shed just to one side of it. Unfortunately, he was careless, for a corner of the roof just protruded onto the course of the flight-path, and the shed was flattened[3]. The Germans more generally had virtual paths they called *Geisterwege* that linked physical cemeteries. In Ireland and other Celtic lands there were fairy paths that while being invisible nevertheless had such perceived geographical reality in the minds of the country people that building practices were adopted to allow them passage. Fairies and the spirits of the dead held a

3 Hinze, Christe, and Diederich, Ulf, 1991, *Ostpreussiche Sagen*, Eugen Diederich, Munich. (Cited in Magin, Ulrich, 'The Flightpath of Corpses', *The Ley Hunter*, no 131, 1999)

Fig 2: This section of a corpse way near the church at Dyrham, Gloucestershire, is said to be haunted by a 'grey lady' ghost.

curiously ambiguous relationship in the peasant mind: American folklorist Evans Wentz was told about paths of the dead in Brittany, for instance, that he could not distinguish from the beliefs about fairy paths elsewhere[4].

Most if not all of these and other virtual spirit paths were conceived of as being *straight* – a factor that intrigues me, as a researcher who long ago cut his teeth on 'leys'. This is even the case regarding fairy paths (an issue that has caused previous debate), as I have now been able to determine[5]. However, the physical features vary between being dead straight and not particularly straight. Straight ones include the Dutch *Doodwegen* (death roads), *Leichenwegen* (corpse roads), or *Spokenwegen* (spook or ghost roads). These latter were officially controlled to ensure their regularity and are rather exact versions of the more relaxed British corpse ways.

4 Evans Wentz, W.Y., 1911, *The Fairy-Faith in Celtic Countries*, Colin Smythe, Gerrards Cross, 1977 (194 and 218).

5 I have recently returned from two research trips to Ireland, where I have been involved with extensive archive and field work. It has now been firmly established that fairy paths were indeed conceived of as being straight. I will be publishing this work – and further research – in due course.

So in Old Europe there seems to have been a 'virtual blueprint' concerning spirit ways relating to physical cemeteries (and certain crossroads) and physical, more pragmatic paths actually used for conveying corpses to burial. The precise relationship between the virtual and physical features is currently fugitive, but it is hoped that this paper can shed some light on the matter.

If we are to ask the basic question as to whether the physical corpse ways came to be perceived as being ways for spirits, the answer is an unequivocal 'yes'. It appears that the physical features, irrespective of the factual historical situation in which they arose, took on some of the key attributes of the 'virtual blueprint'. It may not be a tidy transposition for factual historians, but it is nevertheless undeniable because the documentation is there for those with the wit to seek it.

Apart from there being an abundance of generalised lore about how corpses were to be conveyed along corpse ways to avoid their spirits returning along them, there are specific references. Researcher John Palmer, for instance, found a documented contemporary tradition relating to a *Doodweg* at Aalst in Belgium where mourners used to intone: 'Spirit, proceed ahead, I'll follow you'. This suggests that the spirit connection was alive and well when the roads were being used, and is not some hindsight falsified folk memory. (Incidentally, Palmer also discovered a contemporary document – a Dutch medieval law code – to prove that mourners also recognised the special nature of straightness attached to the death roads. See my *Haunted Land*, p.67.) British corpse ways, although having less rigorous morphology than their Dutch counterparts, were nevertheless also definitely associated with spirits, at least by Elizabethan times, as Shakespeare confirms. In his *A Midsummer's Night Dream*, the Bard has that old land spirit, Puck, pronounce in his penultimate speech:

Now it is the time of night,

That the graves all gaping wide,

Every one lets forth his sprite,

In the church-way paths to glide.

There it is – the secret history recorded for us by the most noble of pens (or was it a quill?). Nor is it surprising that pathways used for such a dread activity as conveying dead bodies should attract spirit lore: as historian Nancy Caciola has remarked, 'spirits seeking bodies haunted the late medieval landscape'[6].

---

6 Caciola, Nancy, 2000, 'Spirits seeking bodies: death, possession and communal memory in the Middle Ages', Gordon, Bruce, and Marshall, Peter, (eds.), *The Place of Dead*, Cambridge U.P., Cambridge, (66).

Corpse Ways and Necromancy

The spirit connection with the physical corpse way has more subtle dimensions. I suspect that there was a link between corpse ways and the strange practice known in Britain as the 'Church Porch Watch'. In this, a village seer would hold a vigil between 11 p.m. and 1 a.m. at the church door or lych (corpse) gate, or at some place in the graveyard, in order to look for the spectres of those who would die in the course of the following year[7]. Typically, this took place on St Mark's Eve (24 April), which was the preferred time, or New Year's Eve, Midsummer Eve, Halloween, or Christmas Eve. The wraiths of the doomed living members of the community would usually appear to the eye of the seer as a procession coming in from beyond the churchyard and passing in through the church door, and then returning back out into the dark night. (What is interesting here, of course, is that this reveals the belief that the spirits of living people while asleep could also wander the land.) My guess is that the concept of spectral processions coming into the churchyard would have been related to the corpse ways or church paths leading there. This is supported in the fact that some seers witnessed spectral funerals rather than the wraiths of living people, and is further hinted at in a record relating to an old woman at Fryup, Yorkshire, who was well known locally for keeping the 'Mark's e'en watch'. She foretold her own death by this means of divination: 'When I dee, for dee I s'all, mind ye carry me to my grave by t'church-road... if ye de'ant, I'll come again,' she warned her neighbours[8].

Haunted Land – Abstract and Literal Cosmologies

In the medieval and early modern periods there was a schism between the Church and the rural populations of Europe with regard to supernatural ideas. It was older motifs to do with the 'unruly dead' and the old gods disguised as Christian saints that held the populace in thrall, not theological constructs. But Nancy Caciola also points out: 'Even as these two systems of thought competed with one another... they over-lapped.' A key aspect of this schism was that the Church taught that the spirit left the body at death and went immediately to another, non-physical plane, while rural communities believed that the dead could return and haunt the locality. The Church abstracted the otherworld – heaven, hell, and purgatory were in places other than the physical Earth. Such abstractions were slow to be accepted by ordinary country-folk; they felt they shared the physical geography

7 Menefee, Samuel Pyeatt, 1989, 'Dead Reckoning: the Church Porch Watch in British Society', in Davidson, H.R. Ellis, (ed.), *The Seer*, John Donald, Edinburgh (80–99).

8 Atkinson, J.C., 1891, *Forty Years in a Moorland Parish*, Macmillan, London (219).

with spirits, as was the case with virtually every other ancient society on Earth. The Church taught an abstract cosmology while country populations stubbornly inhabited a literal one. 'In all tales we find the survival of the medieval connection between ghosts and locality,' historian Bruce Gordon has underlined. (Gordon, Bruce, and Marshall, Peter, (eds.), *The Place of the Dead*, Cambridge UP., Cambridge, 2000, p.93.) Country-folk worried about 'ghostes and spirites walking by nyght'.

The Church Porch Watch custom in Britain may have been a less-structured variant of a Dutch tradition concerning a class of diviners called *voorlopers* or *veurkieken*, 'precursors', who were specifically associated with the death roads (perhaps echoing the more specific morphology of the death roads in Holland compared to those in Britain)[9]. They were seers able to tell who was going to die soon in the community because they had the ability to see spectral funeral processions pass along the death road they visited or lived alongside.

Both the Dutch precursors and the British church seers would seem to fall into the same general class of practitioner as those who perceived the dead by means of trance on St Lucy's Stool in Hungary, or by 'sitting out' in cemeteries or on burial mounds as in Norse tradition (see my *Haunted Land*). Probably another facet of this same class of seership was that described in Icelandic folklore which concerned a medieval practice at crossroads 'where four roads run, each in a straight unbroken line, to four churches', or from where four churches were visible. The seer would go to such crossroads on New Year's Eve, or St John's Day and cover himself with the hide of a bull or a walrus, and fix his attention on the shiny blade of an axe while laying as still as a corpse throughout the night. He would recite various spells to summon the spirits of the dead from the church cemeteries and they would glide up the roads to the crossroads where the seer could divine information from them[10].

Gone with the Wind

Once it is understood that corpse ways had necromantic associations, it is possible to recognise more elliptical references to the matter. Take this folktale from Cornwall: ...a widow who had been deprived of her rights was out walking with a friend when she saw a dog her friend could not see. It transformed into her dead husband who told her to be a ready at a certain time when he would come for her. On the appointed hour, the woman put on her bonnet and went outside her front door. The ghost of her husband appeared and he caught her up in his arms and carried her over the tree-tops to Ludgvan Church, where he set her down on the church stile. There she saw 'a good many spirits, some good and some bad'[11]. The bad spirits wanted her to join them, but the good ghosts gave her information that ultimately was to enable her to retrieve her rights. After this stile divination, the spectral hubby flew the woman home *by the same route*. During the flight, one of the widow's shoes caught in the top branches of a tree.

9 Palmer, John, 1998, 'The Folklore of Death: The Precursors', and 'The Precursors III', *The Ley Hunter*, no. 129.

10 Simpson, Jacqueline, 1972, *Icelandic Folktales and Legends*, University of California Press, Berkeley (176–178).

11 Courtney, M.A., 1890, *Folklore and Legend of Cornwall*, Cornwall Books, Exeter, 1989 (207).

This tale would appear to be a folk-gloss of a corpse way and the spirit divination associated with it. Stiles in Cornwall were often associated with spirits, and stile necromancy was an old tradition. We can now see that it is another echo of corpse way divination.

A Welsh tradition similarly held that living human beings (or their spirits) could be transported through the air by ghosts – it was said that the person was always given the option of flying 'above wind, amid wind, or below wind'[12]. The latter mode often led to collisions with trees and other objects – much as seems to have happened to the Cornish widow. It is essentially the same image as that involving the spirit path between the two cemeteries at Nemen, and this is in turn remarkably similar to ideas about *Geisterwege*. So we can perhaps at last begin to see a widespread conceptual resonance between the 'virtual blueprint' of spirit ways and the physical corpse ways.

Fairy Funerals

Where spirits of the dead are, one might reasonably expect to find those ambiguous entities, fairies. Evans Wentz was told in Armagh that the 'good people' were the spirits of dead friends which cannot be recognized, and another chronicler of Irish fairy lore, Lady Gregory, noted that there was a belief in the west of Ireland that the dead and fairies were different kinds of spirit, but that they mingled with one another, so that when the fairies pass by in a blast of wind we should say some words of blessing, 'for there may be among them some of our own dead'[13].

Residual lore suggests that fairies could be associated with corpse ways. Robert Kirk recorded in 1691 that Scottish Highland people gifted with 'second sight' can see fairies assisting humans in the carrying of the bier or coffin to the grave[14]. In the nineteenth century, Irish folklorist Thomas Keightley recorded an account from an informant who told of seeing a procession of fairies travelling 'acrass the High Field, in the direction o' the ould church'[15]. There was also a tradition of fairy funerals, and Abergavenny museum curator, Frank Olding, has given a number of Welsh examples[16]. For instance, a fairy funeral was seen going down Church Lane to the church at Aberystruth, and another to Llanithel Church. A subtler version of

12 Davies, Jonathan Caredig, 1911, *Folk-Lore of West and Mid-Wales*, Llanerch, Lampeter, 1992 (149–150).

13 Gregory, Lady, 1920, *Visions and Beliefs in the West of Ireland*, Colin Smythe; Gerrards Cross, 1979 (10).

14 Kirk, Robert, *The Secret Commonwealth of Elves, Fauns, & Fairies*, (1691), Rare Text Library of Philosophical Research, Toddington, 1964 (5).

15 Keightley, Thomas, 1892, *The Fairy Mythology*, Wildwood House, London, 1981 (520).

16 Olding, Frank, 'Fairy Lore in 18th-Century Monmouthshire', *3rd Stone*, no 31, 1998 (19–22).

what is probably the same kind of association is attached to Lincoln Cathedral. It is said that when it was decided to build the cathedral, fairies carried the stones from the ancient, Saxon church at Stow 'direct across the fields, where there is still a right of way'[17].

Is the 'Virtual Blueprint' Shamanic?

Through an apparent lack of clarity on my part, I have previously and elsewhere given the impression that I am claiming corpse ways to be themselves of shamanic origin. This is not the case: they are medieval features. What I was trying to suggest is that the spirit lore – the sort of material referred to above – that became attached to them probably has its roots in an ancient Eurasian shamanism, for contact with the ancestral spirits and spirit flight are quintessential shamanic themes.

Due to recent and ongoing scholarly research, it is now possible to detect the context in which mutations of such lore could have survived. Across medieval and early modern Europe, from Hungary to Ireland and Scandinavia, there was a wide range of trance practitioners – village specialists who could enter an ecstatic mode of consciousness for the purposes of divination, or for protecting the fertility of the fields, livestock and vineyards from hostile and evil forces, or for healing (or cursing). These specialists often share discernible characteristics, and the tradition to which they belong seems to be traceable back to an agrarian shamanism of considerable antiquity[18]. There was also a Europe-wide range of 'spirit management' techniques designed to prevent night-flying spirits from entering dwellings or haunting pathways.

Light is just beginning to be shone into the dark, complex secret life of Old Europe which gave corpse ways their hidden (literally occult) dimensions.

17 Dickinson, Bob, 1993, 'Lincolnshire Spirit Lines', *Markstone*, no. 8 (7).

18 Ginzburg, Carlo, 1989/92, *op. cit.*; Pocs, Eva, *Between the Living and the Dead*, (1977), Central European University Press, Budapest, 1999; Devereux, Paul, *Haunted Land*, Piatkus, London, 2001.

Odin's Lost Eye

Alby Stone

Did Odin lose his eye when Irish and Norse traditions of similar gods merged, asks Alby Stone.

Odin, the central figure of Norse myth, is a one-eyed god. This feature makes him instantly recognisable. When the Icelandic sagas tell us that a one-eyed stranger enters a nobleman's hall, we know who it is. If we read in a poem that a traveller meets a one-eyed man along the way, we know that he has encountered Odin. Even more than his ravens, his spear, or his wide-brimmed hat, the lost eye is Odin's defining characteristic.

How Odin Lost His Eye: Literary Explanations

The earliest surviving literary reference to Odin's missing eye is in the poem *Hrafnsmál* (also known as *Haraldskvæði*) by the Norwegian skald Thorbjörn Hornklofi, who died around 945. The oldest parts of *Hrafnsmál* were probably written between 845 and 900. Thorbjörn calls Odin *inum eineygja Friggjar faðmbyggvi*, 'the one-eyed husband of Frigg'. The earliest known explanation of *why* Odin is one-eyed is given in stanza 28 of the poem *Völuspá*.

I know it all, Odin,
where you hid your eye
in the famous well of Mímir
Mímir drinks mead
Every morning

From *Valföðr's [Odin's] pledge.*

Völuspá does not say why Odin hid his eye in Mímir's well. Snorri Sturluson (*Prose Edda: Gylfaginning* 14) who quotes this verse, adds a detail not found in earlier literature: Odin had asked Mímir for a single drink from the well – which bestowed wisdom – and was required to leave one of his eyes in exchange.

It is generally agreed that *Völuspá* was composed toward the end of the tenth century (Nordal 1971, G. Turville-Petre 1953, 56), making it about a hundred years later than the lines from *Hrafnsmál*. These are the earliest known literary references to Odin's lost eye. The earliest full explanation we have for the loss of Odin's eye is from Snorri's thirteenth-century text. There is no guarantee that the explanation did not originate with Snorri, who could have constructed the idea around the *Völuspá* description of the eye as *veðr*, 'pledge' or 'stake'.

Mythological literature gives one explanation. Even if Snorri's tale was based on an authentic tradition, what underlies that myth? Odin's lack of an eye is very nearly unique in Indo-European tradition. There is only one equivalent one-eyed deity anywhere else in Indo-European myth. And, there is evidence that Odin may not always have been one-eyed.

Indo-European Origins of the One-Eyed God?

Dumézil (1973) saw enough parallels with other one-eyed characters to suggest a dual representation of sovereignty in which a one-eyed god of magic was coupled with a one-handed god of law. In Norse myth these were Odin and Týr. Dumézil's theory sounds plausible – but it is not supported by anything more than tenuous associations with minor figures, mostly from Roman historical legend, which are not represented as formal pairs. There are no other one-eyed gods in Indo-European myth, except for the Lithuanian god Velinus, whose one-eyedness is attested only from the sixteenth century and who may well have acquired facets of Odin through close contact with pagan Scandinavians. And although there are dual sovereign gods in Indian myth – Mitra and Varuna – there is no evidence for Odin and Týr being portrayed as a linked pair in Norse myth. Indeed, the more closely Dumézil's idea is examined, the weaker it looks.

An older idea, dating from the nineteenth century but still occasionally given an airing, is that Odin is one-eyed because he was originally, or took over the position of, a sun god – his single eye is the solar orb. For instance, Branston (1980, 114) claims that 'The eye of Odin... is an emblem of the sun and Mímir's drinking mead from it *every morning* a representation of the sun's rising just as the hiding of the eye is the sun's setting'. Branston thinks that Mímir's well is the sea – but is quite clearly one more version of the well or spring at the centre of the world that features throughout Indo-European cosmology. Moreover, this idea would mean that Odin's pledge counted for very little, that he left his eye in the well on a part-time basis but received permanent wisdom in return. The idea has little going for it. There is indeed something about Odin's glance that is directly related to the power of the sun, as we shall see – but he is certainly not a solar deity or a god in the same vein as the old Indo-European sky father. There is nothing to suggest that any other forms of Odin were at any time personifications of the sun or had specifically solar attributes.

Kershaw (2000) argues that the one-eyed god developed from an early Indo-European warrior cult whose members played a ritual game with nuts. This cult was a forerunner of the Germanic war-bands with which Odin has been associated. Like Dumézil's theory, Kershaw's argument suffers from a dearth of genuinely one-eyed deities – the only one-eyed god mentioned in his list of analogues to Odin is Velinus. It is all very well to suppose that Indo-European tales of one-eyed sorcerers and warriors follow the pattern of a one-eyed god, but it falls down when the only known authentic one-eyed deities in Indo-European myth are Odin and Velinus.

Odin as Deified Hero: Hannibal, Sertorius and Civilis

The Norse god Odin, like his English equivalent Woden, developed from an earlier Germanic god whose name has been reconstructed as *Wodanaz[1]. Old Norse

1 Here I use the name **Wodanaz* (the asterisk conventionally denotes a reconstructed linguistic form) in either of two senses, according to context. First, it refers to the early Germanic form of the god before the linguistic diversification that gave rise to *Óðinn* in Scandinavia and *Woden* or *Wodan* in West Germanic (Old

Óðinn and Old English *Woden* and other forms of the name known from Germanic texts and inscriptions all come from an older form *Wodanaz that must have been current before the Germanic languages diverged, and before the Germanic migrations began. There is a widely held view, first aired in 1876 by the Danish archaeologist Karl Nikolai Henry Petersen, that *Wodanaz may not have been one of the original Germanic gods. According to this school of thought *Wodanaz was a relative latecomer to Germanic religion, who somehow managed to usurp the position and many attributes of the original Germanic sovereign god – the 'sky father' *Tiwaz, who survived in Norse myth as the diminished Týr.

One branch of the theory suggests that *Wodanaz was originally a Germanic adaptation of the Gaulish Mercury, Lugos – the god known as Lug in Irish myth, and who is also known from Roman Britain. The only factor that could realistically argue for this is that Lugos appears in Romano-Celtic inscriptions before the later forms of *Wodanaz appear in writing – which proves nothing except that the Gauls and Britons were dominated by a literate society while most of the Germans were still illiterate. Take away the inscriptions and one could just as easily argue that Lugos was a Celtic adaptation of *Wodanaz.

Until recently none of the arguments for a late *Wodanaz gave any clue as to why Odin has only one eye. An intriguing explanation of the rise of *Wodanaz was proposed by Africa (1970), and recently revived and expanded by Enright (1996, 217–40). Enright argues that *Wodanaz developed from a cult arising from three historical figures: the famous Carthaginian general Hannibal; Quintus Sertorius, a first century BCE Roman governor of Iberia who rebelled against Rome; and the first-century Batavian chieftain known as Julius Civilis. Because of his Germanic connections Civilis may be the most important. Tacitus (*The Histories* 13–14) says that Civilis shared a facial disfigurement with Hannibal and Sertorius. They were all one-eyed. Tacitus tells how Civilis, who consciously imitated Hannibal and Sertorius, stirred up a rebellion against Rome. In the process, he deliberately invoked his ancestral traditions. During a lavish feast he addressed the most prominent of his compatriots in a sacred grove, invoking the past glories of the Batavi and obtaining an oath of loyalty cemented by barbaric ritual and traditional curses.

Sertorius and Hannibal were both said to have been masters of disguise; Sertorius in particular was noted for disguising himself and infiltrating his enemies to find out their plans. Furthermore, Sertorius had a strong interest in locating the Celtic version of the Elysian Fields, which he believed to be on an island in

English, Old Saxon and so on). Second, to the entire range of manifestations and names of the god: *Óðinn*, *Woden* and *Wodan* (including Longobardic *Guodan*, and so on).

Fig. 1: Illustration of Woden, from a 13th Century English genealogy.

the Atlantic. Enright suggests that 'one-eyedness, disguise, war leadership and a possible connection with a cult of the dead are simply too specific and too arresting to easily be dismissed as coincidental' (Enright 1996, 220).

Was Sertorius the source of the idea of *Wodanaz as a master of disguise? Enright bases this largely on the Odin's nickname Grímr 'the masked one' and the occasional failure of characters in Norse literature to recognise the god when he appears. But in Norse literature Odin does not usually assume a disguise in the sense of changing his physical appearance. Odin normally appears as himself.

Fig. 2: Bracteate from Zealand, Denmark. The runic inscription reads: hariuha haiteka farauisa gibu auja, *'I am called Hariuha, who knows dangerous things. I give luck', followed by a threefold ↑-rune. While the final rune might be thought to indicate *Tiwaz, the rider's spear and accompanying raven would rather suggest Odin as he is known from Norse myth, as would the association of dangerous knowledge and luck (presumably in battle). The name Hariuha also supports the idea that this is a depiction of Odin – the compound from* Her- *'army, host' is a common feature of Odin's nicknames.*

Indeed, it is remarkable that anyone could fail to recognise that famous grey-haired, bearded, one-eyed man carrying a spear and wearing a hood or broad-brimmed hat. But Odin does not normally go in disguise – he travels incognito, and even then he usually uses one of his well-known nicknames. Paradoxically, Odin is usually disguised as himself. The idea that a character is not recognised despite being eminently recognisable is clearly a narrative device.

The connection between Sertorius' strong interest in the Celtic otherworld and the role of *Wodanaz in a cult of the dead is far too tenuous to be taken as supporting evidence. Enright shows that Sertorius went to great lengths to demonstrate supernatural knowledge, even claiming to receive messages from his pet white doe. This, Enright suggests, is the source of Odin's oracular ravens and wolves. It is hard to take seriously. Enright also suggests that Odin's spear Gungnir can be traced to the Celts and Celtiberians with whom Sertorius associated, and he points out that Sertorius was involved in javelin attacks on Roman troops, supposedly presaging Odin's favoured method of starting battles. But this does not take into account the occurrence of magical weapons in nearly all branches of Indo-European myth. Furthermore, a spear-wielding figure, arguably a divinity, is clearly depicted in the Bronze Age rock carvings of Scandinavia.

Sertorius may well have been accorded the divine or supernatural status he so carefully cultivated, but does that mean the Germans would have adopted him as a god? Other warlords had a powerful impact on the Germans but were accorded no more than heroic status – Attila, for example. Augustus Caesar, hailed as a god in his own lifetime by the citizens of Rome, and a formidable foe to the Germans, did not attain divinity in Germanic eyes. In historical times the Germans' own great leaders were not revered as gods. Offa of Angeln, ancestor of the Mercian kings, was a major heroic figure – but he was not portrayed as a god. In any case, if Sertorius was ever considered a god it would more likely have been among his Celtic followers. As a German, Civilis would be a much better prospect. But how much of the legend surrounding Sertorius did Civilis knowingly appropriate? The literary evidence suggests that it was not much.

The hypothesis advanced by Africa and Enright is the only incarnation of Petersen's idea that offers any kind of realistic process by which a latecoming *Wodanaz could have become chief god of the Germanic peoples. It is also the only hypothesis that even attempts to explain why Odin is one-eyed. But it has a number of serious weaknesses. Apart from those discussed above, the obvious objection is that it requires a prior assumption that *Wodanaz really did usurp the position of an earlier sovereign Germanic god. Dumézil has shown that the basic structure of Indo-European religion is remarkably constant. While Odin may indeed have taken on some attributes of the old Germanic sky god, there is little doubt that he mainly occupies another position altogether. He is primarily the representative of magico-religious authority, reflecting one of the three strata into which the Indo-European cosmos was partitioned – including a ritual division of society into priests/kings, warriors, and farmers/workers. The names of the gods who embody each of these functions vary from one Indo-European people to the next, but the functions remain constant. The god who represented the first function among the Germans might not always have been called *Wodanaz, but the position was surely there long before the time at which the alleged usurpation took place[2].

2 Too much has been made of the fact that *Týr* is linguistically cognate with *Jupiter* and *Zeus*, who occupy the same place in the Roman and Greek pantheons as Odin does among the Norse gods. In Indo-European myth structure is primary – deep linguistic connections do not guarantee exact equivalence of position in the divine hierarchy. Except in Greece and Rome, the Indo-European sky god is a *deus otiosus*, a god without function. That is already apparent in the oldest Indian religious texts, where Dyaus Pitar is an insubstantial figure. It is difficult to say exactly why the same status did not apply to Jupiter in Rome and Zeus in Greece. There is not space here to discuss this in any detail, but the likelihood is that in Greece the Indo-European trifunctional framework was superimposed on an older, deeply entrenched system that placed greater emphasis on the sky father.

When Did Odin Lose His Eye?

The loss of an eye is often associated with sorcerous powers in Indo-European myth and tradition. While Odin has sorcery to spare, he has little else in common with any of those other one-eyed sorcerers. For instance, some of the Fomoire of Irish tradition were not only one-eyed but also one-armed and one-legged. One of them, Balor, whose eye is a potent weapon, is cast as the opponent of Lug, but it is the two-eyed Lug who resembles Odin. In general, one-eyed figures tend to play fairly minor parts in myths and legends, and are normally cast as outright villains. One cannot imagine much of a cult growing up around any of them. It is indeed possible that one or more of these could have merged with *Wodanaz, but unlikely that the god could owe his origin to any one of them.

There is another problem with the missing eye. In Norse tradition, the lost eye is an important part of Odin's myth. Yet there is no mention of *Wodanaz being one-eyed in Germanic traditions outside Scandinavia. Admittedly, there is so little material relating to the non-Scandinavian manifestations of *Wodanaz that the absence of textual references should not be treated as a definitively negative statement. Yet no Greek or Latin source of any date mentions a one-eyed Germanic god. As Kershaw (2000, 6) observes, 'a god so maimed is enough of an oddity that one of the classical writers would have heard of it from his informants and remarked upon it'... The silence extends through the years to the Middle Ages. Furthermore, the only certain English depictions of *Wodanaz are illustrations of Woden in medieval manuscripts (Joan Turville-Petre 1988) – and they show him with two eyes (Fig. 1).

The earliest Germanic images that may be interpreted as a one-eyed deity occur on bracteates of roughly 500 to 700 CE. These thin gold discs, worn as pendants, were modelled on Roman personal decorations. Most finds are Scandinavian, but they have been found in much smaller numbers in England, Germany and elsewhere. The bracteates fall into several main types: the important ones in the present context depict a horse surmounted by a human head in profile. These have been associated with the cult of *Wodanaz (Fig 2). Karl Hauck, who has been studying the iconography of bracteates for many years[3], has shown that there are variations. The human heads are shown in profile facing to the left or to the right. Most have a large, clear eye – but others seem to have no eye at all. Some

3 Hauck's many studies of bracteate iconography have appeared regularly as instalments of a series *Zur Ikonologie der Goldbrakteaten* in a number of journals and books. Detailed studies of bracteates in English are hard to find, but Gaimster (1998) includes a useful survey of theories of bracteate iconography, with particular emphasis on Hauck's ideas.

Fig 3: Metal die from Torslunda, Öland, Sweden.

show an exceptionally large eye. A sixth-century die for making helmet plates, from Torslunda on the Swedish island of Öland, shows a 'dancing' warrior in a horned helmet, with a spear in each hand. This figure has been associated with the cult of Odin, largely because of a bear-like figure shown next to him. Kershaw thinks the warrior is Odin himself because when magnified the warrior's face seems to have an empty eye socket (Fig. 3). However, if one looks closely there is a suggestion of the outline of an eye. The seemingly empty socket may just be a manufacturing defect.

The Torslunda figure and the bracteates that show eyeless faces might be good evidence for a Germanic one-eyed god in the sixth century – if we could take them at face value. But the Torslunda figure is of doubtful value. The eyeless heads on the bracteates might have been designed to convey the idea of a one-

Fig. 4: Helmet plate from Välsegarde, Sweden.

eyed or blind god. Or the designs may have been defective or not fully realised. If the bracteates were intended to show a one-eyed god their makers took no steps to make it obvious. Later images of Odin offer no help – there is no medieval consensus as to which of Odin's eyes is missing.

But there are a number of images from the sixth and seventh centuries that seem unambiguous. These are from a variety of objects. They show a mounted warrior armed with a spear, which is being guided from behind the rider by a smaller figure. This is related to the Roman motif known as *sustentatio*, where a divine figure is depicted guiding the actions of a human one. It is also a clear image of divine assistance or intervention in battle, a function of Odin in Norse myth – and the smaller figures have been identified as epiphanies of Odin (Gaimster 1998, 57). Two of these, helmet-plates from Välsegarde in Sweden, show the smaller figure wearing horned headgear, indicating that he is indeed a god. In these particular images the deity also holds a spear of his own. But the important thing about the Välsegarde figures is that their whole faces are depicted. And they clearly each have two eyes (Fig. 4).

There is no solid evidence for a one-eyed *Wodanaz outside the Norse lands. There is no trace at all of a one-eyed god in Scandinavia before around 500 CE, and even then the evidence from sixth- and seventh century artefacts is weak. The strongest evidence of all is from the Välsegarde images, which show a two-eyed god. All extant images of an unequivocally one-eyed Odin are significantly later than the latest date that can be assigned to *Hrafnsmál* (Figs. 5–6). Somehow, by about 845 CE (the earliest possible date for those lines in *Hrafnsmál*), *Wodanaz became Odin and in the process he lost an eye. Prior to that date there is no textual or indisputable archaeological evidence for a one-eyed god anywhere in Germanic culture.

The evidence is not conclusive but it does tend to suggest that in Scandinavia the one-eyed Odin familiar from the Eddas and later representations evolved from an earlier *Wodanaz who had two eyes. Meanwhile, Woden, Wodan and so on may have developed in a way that left them with both eyes intact. Possibly the single eye of Sertorius or Civilis became grafted onto the cult of *Wodanaz in the first or second centuries. But if *Wodanaz does represent a deified Sertorius or Civilis, his one-eyedness should have been a major iconographic theme among the Germanic tribes of the Rhineland from the first century onward.

We can almost certainly discount Civilis and Sertorius as direct sources of Odin or his one-eyedness. Textual references to Odin and his cognates, along with images in medieval manuscripts, carvings, tapestries and so forth, suggest that the lost eye was a Norse innovation. The complete absence of traditions pertaining to a one-eyed Woden or Wodan would seem to support this conclusion. Alternatively, the missing eye could have been part of the *Wodanaz tradition all along but disappeared among all but Norse myth. But that is most unlikely. The disappearance of such a major physical characteristic throughout the remaining Germanic world would be even harder to explain than its sudden appearance in Scandinavia.

Fig. 5: Carved head, probably Odin, from the church at Hegge, Norway (after c.1200).

Names, Roles and Themes

Could the explanation for how the Norse version of *Wodanaz came to lose his eye be found among Odin's many nicknames? These include Hárr, Báleygr, Bileygr, and various compounds with *blindr*, 'blind'. In Old Norse *hárr* means 'grey (-haired)'. One suggestion is that when applied to Odin *hárr* is from a different source, Proto-Norse **haiha-hariR*, 'one-eyed hero'; another is that *hárr* must be the regular Old Norse cognate of Gothic *haihs*, 'one-eyed' (Kershaw 2000, 3–4). However, Lehmann (1985) asserts authoritatively that *haihs* has no cognates in other Germanic languages – it only occurs in the Gothic translation of Mark 9.47 – the implication being that it is a loan, perhaps from Latin *caecus* 'blind, one-eyed' or Irish *caech*. If *haihs* is not a Germanic word, there is no reason why it should have a regular form in Old Norse. There is no support here for *Wodanaz having one eye early on in Germanic tradition.

The meanings of *Bileygr* and *Báleygr* are clear: 'Weak-eyed' and 'Flaming-eyed'. It is tempting to relate these to the faces on the bracteates. *Báleygr* recalls the Irish hero Cú Chulainn whose battle-rages involved bizarre physical contortions in which one eye would recede deep into his skull while the other bulged out like a cauldron. As patron deity of the berserks, Odin might be expected to undergo similar contortions. The names compounded from *blindr* might also be an allusion to unseeing frenzy – for instance, *Gunnblindi*, 'war-blind'. This would also be in keeping with the name *Wodanaz ('ecstatic', 'mad', 'furious'). On the other hand, the *blindr* names could refer to one who blinds rather than one who is blind, perhaps reaffirming the power implied by *Báleygr*. Not one of Odin's nicknames definitively signifies one-eyedness, nor do any seem likely candidates for any kind of misapprehension that could lead to the god being imagined as one-eyed.

Interestingly, Kershaw (2000, 5–6) observes that in Snorri's *Ynglinga* saga and the *Prologue* to the *Prose Edda*, and in his contemporary Saxo Grammaticus' *Gesta Danorum*, there are two distinct ways of treating Odin. When these writers portray Odin as a human king the lost eye is never mentioned. Indeed, far from being disfigured the euhemerised Odin is described as fair of face. In Snorri's *Gylfaginning* Odin appears in triplicate as three kings named Hár, Jafnhár and Þriði – but an early manuscript illustration of the *Prose Edda* depicts each of these with two normal eyes. When Odin appears in his supernatural form, his one-eyedness is usually to the fore. This suggests that the lost eye was only apparent when Odin acted as a god. When Odin practised sorcery, or concealed his identity, or acted as cause or arbiter of conflict, he was one-eyed.

Fig. 6: Detail of a tapestry of about 1100 from Skog church, Hälsingland, Sweden. These three figures almost certainly represent Odin, Thor and Freyr. Odin, on the left, is recognisable by his single eye.

The Irish Connection

Parallels to the myth of Odin's eye are found in Irish stories that link eyes with wells or springs. For instance, the well of Segais was associated with knowledge – but it would blind anyone who approached it. Another parallel describes how St Brigit destroyed one of her eyes to avoid marriage: where she planted her staff a stream miraculously appeared so that she could wash the wound. One version of the story tells that the water restored the lost eye. Carey (1983) suggests that these tales derive from the same source as the story of Odin's eye, and that originally the sacrifice of the eye caused the waters of knowledge to spring forth.

There is evidence that eyes and wells have been closely associated in Celtic belief for a long time. Several sites in Roman Gaul and Britain offer clear indications of a belief that springs could cure blindness or ease eye diseases – at Bath, Lydney and Dijon, for instance. At the root of this is an ancient metaphor in which eyes are likened to bodies of water. In Indo-European tradition lightning, a homologue of fire and the sun, resides in water. This is related to belief in the evil eye, the look that can blind, kill, paralyse, sear and destroy (Stone 1993; 1995). This would explain Odin's nickname *Báleygr* – 'flame-eyed' – and the destructive gaze attributed to figures like Balor.

Although this may illuminate the distant origins and early shape of the motif, it only partly explains why Odin was one-eyed while his counterparts show no sign of that trait. Once again, we must look to Ireland. At the Second Battle of Mag Tuiredh, Lug defeated his grandfather Balor not only by destroying Balor's single eye, but also by employing sorcery. His method was to cover one eye with one of his hands, and chant a spell while hopping on one foot. In other words, when he performed his magic, Lug was one-eyed. Furthermore, Cú Chulainn was thought of as Lug reborn as a mortal. In his battle rage, Cú Chulainn too was effectively one-eyed. Cú Chulainn's facial contortions are echoed in chapter 55 of the thirteenth-century saga of Egil Skallagrimsson, an Icelandic poet and sorcerer who was a devotee of Odin. Grieving and angry at the death of his brother, Egil sat 'with one eyebrow sunk down right to the cheek and the other lifting up to the roots of the hair'.

Odin is mainly preoccupied with magic and war. It is when he performs in either of these capacities that he is one-eyed. Furthermore, Odin's devotee Egil Skallagrimsson had more than a grimace in common with Cú Chulainn. Like the Irish hero, Egil was uncommonly big, quick-tempered and aggressive, and each killed a competitor in a fit of rage during a childhood ball game. Egil was a real person around whom a number of folkloric themes accumulated. Could some of these themes have been taken from Irish tradition? There is every reason to believe that they could. Vikings began raiding Ireland toward the end of the eighth century, and settled there from around 830. If the earliest literary reference to Odin's lost eye is the line in *Hrafnsmál* then it dates from fifteen to seventy years after parts of Ireland began to be colonised by Norsemen. Most of Iceland's settlers came from Norway, but others came from Norse colonies in Ireland. Many who came from Ireland had married Irish women, and had Irish servants. There is even one account, in *Laxdæla saga*, of an Icelander's Irish wife teaching their son to speak Irish. The strong Irish element among the Norse settlers is borne out by the number of Irish place-names in Iceland and the frequency with which Irish personal names occur in Icelandic history (G. Turville-Petre 1953). It would be unwise to suppose that they were the only traces left on Icelandic culture by the Irish element.

Could Snorri Sturluson have known of an Irish tale, such as the stories of Lug and the well of Segais, and incorporated them into his *Edda*? Snorri was renowned as a man of learning, and he certainly knew of the Trojan War, and seems to have been familiar with Virgil's *Aeneid*. And if Snorri was the author of *Egils saga skallagrimssonar*, as a number of scholars believe, then we might suspect that he was also familiar with the deeds of Cú Chulainn and other Irish material.

Conclusion

Variant forms of *Wodanaz clearly existed among the Germanic peoples long before Norsemen began to colonise Ireland – but the one-eyed Odin cannot unequivocally be shown to have existed before then. The implication is that Odin's missing eye may derive from Irish tales, specifically those concerning Lug. It is easy to imagine Irish people in Iceland telling stories of their own god Lug to Scandinavian audiences and perhaps substituting the name of the Norse deity who most resembled him. There may have been existing traditions of Odin having the power of the evil eye. We know that there was a widespread association of eyes with wells, and that there was a widespread Indo-European myth of a body of water that gave wisdom and inspiration in the form of a fiery radiance also associated with sovereignty. Such a convergence of themes could have been enough to found a tradition in which Odin was a one-eyed god whose lost eye was hidden in a well of wisdom. And alongside it an older tradition may have run, one in which Odin was fair to look upon.

Like all hypotheses, this one should be treated with a healthy degree of caution. The old adage, that absence of evidence is not evidence of absence, applies particularly well to non-Scandinavian Germanic myth, of which we know so little. Yet in the case of *Wodanaz the absences may be significant. *Wodanaz is mentioned quite often in genealogies, histories and other texts throughout the Germanic world. But only the Norse Odin has a missing eye, and all the undoubtedly one-eyed depictions of Odin in Norse art are later than the tenth century. The only known depictions of Woden in English art show him with two eyes. Could Woden have had a missing eye that was forgotten after the English became Christianised? Perhaps: but in Norse tradition, Odin's lost eye seems to have become a more popular theme as time passed. And it survived Christianity. In the Eddic poems, most of which are believed to date from the tenth century, the lost eye is mentioned only in *Völuspá*. It occurs rarely in other skaldic poetry. Indeed, until Snorri and Saxo, the lost eye is hardly mentioned at all. Most references to Odin's lost eye occur in the Icelandic sagas – and the earliest saga dates from the twelfth century.

A one-eyed *Wodanaz could have influenced the Irish myths and traditions. But the plethora of one-eyed figures in Irish lore suggests that the one-eyed villain has been a stock figure for a very long time. The story of Nuada – who lost his kingship when he lost a hand – shows that in ancient Ireland physical disfigurement excluded a man from kingship. A missing eye would have similarly disqualified Lug, but his sorcery involved the simulated loss of limbs and an eye. This was a frank impersonation of a character type that must have been current when the story came into being: the one-eyed, villainous sorcerer. No such model exists in Norse myth and legend. This suggests that Odin's missing eye was a motif that came from outside Scandinavia, and ultimately from outside Germanic tradition. Exactly why the one-eyed sorcerer has been such a firm favourite in Irish tradition is anyone's guess. Maybe there is a connection with Quintus Sertorius after all, given the almost divine status he enjoyed among his Celtic followers, and the Irish tradition of migrations to Ireland from Spain.

The evidence is ambiguous and fragmentary, but we should not speculate too far outside it, no matter what the quality or quantity. Like any other hypothesis, this one is only as good as the supporting evidence, and it is possible that something may turn up to disprove it entirely. But for the moment the suggestion is that Odin lost his eye as a result of the merging of Irish and Norse traditions of similar gods, probably in Iceland, some time between about 800 and 900. At the very least, this should be entertained as a serious possibility.

References

Africa, Thomas W., 1970, 'The One-Eyed Man Against Rome: An Exercise in Euhemerism.' *Historia* 19.

Branston, Brian, 1980, *Gods of the North*. 2nd ed. London.

Carey, John, 1983, 'Irish Parallels to the Myth of Odin's Eye.' *Folklore* 94:ii.

Dumézil, Georges, 1973, *Gods of the Ancient Northmen*. Berkeley, California.

Enright, Michael J., 1996, *Lady with a Mead Cup: Ritual, Prophecy and Lordship in the European Warband From La Tène to the Viking Age.* Dublin.

Gaimster, Märit, 1998, *Vendel Period Bracteates on Gotland: On the Significance of German Art.* Lund.

Kershaw, Kris, 2000, *The One-Eyed God: Odin and the (Indo-) Germanic Männerbünde.* Washington DC.

Lehmann, Winfred P., 1986, *A Gothic Etymological Dictionary.* Leiden.

Nordal, Sigurður, 1971, 'Three Essays on Völuspá.' *Saga-Book* 18/I-2.

Stone, Alby, 1993, 'The Eye in the Well.' *Talking Stick* 13.

Stone, Alby, 1995, 'Looks that Kill.' *Talking Stick* 20.

Turville-Petre, G., 1953, *Origins of Icelandic Literature.* Oxford.

Turville-Petre, Joan, 1988, 'Illustrations of Woden and his Sons in English Genealogical Manuscripts.' *Notes & Queries* 223/2.

Thunderstones

Jennifer Westwood

Jennifer Westwood looks at the folklore and use of these fabled stones from the sky. Main illustration by **Ian Brown**.

> *If thunder is the atmosphere's noisiest production, lightning is its most dazzling' (Ludlum 2001, 97). Lightning heats the air almost instantaneously 11,100°C (20,000°F) or more, hotter than the surface of the sun. This channel of hot air manifests itself as the lightning flash, while the thunder is the explosion of air along the length of the flash caused by the sudden heating. The noise of the explosion has been heard as much as 100 km (60 miles) away*
>
> (Ludlum 2001, 517).

Outside regions of violent seismic activity, thunder and lightning are often the most alarming natural phenomena that people ever experience. Against the devastating effects of lightning-strike in the early modern period and later there were many and various magical insurances, whether these were thought of in their day as 'magic' or, as they derived from learned authorities, 'science'. The most written-about lightning charms are the so-called 'thunderstones', variously Neolithic flint tools or weapons, naturally occurring stones and fossils. The best evidence for these comes from Denmark, where it was systematically collected by Christopher Blinkenberg in *The Thunderweapon in Religion and Folklore* (Blinkenberg 1911, 68–122; hereafter Bl. # indicates item number).

The Written Record

People have been collecting fossils since Palaeolithic times (see Oakley 1975). The beliefs attached to those fossils, and to other kinds of stone, must be a matter for speculation until the period of written records. And the intervention of the written word, from the Roman period on, brings its own problems. How far, when we see a European peasant of the 18th century collecting the same kinds of stones and fossils for use as amulets and talismans as we know Romans did, can we assume a belief transmitted orally through time? Or should we suspect that it passed to that peasant direct or through a literate third party via the agency of print?

And print, or at least writing, there was in abundance – the properties of precious, semi-precious and sometimes to us perfectly ordinary stones were described by classical authors, notably Pliny the Elder (d. AD 79). In the Middle Ages this information was perpetuated by St Isidore, Bishop of Seville in the early 7th century, and by Marbode, Bishop of Rennes between 1067 and 1081 (Evans and Serjeantson, 1933; repr. 1960, xi). From the lapidaries, the information passed into other channels, including literature. When Shakespeare, in that famous song from *Cymbeline*, 'Fear no more the heat o' the sun', says:

Fear no more the lightning flash

Nor the all-dreaded thunder-stone...

we do not actually know if he picked up this idea of the 'thunder-stone' from oral tradition in his native Warwickshire, or had simply read his Pliny.

The Underlying Concept

Only comparatively recently have people in general understood that the word 'thunderbolt' refers to an idea and not a thing – indeed, as late as 1992 I heard a well-spoken member of a Norfolk local history society express surprise at the idea that 'thunderbolt' was just an abstract notion and not a tangible object.

Blinkenberg's research indicates that the thunderstones 'were supposed to have fallen from the sky in thunderstorms' (Bl. #3). 'About 1850, when I was a child, I was often sent out in the fields, after a thunderstorm, by a servant from Kjeldby vicarage (island of Mön) to look for thunder-stones' (Bl. #17; cf. 21, 22, 32a). A headmaster reported for Vonsild near Kolding: '...only when a crashing thunderclap followed the lightning did we think that a stone had fallen, and it was precisely its fall and great speed which produced the crashing sound' (Bl. #67).

A belief held in Sweden, though 'hardly in the Danish tradition', was that the thunderstone on striking dives seven fathoms into the ground, afterwards rising one fathom a year until, after seven years, it again reaches the surface (Blinkenberg 1911, 4). In Italy, though the magical number seven is normally a constant, the spatial measure might be different or it could be a measure of time: 'The thunderstone darts seven spans into the earth and rises a span every year'; 'With the lightning a stone descends which after seven years, seven months, and seven days comes up again out of the earth into which it has sunk' (Bl. #113). In Wales the magic of 'nine' was similarly admitted into the formula. Marie Trevelyan writes: 'A very old man... said there was an old belief that the thunderbolt dived into the earth – it was in the shape of a black wedge – and remained in the earth for seven or nine years, when it returned to the surface again. Every time it thundered the bolt ascended nearer the surface' (Trevelyan 1909, 42; cf. Bl. #110).

In the Pays de Luchon (Pyrénées), people sought the thunderstones both before and after emergence: 'When the lightning had struck the spot was visited and an attempt was made to dig out the thunderstone; if it was not to be found, the place was marked, as the thunderstone comes up to the surface after seven years and can then easily be found' (Bl. #110). In Calabria, they were afraid of them: 'when a peasant finds one he dare not touch it for fear' (Bl. #113; and see *Folk-Lore* 14 (1903), 142).

This business of the re-emergence of the thunderstone after seven years is not in fact a bad way of describing the reality of the situation: the apparent sudden appearance of objects after thunderstorms may be explained by heavy rains washing away the overlying soil. But things do also come down. The Elder Pliny, writing on lightning in the first century AD, was firm on the subject: 'It will not be doubted... that stones often fall from the sky. A stone of moderate size indeed is worshipped for this reason today in the gymnasium at Abydus... I myself saw one that had fallen a little while before in the territory of the Vocontii' (Pliny II: 149–50; trans. Healy 1991, 29). As well as meteorites, the occurrence of fulgurites was probably a contributory idea (Wright 1912, 123).

What Objects Were Identified As Thunderstones?

The words 'thunderbolt' and (from 1598) 'thunderstone' in Britain were applied to three main categories of object: Neolithic stone axes, belemnites, and fossil sea urchins. Sometimes nodules of iron pyrites were also identified as thunderstones.

1. Neolithic Axes

In the first half of the fifteenth century the *London Lapidary* describes the stone Teramus (for *ceraunias*, the classical name for a stone axe). 'Teramus is a stone þat fallith with þe thondre; & he that berith hit clenely, þe thondre shal neuer smyte hym in house ne in fire...' (Evans and Serjeantson 1933; repr. 1960, 33).

This information, derived via Marbode (cap. 28) and other lapidaries from classical authorities, pretty much states the case for the Middle Ages. The same belief was popularly held in the 19th century: 'If a thunderbolt or wedge was preserved indoors, the house would be proof against damage by lightning' (Trevelyan 1909, 42). The use of the word 'wedge' makes it clear what category of thunderstone is in question.

The rationale may have been something like that reported to Blinkenberg in 1908. A schoolmaster remembered that, during his childhood in the parish of Stadil in Ringkjöbing, it was believed that 'thunderstones' (though in this case fossilized sea-urchins) served as a protection against lightning because 'where it had once struck it was not worth coming again' (Bl. #62). This is of course the same belief as in the English proverbial (though factually incorrect) expression 'lightning never strikes twice in the same place'.

In parts of Germany, it was believed that thunderstones could be tested by wrapping a string round them and throwing them into the fire: if they were genuine, the string would not burn. A Silesian peasant performing this experiment in the presence of the informant was sufficiently convinced of its success as to refuse to sell the axe (Bl. #94 I). In Denmark, Blinkenberg found instances of axes being kept under the eaves; on the underside of the roof, often near the chimney; under the ceiling; on top of a four-poster bed or actually in the bed; immured in the wall of the house or in a chimney-breast; under the floor; under a chest; fixed behind a lath near the rafters; on the hearth; behind the wainscot (Bl. #6, 7, 12–16, 18, 19, 23, 26, 27, 29, 34, 35, and cf. 37).

The object was evidently to avoid touching it and this is sometimes emphasized in the records (Bl. #51, 53).

In Germany, a large jadeite axe-head found in the floor of the granary of a ruined Cistercian nunnery at Bonn is presumed to have been placed there as a lightning-deflector not earlier than the twelfth or thirteenth century, perhaps much later (Merrifield 1987, 13). Sometimes lightning-protection in Germany is more visible, as for example two stone axes placed near the apex of the roof at one gable of a relatively recent farm building at Rothemühl, Kries Ueckermünde (Holtorf 2001, 1).

As for Great Britain and Ireland, the folklore collector Edward Lovett reported that, in the north of Ireland, where they kept polished diorite axes, there was a time when every cottage kept one on the rafter as a safeguard against lightning (Skeat 1912, 65). A perforated stone hammer-head was found under a layer of burnt clay – evidently the remains of an earlier hearth – beneath an Elizabethan fireplace at Chaplins Farm, Langham, Essex (inf. courtesy Sealey, 2002). Also in Essex, a small, polished flint axe was found under a cottage hearth at Fingringhoe and a round stone, 'probably a pestle', under a cottage oven at Lamarsh (Rudsdale 1938, 48–9). The Lincolnshire folklorist Mabel Peacock writing in 1901 says: 'My father has a fine neolithic stone hammer with a perforation for the handle, which was discovered in a little square chamber contrived beneath the door-stone of an old house which used to stand opposite to the Methodist chapel at Messingham' (Peacock 1901, 175). I have heard of an example found in the roof of a post-mediaeval house in North Walsham, Norfolk. Many have no doubt gone unreported for superstitious reasons.

Merrifield suggests that, because they were valued for magical purposes and no doubt commanded a good price, axes in the mediaeval and early modern period tended to drift out of the hands of their finders to centres of population, in particular London (Merrifield 1987, 11, 13–14). For whatever the reason, this is not what we generally see in more recent times. Danish collectors of antiquities were frequently turned away empty handed. 'I visited the peasants in search of stone antiquities', one writes. 'At a farm where I went for that purpose the farmer's wife showed me a stone axe fixed under the thatched roof; but she would not sell it, as according to her it protected the house against lightning' (Bl. #7). One Thue refused to sell for a 'daler' (two shillings in Blinkenberg's time) the flint wedges found on his allotment. 'It's all the same to me whether I get that daler or not,' he said (Bl. #8). Another woman turned away one of the local vicar's sons, who wanted to buy her husband's collection of stone axes, saying 'No; as long as we have them we need not insure our house against fire' (Bl. #29; see also 14, 34; cf. Rudsdale 1938, 49).

2. Belemnites

The belemnite is the fossilized guard on the internal skeleton of an extinct cephalopod mollusc (Taylor 1998, 142). In the 17th century, Dr Robert Plot in his account of Oxfordshire mentions the folk interpretation of fossil sea-urchins as 'thunderbolts' (Bassett 1982, 16), and Skeat records J. Walcott in 1779 as saying that 'the Belemnite receives its English name thunder-bolt from the vulgar, who suppose it to be indeed the darts of heaven' (Skeat 1912, 62). This may or may not be a 'folk' belief in the sense of a native oral tradition: Greek belemnon, which gives the fossil its name, means a dart.

Fig 1: Zeus with thunderbolt, from an early Greek vase.

In East Anglia and elsewhere belemnites are still known as 'thunderstones' or 'thunderbolts', though some people in Norfolk thought they were the ends of shooting stars (elderly fossil hunter, Bacton Beach, Norfolk, collected 13/3/65 Loveday). A similar belief was held in Denmark, though there the 'stars', which came down with shooting stars, were fossilized sea-urchins (Bl. #44).

Belemnites, in Denmark known as 'finger-stones' or 'thunder-arrows' as well as 'thunder-stones', prevented lightning-strike ('If you have a fingerstone in the house lightning will not strike it', Bl. #41). It seems likely that it was as a lightning charm that a belemnite was concealed under the floor of an early modern farmhouse in Norfolk that also showed other signs of anti-lightning activity (Lloyd, Dean and Westwood 2001, 61–3).

Above top: Jeremy Harte and Neil Mortimer, viewing the solar eclipse, 11 August 1999, Portland Bill, Dorset.
Above second from top: Jo-Anne and Danny Sullivan, late 1990s.
Above third from top: Hilary Schrafft-Mortimer, Neil, Jayne Pilkington and George Nash, June 2000 at Silbury Hill, Wiltshire (photo: Jeremy Harte).
Above: Salisbury Plain field trip, 7 September 2002.

Above top: Editorial/family outing to the Devil's Den, Wiltshire, summer 2001.
Above middle and bottom: Salisbury Plain field trip, 7 September 2002.

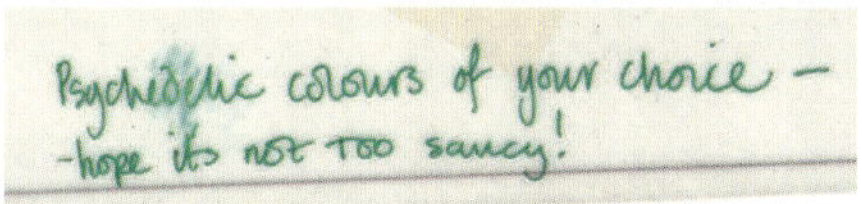

This page and next, previously unpublished artwork by Davina Ware.

Above top: Trethevy Quoit, Cornwall.
Above: Unused t-shirt design, with Davina's additional comment...
Above right: 'Henge'
Right: 'The Third Stone'.
Opposite page: 'Stonehenge'.

Davina Ware's original artwork of William Stukeley, reproduced on the bestselling *3rd Stone* t-shirt.

Previously unpublished illustrations by Ian Brown.

Ian Brown's original, uncropped full page artwork for the cover of issue 44, featuring Pan in a stone circle.

Pan also features on this postcard sent by John Balance of the band Coil, after accepting an invitation to appear at our *Megalithomania!* event, held at Conway Hall, London, in October 2002. Interestingly, the postcard also mentions Babyface Cave: "My gardener's brother apparently re-discovered it in the 70's." (See 'Babyface Cave: A Personal History' by Paul Newman, pages 36–47 of this volume.)

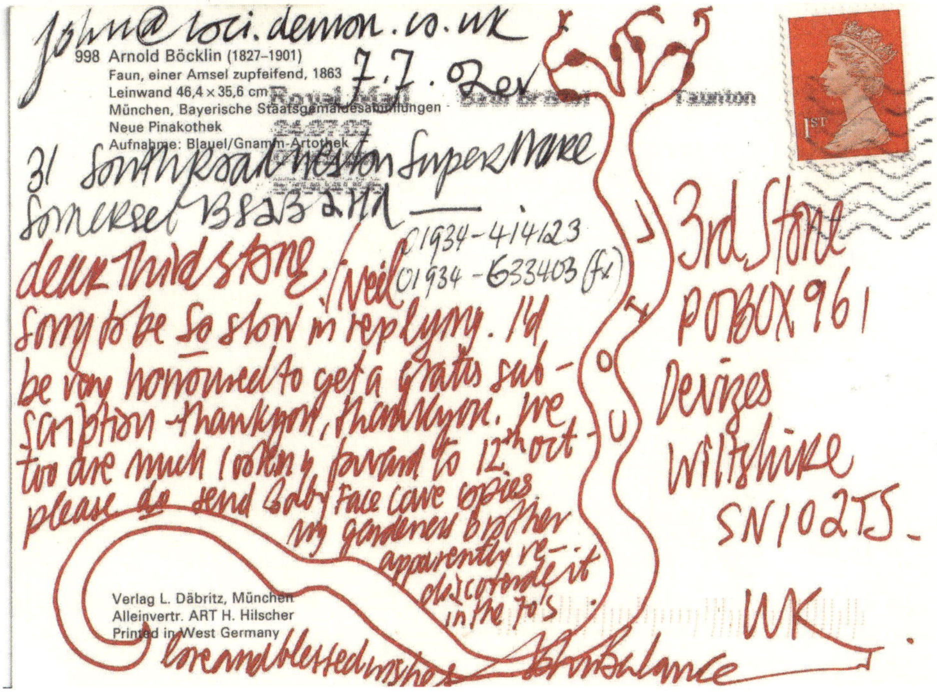

3rd Stone & Strange Attractor present

Megalithomania!

October 12th, 2002 10am - midnight

The Conway Hall, 25 Red Lion Square,

London WC1R

www.thirdstone.demon.co.uk www.strangeattractor.co.uk

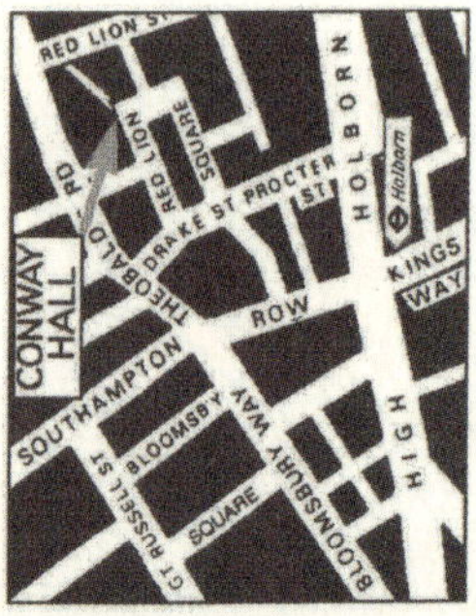

The Conway Hall is situated a few minutes north of Holborn Underground station which is on the Piccadilly and Central Lines. Buses 8, 19, 25, 38, 55 68, 91, 98, 168, 188, 242, 501 and 521 all stop within a 5 minute walk of the venue.

24/500

Jeremy Harte appeared on the front of the *Megalithomania!* ticket (above), surveying the Avebury Down stone circle, or cairn circle or bell barrow, the previous summer.

Meanwhile, John Michell (right) discovers mid-sentence that he can attend *Megalithomania!*...

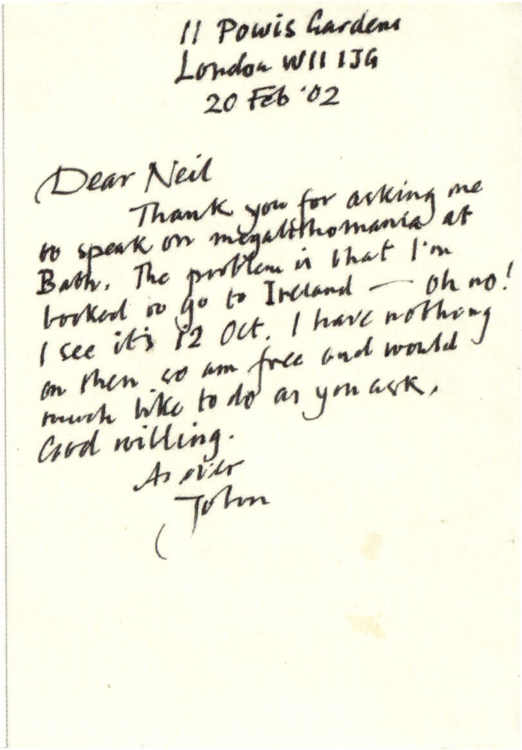

11 Powis Gardens
London W11 1JG
20 Feb '02

Dear Neil

Thank you for asking me to speak on megalithomania at Bath. The problem is that I'm booked to go to Ireland — Oh no! I see it's 12 Oct. I have nothing on then so am free and would much like to do as you ask, God willing.

As ever

John

3. Fossilized Sea-Urchins

In both Britain and Denmark, as well as in other parts of Scandinávia and in Germany, fossilized sea-urchins were also called thunderbolts or thunderstones. In Denmark, Blinkenberg judged this belief typical of western and southern Jutland (Bl. 2, #49–70). In some places within this area, the usage was exclusive: 'The only stones that pass for thunderstones in these parts (North Salling) are the fossilized sea-urchins' (Bl. #52, 66 and 67).

In Denmark, echinoids were used as lightning-averters in exactly the same way as stone axes. 'In Fur, old people still cling to the belief that when a thunderstone is laid in a place 'where no one can set foot,' the house is guarded against strokes of lightning' (BL. #51). 'When they were kept in the house in an unfrequented place, they protected the house against strokes of lightning; the general custom was, I think, to hide them under the far side of the bed. This we did in Nörbæk, district of Viborg, about 30 years ago' (Bl. #53).

Oakley says that at a number of localities in southern England fossil echinoids 'are' (in the 1960s) traditionally placed on dairy shelves to keep milk from going sour (Oakley 1965, II, 117). Such a practice chimes precisely with what was going on in Denmark around Davbjerg and Mönsted in the district of Viborg as communicated to Blinkenberg: 'The... fossils were laid on shelves in the pantry as they 'kept the milk fresh and caused plenty of cream.' The belief in these stones is said to be extinct, but I have seen... the fossils laid in pantries as late as February, 1908' (Bl. #55; and cf. 56).

4. Ætites Or Eagle-Stone

The ætites could be 'any kind of hollow stone containing loose matter, a smaller stone or sand, which rattles when shaken'. It might also be a solid nodule of pyrites 'like those common in parts of the chalk in England and sometimes called thunderbolts by the ignorant' (Bromehead 1947, 16–17).

Why were these stones also known as 'thunderbolts'? The name in itself suggests that it was thought to descend with the lightning, like other thunderstones. Another clue is in the name 'eagle-stone', which Barb suggested originated in an Assyrian pun on the words 'pregnant stone' (because it had another inside it) and 'eagle' (Barb 1950, 318). Once the name reached the west, it had to be explained. According to Pliny, writing on the effects of lightning: 'The eagle is the only bird that is not struck and is represented as armed with a thunderbolt for this reason' (Pliny II:146; trans. Healy 1991, 28). Elsewhere (XXXVI, 39), Pliny writes that the

Fig 2 Teshub, the Hittite storm god, with club.

ætites were found in eagles' nests. Why eagles had such stones in their nest is variously accounted for by subsequent writers, but Pomet's *Compleat History of Druggs* (original French edition 1694) mentions as being sold in shops 'a Kind of Stone that is found at the entrance of the Holes where the Eagles build their Nests to preserve their Young from Lightnings and other Injuries of the Weather' (Bromehead 1947, 19). As with the nests of eagles, so with human homes. It seems likely that it was in accordance with this tradition that lumps of iron pyrites were found embedded in the plaster of some old cottages near Newbury (Williams 1933, 236).

What Have They In Common?

Apart from all being wonder-working stones, what have Neolithic axes, belemnites, fossilized sea-urchins and eagle-stones in common? Why were they singled out from so many others as charms against lightning? The answer seems to be that they are or resemble tools and weapons. Sea-urchins and globular stones resembled slingshot; the 'bolt' of 'thunderbolt' is the same word as is used for the shaft of an arrow, and 'elf-shot' is part of the same idea; belemnites might have been compared with arrow-heads just as later they were with bullets.

Now, according to Ralph Merrifield, stone axes were sought after and collected for magical purposes 'long before their true nature was understood... It was only with growing knowledge of recently discovered peoples in America who... used precisely similar polished stone axes, that it came to be realised by a few European scholars in the sixteenth century that these rather beautiful objects... were tools made in a remote past' (Merrifield 10; and cf. 15).

This seems to me a very academic view. I do not think it can be taken as read that no-one before a 'few European scholars' recognised these objects as tools and weapons. Some clearly did. Probably any farmer or soldier would. Merrifield himself remarks that the occurrence in pre-Roman levels under the Romano-Celtic temple at Mont-Beuvray (Saône-et-Loire) of both a bronze axe of the Bronze Age and one and a half polished jadeite axes 'gives food for thought' (Merrifield 1987, 15). Surely that thought is that stone axes were known to be artefacts and that is why they were treasured or revered – as relics of ancestors or Otherworld beings; or for themselves as weapon-fetishes (see Blinkenberg 1911, 39–40).

Blinkenberg was certain that recognition was a factor. 'The peasants of earlier days often formed a remarkably accurate view of the nature and purpose of the antiquities, in spite of all the changes in the normal shape of implements that had taken place in the course of time' (Blinkenberg 1911, 37). And the proof of this is that the tool/weapon nature of the thunderstone is often embedded in the languages of the countries where belief in it is found. In the West Country, a thunderstone is called a 'thunderaxe' (Skeat 1912, 65). The ordinary modern Danish word for a thunderbolt is *tordenkile – kile* itself being the ordinary word for a wedge (cf. Bl. #5, 21, 22, 24, 27, 47). In Sweden, the thunderstone may be known as *thorvigge* (Thor-wedge) or *okspil* (thunder-arrow). In Dutch, it is called *donderbeitel* (thunder-hammer) and *donderkeil* (thunder-wedge), as well as the self-explanatory *dondersteen* (Bl. #108). In France, an alternative for the *pierre de tonnerre* is *coin de foudre* (thunder-wedge) (Bl. #110). In Hungary, stone axes were sometimes known

Fig 3: The Hammer of Thor.

as *Iften mjila* (god's arrows) (Bl. #96). The stroke of lightning in modern Greek is *astropeléki* (sky-axe) and the same name is applied to small stone age axes (BL. #114). What these names are telling us is that the thunderstone idea is not an uninformed attempt to explain mysterious stone antiquities, but an explanation of a natural phenomenon by analogy.

Continuity

How far is the thunderstone an old idea that has remained in currency? We know from literature that the Greeks and Romans regarded Neolithic stone axes as thunderbolts or *ceraunia*. Archaeology supports the written statements that such *ceraunia* were collected in Roman times. Stone axes were in both ancient Italy and Greece made capable of being worn as amulets, sometimes with the addition of engraved figures and inscribed charms (Bl. #115b).

Ralph Merrifield suggests that the belief in thunderstones dates back to the pre-Roman Iron Age, since a number of axes have been found in Iron Age contexts. At Mont-Beuvray archaeologists have deduced that there was a pre-existing Iron Age shrine and that the axes were probably deposited there in the first century BC as votive offerings (Merrifield 1987, 15). Not only am I uncomfortable with a house-of-cards interpretation – 'This was a temple, so that must have been a shrine, therefore this was an offering' (cf. Eddie Izzard on 'a series of small walls' in *Glorious*, Ella Communications Ltd 1997) – but there seems nothing to suggest how the Mont-Beuvray axes were thought of by their depositors other than that they were worth preserving.

The same applies to axes found in later contexts (e.g. Merrifield 1987, 10). Often all there is to connect them with thunderstones seems to be a best guess based on Pliny and the back-projection of later folklore. A rescue excavation on the site of Treasury Green, Westminster, 1962–3, uncovered the eastern end of a Saxon hall, datable by associated finds to the Middle Saxon period. A flint axe lay on the floor of the hall, evidently brought from elsewhere. 'There is little doubt that this 'thunderstone' was installed as a protective talisman, perhaps originally in the roof...' (Merrifield 1987, 12–13; cf. the Beddington axe, 10).

I wish I felt as confident. Kenneth Oakley, too, speaking of the fact that fossil sea-urchins were once called 'thunderstones' in Sussex, says: 'This practice is clearly linked with the ancient idea that these fossils are thunderstones' (Oakley 1965, II, 117). That the collecting of echinoids is 'ancient' is certainly true (see Oakley 1965, II, 117; and cf.118). The rest is surmise. The occurrence of fossil sea-urchins and belemnites (separately) in both Bronze Age and Anglo-Saxon graves might be susceptible of many interpretations (Oakley 1965, part I, 14; Griffiths 1996, 112).

Perhaps only when we find objects in association which at various times have been identified as 'thunderstones' are we entitled to suspect that something is going on. Neolithic axes and fossil sea-urchins were found together with flint arrow-heads in the *cella* of a Romano-Celtic temple at Cracouville (Eure) (Merrifield 1987, 16; and cf. Oakley II, 1965, 118). This is indeed beginning to look like the collecting of 'thunderbolts'. Suggestive, too, are the Iron Age and Roman instances of stone axes built into walls reported by Leslie Grinsell (Harte, pers. comm. 18 Feb. 2002).

Of course, these cases do not prove continuity of belief between the pre-Roman Iron Age and the post-mediaeval period, much less the threshold of the present day. I am still half-inclined to think that West European peasants learned their thunderstone lore in a roundabout way from Pliny. Like most people, though, I'd rather believe that the 'fairy loaf' that sat by my grandmother's fire and now sits by mine is part of an ancient and continuous tradition.

References

Barb, A.A., 1950, 'Birds and medical magic', *Journal of the Warburg and Courtauld Institutes 13*, 316–22.

Blinkenberg, Christopher, 1987, *The Thunderweapon in Religion and Folklore: A Study in Comparative Archaeology* Cambridge, 1911; repr. New Rochelle, N.Y.

Bromehead, C.N., March 1947, 'Ætites or the eagle-stone', *Antiquity* 21, 16–22.

Bassett, Michael G, October 1982, *'Formed Stones', Folklore and Fossils*, National Museum of Wales Geological Series No. I, Cardiff.

Evans, Joan, and Serjeantson, Mary, 1960, *English Mediaeval Lapidaries*, EETS OS 190, London etc., 1933; repr.

Griffiths, Bill, 1996, *Aspects of Anglo-Saxon Magic*, Hockwold-cum-Wilton.

Harte, Jeremy, 2002, Bourne Hall Museum, pers. comm. 18 Feb.

Holtorf, Cornelius, 2001, (update 10/07/01), 'Earlier artefacts at later prehistoric sites'.

Lloyd, Virginia, Dean, John, and Westwood, Jennifer, 2001, 'Burn marks as evidence of apotropaic practices', in R.J. Wallis and K. Lymer (eds), *A Permeability of Boundaries? New Approaches to the Archaeology of Art, Religion and Folklore*, BAR International Series 6, Oxford.

Loveday, Ray, *Folklore Cuttings and Notes 1960s–1970s*, FLS Archives.

Ludlum, David M., 2001, *Weather*, London.

Merrifield, Ralph, 1987, *The Archaeology of Ritual and Magic*, London.

Oakley, Kenneth, 1965, 'Folklore of fossils', *Antiquity* 39, part I, 9–16; part II, 117–25.

Oakley, Kenneth, 1975, *Decorative and Symbolic Uses of Vertebrate Fossils*, Pitt Rivers Museum: Occasional Papers on Technology 12, Oxford.

Peacock, Mabel, 1901, 'The folklore of Lincolnshire', *Folklore* 12, 161–80.

the Elder, Pliny, 1991, *Natural History: A Selection*, trans John F. Healy, Harmondsworth.

Rudsdale, E.J., 1938, 'Thunderbolts', *Folklore* 49, 48–9.

Sealey, Paul R., 13 May 2002, Asst. Curator of Archaeology, Colchester Museums, pers. comm. citing Colchester Museums Annual Report 1937–44.

Skeat, Walter W., March 1912, '"Snakestones" and stone thunderbolts as subjects for systematic investigation', *Folklore* 23:1, 45–80 (read at Meeting 28 June 1911).

Taylor, Paul D., July–August 1998, 'Fossils in folklore', *Geology Today*, 142–5.

Trevelyan, Marie, 1909, *Folk-Lore and Folk-Stories of Wales*, London.

Williams, P., 1933, 'Thunderbolts', *Folklore* 44, 236–7.

Wright, A.R., March 1912, review of C. Blinkenberg, *The Thunderweapon in Religion and Folklore, Folk-Lore* 23:1, 122–3.

Marden: A Not Very Secret History

Pete Glastonbury, Neil Mortimer and Brian Edwards

Pete Glastonbury, Neil Mortimer and Brian Edwards describe the Wiltshire henge monument at Marden, a site considerably less frequented than its much more famous neighbours.

> *I shall make a long paper of Marden, and giving my opinion, I hope I shall do it modestly, and leave others to think as they please... Mr (Revd. Francis) Wise says 'Where history is silent and the monuments do not speak for themselves, demonstration cannot be expected, but the uttermost is conjecture supported by probability.*
>
> William Cunnington, October 1807.

Magazines of the sort George Orwell once perused in a town newsagents are fond of announcing that Avebury is 'hardly known', or perhaps even Wiltshire's 'secret'. Avebury is of course no secret to anyone, let alone readers of *3rd Stone*, and is 'secret' only in respect of receiving far fewer visitors than Stonehenge. But if Avebury, with 400,000 visitors a year, is made out to be a secret, what does that make Marden?

I have just received a letter from Mr Mayo, the clergyman who lives near Marden, ... His account somewhat staggered me...

Richard Colt Hoare, September 1807.

You know Marden – Wiltshire village approaching midway between Avebury and Stonehenge. Has a huge henge that is larger than Avebury. The henge has a unique feature of two entrances at right angles to one another on the north and east sides, and a ditch 40 feet wide. Had a 'Giant' mound that John Aubrey claimed was second only in size to Silbury Hill. Has a 12th century church, and a 16th century manor. The geologist and Keeper of the Ashmolean Museum John Phillips (1800–1874) was born there. The actor David Niven lived at the manor, and a wartime radar station was secreted at Marden Clump, where someone was captured signalling 'enemy aircraft'.

Marden Earthwork... Late Neolithic henge monument roughly oval in plan enclosing 35 acres. On the S and W it is defined by the River Avon, elsewhere by a massive bank and ditch, now reduced by ploughing. There are at least two entrances, on E and NW. Excavations at the latter in 1969 produced quantities of Grooved Ware, flints, antler picks, and animal bones. Remains of a small circular timber structure were found just within the entrance.

Nikolaus Pevsner, *The Buildings of England: Wiltshire*, 2nd ed, 1991.

As a reader of *3rd Stone* you probably know something of Marden, but if you didn't you would not be alone, and you could include most of the inhabitants of the village until the 'Millennium' reminded them of local history in terms of hundreds and thousands of years. The few surviving older indigenous locals would recall Marden henge being investigated and written-up by Geoffrey Wainwright in the late 1960s, and weekenders and incomers may come across Marden in gazetteers, guides, and a few popular archaeology books.

So in the summer of 1969 the team were back together at the Hatfield enclosure, an all but ploughed flat and little known earthwork near the village of Marden, about halfway between Durrington Walls and Avebury. It was not the sort of place that normally attracted the modern archaeologist.

Mike Pitts, *Hengeworld*, 2000.

Secret or hidden history when featured in a rural living style magazine, usually translates to enthusiasts knowing about something that the public do not. The subject can be freely accessed by those who look hard enough for it, albeit the detail may be secreted in specialist books that the greater public rarely access. Knowing the public would be entertained by any TV programme or newspaper column in which this sort of knowledge was revealed to them, programme makers and editors make hay with knowledge as entertainment at opportune moments. Hence Avebury being a 'secret' and the media celebrating the 'Millennium' by giving the public the 'news' that Avebury and Stonehenge had undergone restoration with stones fixed in concrete – which of course was no-news to *3rd Stone* readers.

Fig 1: Marden Henge, Wiltshire.
Sections of the much-reduced bank and ditch can be seen in this aerial photograph, running from middle right to middle top. The River Avon can be seen at the bottom of the photograph (Pic: Brian Edwards).

Marden is secret, in that it has not regularly featured in monthly magazines or newspaper columns. Marden thereby sees few visitors, other than those who holiday in Alton Barnes' caravans drawn by horses that feed on the unmowed lawn of Marden's boarded-up pub. It would surprise some of the former regulars to learn that the pub garden formed part of the divide between historic village and prehistoric site. At least it was like that until the district council built municipal houses into part of the earthwork.

> *The whole site is now in a rather poor condition, and part of the interior has recently been built upon.*
>
> Leslie Grinsell, *The Archaeology of Wessex*, 1958.

What makes the local authority despoliation of Marden all the more incredible, is that it was instigated at the same time that same local authority was condemning existing homes inside Avebury henge and building municipal replacements outside Avebury village to free the henge of modernity.

> *'I suppose,' said Miss Whissitt, calling early one morning about some old cottages the Rural District Council proposed pulling down, and which she was determined to keep up, 'I suppose you're doing Avebury as soon as you've finished with Marlborough?' ... 'That marmalade reminds me,' she said, pointing to a jar of Keiller's Dundee marmalade on my table... 'Because at Avebury Mr. Keiller is doing really marvellous work. He is digging out and re-erecting all the Sarsen stones...'*
>
> Cecil Roberts, *And So To Bath*, 1940.

If you were to think that this would not happen at Marden today you might be wrong, for only last year Wadworth brewery was granted permission to greatly extend the aforementioned pub – The New Inn at Marden. This could be equated to building a tourist attraction where the Beckhampton Avenue meets Avebury henge. It would not only see a large section of a still recognisable prehistoric landscape infected with bricks and mortar, but would attract more people to the site.

The most surprising thing about the Marden planning application was the lack of objection from the official heritage industry. Being immediately south of the River Avon and adjacent to the road exiting the complex, the pub actually borders, overlooks, and is possibly founded on part of a known prehistoric site, so objections might be expected. It was noted by the district council and a watching brief would probably be deployed during any digging, but no major objections were raised, which is surprising as Marden is a very special site.

The precise plan is not certainly known, but it is possible that the earthwork extends south of the River Avon and that part of the river runs through it.

Leslie Grinsell, *The Archaeology of Wessex*, 1958.

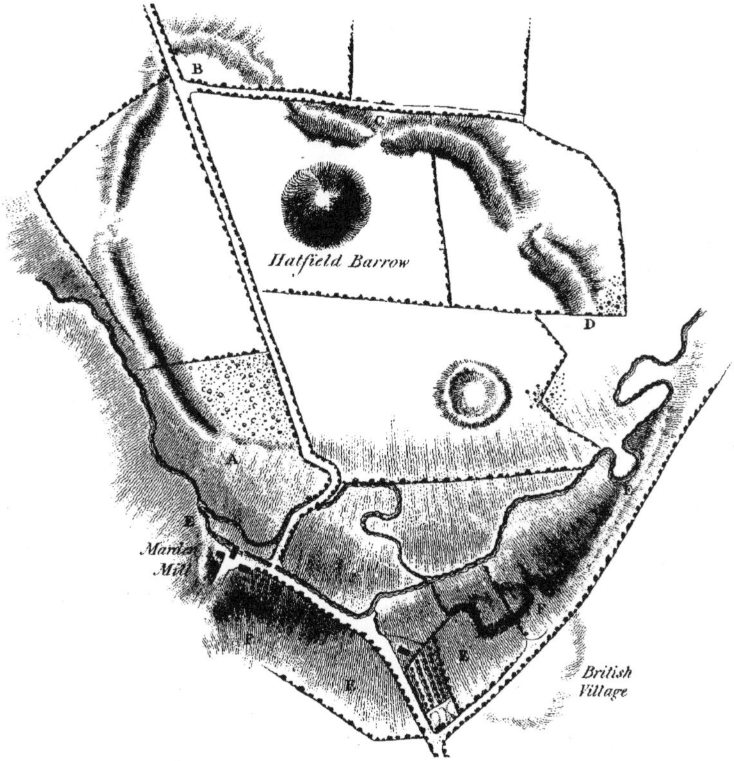

Fig 2: 'Works at Marden', from The Ancient History of Wiltshire Volume II, by Sir Richard Colt Hoare (1821).

Being on a tributary to the Avon, Marden henge links with Durrington Walls and Stonehenge, and like the former there is evidence of considerable Neolithic occupation at Marden, where the remains of a wooden building over 30 feet across were found inside the henge. Although larger in size, Marden also has similarities with Avebury, and apart from being almost mid-way between Avebury and Stonehenge, Marden's historic landscape development is rather reminiscent of Avebury.

Even a walk through Marden can remind you of Avebury, minus the traffic that is. If for the moment you imagine yourself on the footpath from Little Avebury (Truslow, Truslowe or Trusloe) heading in to Big Avebury, you come across a Manor House and grounds on your left, then you walk among village houses for quite a distance, then there is a church on your left, then you are inside the henge then after quite a lengthy step it all of a sudden disappears. That is what it is like at Marden too.

> *You will find every farmer in the parish an antiquary, who will not only tell you who erected these works, but who almost remembers the battle that was fought under Broadbury Banks, to which events these works at Marden are connected!*
>
> Philip Crocker, 14 March 1805.

If we consider where the tributary to the River Kennet is at Avebury, and compare it to the stream at Marden which runs into the Christchurch Avon, the comparison proves quite a coincidence. Where Avebury has a Saxon settlement beneath the south car park, Marden has a settlement adjacent to The Glebe. Both sites have communities similarly positioned relative to their respective churches. The church at Marden is dedicated to All Saints, as was Avebury church until it was changed to St James, and the similarity doesn't end there.

> *The evidence from Marden, so close to Avebury, the silting at Waulud's Bank (Beds), and the absence of waterlogging at Avebury all argue against the theory that its ditch had ever been a moat, and an alternative explanation must be sought for its depth.*
>
> Aubrey Burl, *Prehistoric Avebury*, 1979.

The present-day villages at Marden and Avebury share a similar layout along a route out of their henges. Where Avebury expanded along its main street and into the henge, Marden similarly expanded along a road without it being such a main thoroughfare. In the case of Marden, the village expanded away from the henge, but perhaps more pertinently away from the river and on higher ground. Avebury would have increasingly got its feet wet by expanding any further away from the henge, so perhaps encroachment on the henge was inevitable once a street developed along the path of a stone avenue.

> *I am of opinion it had a circle or circles of stones set round the area on the verge of the ditch similar to Abury; for in passing the narrow bridge and horse path from the Mill to the Work, you perceive a great many sarsen stones in the water. These stones are not so large as those in the outer circle of Stonehenge, yet several of them are as large as those in the inner circle of the latter place. A farmer told me he thought they were probably brought from Kennet and placed there to protect the banks of ye river from being washed down by the stream; but this is by no means probable. On the road a little way from the Mill is a sarsen much larger than those in the water.*
>
> William Cunnington, May 1806.

Standing stones are noticeable by their absence at Marden, despite the location being midway on a route between Avebury and Stonehenge. Although a few small examples of sarsen stone can be found in the bridges and in Marden church, there is nothing obviously suggesting there were sarsens standing in the vicinity. A large sarsen was recently recovered from the foundations beneath a thatched wall, built presumably before the nineteenth century, and therefore is not one of those stones seen by William Cunnington in 1806. There are also sarsen shards in fields to the west and several large stones were found when trees and hedges were planted for the 'Millennium', but although Marden henge is contemporary with Avebury henge it is not similarly located adjacent to a natural source of sarsen. We therefore may not expect to find as much sarsen in later buildings, but as Marden is on greensand a large sarsen may 'sink' if it wasn't supported on a very wide base. Perhaps this is why there are large stones at Avebury and Stonehenge, but not at sites in between.

> *The Ridgeway coming from Streatly in Berks, and Liddington Castle, Wilts, passes between the Castle and these works in the bottom. Mr Leman thinks it is continued to Abury; and I think very probably to Marden and Stonehenge.*
>
> Richard Colt Hoare, 22 March, 1806.

It is not the lack of stones that sees Marden fall outside the ranks of Avebury and Stonehenge, however. William Cunnington thought Marden was the most important site next to Stonehenge and Avebury, but Marden is not ranked alongside the two stone circle sites in terms of World Heritage Site status because less survives.

At Marden also we have made an accurate survey... it consists of a large barrow (about four chains over) in the area of some works which is now much destroyed.

Philip Crocker, 14 March, 1805.

We have also taken sections, etc. of the gigantic tumulus, which I think had a connection with Silbury hill, for before its summit was levelled, they must have been seen from each other.

Richard Colt Hoare, 22 March, 1806.

Similar to Silbury in shape but not in construction, the Marden 'Giant' barrow was investigated by William Cunnington, who abandoned the mound to the elements after opening it in 1807. Subsequently pummelled by the weather, and with the messy remains flattened by the farmer, the great barrow disappeared inside a decade. This is not very encouraging when considering that the Silbury 'hole' was open to the elements for over a year [this 'hole' refers to the collapse discovered in the summit of Silbury 29 May 2000]. Marden mound was of course a rather different species to Silbury, but the weather does not trouble to differentiate between the greensand of a Marden mound and the chalk of a Silbury Hill.

Fig 3: A Sarsen, recently recovered from a wall foundation in Marden (Pic: Brian Edwards).

> *...said to be the largest barrow in these parts except Silbury it is situated near a village called Marden... There is a great reason to suppose that there is a cavern in the great barrow, for the top or vortex of it is sunk into a hollow. I have conversed with old people in the neighbourhood, and they all think it is considerably sunk within their remembrance.*
>
> *Salisbury and Winchester Journal*, 2 December, 1776

> *Mild and fine day. Went in a chaise to Marden. Our workmen had a most providential escape by being taken off to another spot by Mr Cunnington, when, during their absence, several ton weight of earth fell at a time when the floor of the barrow was nearly uncovered... The manoeuvres for the day being interrupted by the heavy fall of earth, I left Marden and ascended the chalk hills.*
>
> Richard Colt Hoare, October 10th, 1807.

Marden lost its 'Giant' mound when the weather flattened its remains, lost its ditch when it was filled up by the plough, and its pub closed its doors on 7th January 2000 when the landlord retired after 35 years. On the other hand, Marden has not suffered the ravages of the heritage industry, and the subsequent annual toll of tourism.

Marden has much of that which is longed-for at Avebury and Stonehenge. It has the solitude sought at Stonehenge, fewer buildings than Avebury, and far less traffic than either stone circle site. This is because there is much less to see. Much less to see means no World Heritage Site status, no WHS means less tourists, less tourists mean less attention, less attention means secret, secret means the public doesn't know about it, and what the public doesn't know about is the domain of activists – like readers of *3rd Stone*. Long may it be so.

A Living Landscape? Pagans, Archaeology, and Spirits in the Land

Jenny Blain, Robert J. Wallis

Jenny Blain and **Robert J. Wallis** consider landscape, indigenous spirituality and today's paganisms. This article is a condensed version of a paper presented at the Landscapes and Seascapes Conference at Sheffield in February 2002.

Our exploration in this article begins with place, landscape and interpretation, in the Peak District. Above the cliff a path leads through a birch wood, alive in the spring with birdsong, to a place where a small stream emerges, rushing among the birches and the rock to find its way as a torrent down the cliff face to the river below: but the path rises slightly onto moorland and from the nearby stone circle you can look across the valley to the peaks, or behind to the highest point of the near horizon of the moor. The components of earth, water and sky come together at a point where today moor meets woodland and stream, and where the imagination of the present may meet the builders of that circle and the associated cairns of this edge – and others around – within sight of village and farm on the far side of the river.

While it is possible to view this landscape as its component parts – circle, stream, moorland, bird-life and plant-life, cliffs covered in abseilers on a bank holiday –

Fig 1: A Peak District circle in its landscape, under snow on the winter solstice.

or as lines on a map, theoretical relationships between points, or disaggregated time periods, it is equally possible to view it as the coming together of all of those, a point at which pasts and presents meet. Multiple possibilities are inherent in the ways people approach the area: and whatever their purposes, all must walk through wood and moor, and experience, in some way, birdsong, stream, view, and rocky path. Can *any* experience of the site be separated from the movement through the landscape, that precedes and follow it?

Today, 'landscape' is fashionable in the thinking of archaeologists and heritage managers, and, differently, among those people – including contemporary pagans – who see the earth around as 'living'. In some ways these views conflict, but in others, they may align. Here we take account of popular/pagan discourses of 'sacred sites' in which land, water and other components of landscapes are perceived as dynamic, living entitles; archaeological approaches to ancient landscapes which are to a certain degree 'sterile' and unpopulated, and which disengage landscapes and their components (including water, sky, etc); and some relations between these different approaches. Positions are not clear-cut. Concepts of the living landscape are discursively constituted in some archaeologists' talk (though less so in published archaeological accounts) and some pagan accounts focus on an inability to know or document precise 'reasons' why sites and landscapes might have become important. On the whole, however, pagan discussions can make use of speculative and imaginative elements which are taboo to most academic constructions, and invest landscape with the agency suggested by our title: a living landscape.

'Sacred site' is likewise becoming a popular term – yet, why and how is 'site' specified, and how is 'sacredness' constituted and applied? Often, research literature (e.g. Carmichael et al 1994, Saunders 1994) suggests that a site is sacred because people honour it, or treat it as sacred, i.e. landscapes are cultured. Some indigenous and western pagan understandings reverse that. Sites are spoken of as 'sacred' because people feel touched by a 'sacredness' or a connection that emerges more strongly than elsewhere, which is embedded *a priori* in the site: a site is a point in the landscape at which people seem more likely to acknowledge that living presence. The stories in the land may be those of how sacredness becomes known, rather than how people have constructed it.

> *Always changing, this landscape was alive on many levels, natural, historical, personal. The landscape was explicitly shared and socialized. It was also known at a most intimate level, and it was only through shared moments of intense silence or through equally intense bursts of poetry... that I came to glimpse the passionate longing that linked each of my instructors to the world around them. My instructors did not seem to separate the stories from the landscape... included in the definition, both as a carrier of traditions (as content), in the forms of resources, life style, and landmarks, and as a medium (as process) through which the Dene ways could be transmitted and created. All my Dene experiences lead me to conclude that the Dene territory is best defined not as 'cultured' but cultural. From this perspective the land is perceived as a process and as an unfolding story.*
>
> (Guédon, 1994: 47)

Thus ethnographer Marie-Françoise Guédon described landscape in northern Déné culture, referring to her own attempts to learn to 'be' Déné, to walk in the landscape and see it as 'alive'.

Coming closer to home, we can further explore this understanding of 'sacred site' before relating it to 'landscape'. Jörmundur Ingi Hansen, head of the Ásatrú religion in Iceland where Jenny interviewed him in 1998, refers to the Vættur or land-spirits (in English, 'wights') of Icelandic folklore.

> *...this is usually the idea in Iceland, that the land wights are tied to a spot in the landscape, to a huge rock, to a mountain, or to a specially beautiful place. A friend of mine has given a definition of how you can know where there is a land wight, or at least a particularly strong one... you will know*

> *where it is because there, things are a little better. The grass is a little greener, all the colours of the flowers are a little bit ah, brighter, and the bird song is more lilting and beautiful, than just a few yards away.*

Near this spot one might, honouring the wight, enter into negotiations about the use of other areas of the land. Within Jörmundur's worldview, the earth, the rocks, the landscape are alive, guarded, and the definition of 'sacred' here does not stem from only the human participant.

In another example, some involved with Irish druidry speak of various kinds of 'power' in the landscape. This seems far from the definitions of landscape in today's society in which commodification is paramount: but in our post-modern society such a concept of the living landscape forms part of the ways in which at least some people interact with both that landscape – and its 'official' guardians: heritage management, local councils, and so forth. These latter, though, work in general from a different view. How are decisions made about which land is 'heritage', what is 'important', what should be 'protected' or conserved, and which viewpoints need to be balanced to accommodate maximum utility?

Indeed, we start to glimpse such multiplicity of possibility in, for example, Cooney's discussions of Irish sacred landscapes (1994, 2000) holding multiple meanings at least in the past, also notable in Edmonds and Seaborne's (2001) *Prehistory in the Peak*, in which multivocality is foregrounded. Still, much heritage literature deals in the discourse of 'site', 'visitor', and the ideal 'visitor experience' of the informed consumer who accesses places and information in prescribed ways, usually avoiding direct physical engagement with sites and based around the idea of a specular observer. Yet people who frequent a sacred landscape are not necessarily going somewhere 'new' to be 'informed', nor somewhere to observe and record their looking experience on film, but may be journeying by various means to reach a known point, or a point at which connections are felt.

Here we explore multiplicities and contestations of meaning in landscapes of past and present, becoming future, narrativised as 'sacred sites' in today's competing discourses. We examine several 'sacred landscapes': (the almost obligatory) Stonehenge, and its environs and current controversies around the proposed tunnel; Avebury and perceptions of the relations between its components; and Stanton Moor.

Sacred Landscapes in Today's Constructions: Stonehenge

Those approaching Stonehenge as a sacred site arrive with a variety of interpretations already in place: these include glimpses of history and prehistory, whether gleaned from guidebooks, websites or archaeology books, or the vast amount of promotional material in which 'the stones' appear as an icon of Britishness. During a standard 'visit' these interpretations are reinforced: thus, tourists today are given snippets of information, which, transmitted, become a 'new folklore' – complete with stories which purport to come from Wiltshire shepherds, as part of the narrativised presentation of the archaeology, packaged (via handsets) for non-interactive consumption. Tourists are directed over a path – varying seasonally to allow regrowth of grass, with no direct approach to the stones possible. Despite the encircling downs with their barrows and song of skylarks, the tourist focus is almost all towards 'the stones'.

Fig 2: Waiting for the magic of summer solstice dawn, at Stonehenge 2001.

Not too dissimilarly, of those we interviewed at 2001's summer solstice, most interpretations focussed only on the immediate, the stones as 'home'. Yet landscape was inherent in approaches. The previous year (2000) the summer solstice event was preceded for some by a processionary walk from Woodhenge, accompanied by some ritual at its start. People walked through lanes and field, past barrows, finally joining the last part of the Avenue, and experiencing the monument rising up before them as they walked the last uphill metres, only to have to turn aside at the last moment because of the separation of Avenue and monument by the A344 and two fences. At the 2001 event, foot and mouth restrictions prevented such processions. The monument existed for attendees within a context which was restricted and politicised – by the festivals of the 70s and the confrontations of the 80s and 90s, and again by foot and mouth regulations in 2001.

For the night of the solstice, the context for many narrowed to the immediate area of the stones – and the approximately 14,500 people there caught within the brightness of the lighting – intrusive floodlights brought in by English Heritage – and the darkness 'outside'. The artificiality of this context was demonstrated as dawn neared and increasingly celebrants stood in the growing daylight to watch for a 'main event' that was most definitely outside – sunrise over the escarpment to the north-east. For though some interpretations – in past or present – have focussed narrowly on specifics of Altar Stone and Heel Stone, now many (human people and 'stone people') stood waiting as sky, mist, stones and celebrant became part of an experience that was deeply moving (while some participants continued to drum within the circle).

Sunrise is, within the anthropology of religion, a liminal time: even more so a solstice sunrise, when the land appears to wait for change. Stonehenge may be today an 'icon of Britishness', but for those celebrants it became located within dimensions of time as well as space, a point of connection with 'ancestors' real or imagined, with the white mist of the dragon's breath rising.

The proposed Stonehenge tunnel – to take the traffic off the A303 – is seen by many of those celebrants not a removal of intrusion, but as intrusion, a gash within sacred landscape, a massive trench scooped out of land (and archaeology) which, according to some, would break lines of energy, to others would destroy links with the past they would rather were left *un*excavated, and to still others would destroy the relationships constructed over millennia between ancestors, stones and people. Commenting on a recent (28 March, 2002) press release from English Heritage, ASLaN spokesperson Andy Norfolk saw the plans as:

> *...partially reuniting some of the landscape, further severing other large bits, and destroying irreplaceable scheduled monuments, which are an integral part of the WHS landscape in the process.* (29 Mar 2002)

Consideration of the Stonehenge landscape, therefore, for many of today's pagans, includes both a sympathy to seeing 'the monument within its landscape', and a concern over the process by which this can be achieved (and not merely the achieving of a cosmetic end product). Some (including many archaeologists and heritage managers) point out that the proposed changes cannot (in any case) return Stonehenge to how 'it was' and that the devastation already accomplished by not only the current A303, but by excavation and concrete, would not be somehow 'cancelled' by the current plans. This concern for landscape, earth, water, appears to be uniting some hitherto opposed factions.

However, for archaeologists, pagans, and others to work together here, there is need to avoid devaluing the discourses of others. While there is evident common cause, this is not perceived when some pagans view archaeologists as saying only that 'we cannot know the purpose' of a monument, and removing or sterilising any spiritual element; or some archaeologists view pagans as irrationally 'appropriating' the landscapes of the past to avoid a less romantic present. Neither group is monolithic and there is need to move between, to translate archaeological discourse into something which becomes accessible but not patronising. A reminder comes from a druid interviewed at Stonehenge at the summer solstice, 2002, who said that:

> *There's all sorts of people here. There's crusty traveller hippie types, there's little old ladies, there's – everybody's here... And yeah, they're here for one reason, because it's a place to be on the summer solstice... this is a holiday, it's a Holy Day, it's special, and people I think feel it's special. And I think the site likes us to be here, as well. Stonehenge wasn't built as a museum. It was built as a place for people to come, for worship, to use it... Come here at other times, and it's quite quiet, and still and peaceful... but I always think this is like New Year's Eve or Christmas or your birthday, all rolled into one. And it is about – a lot of people partying. There's nothing wrong with that, that's a spiritual thing too, or can be.*

Places, Stonehenge and others, have meanings which are constructed from other involvements: whether we be archaeologist, traveller, druid, press reporter, or the world watching on TV. For many, the past echoes within the present and archaeological discourse does not permit or express all questions that may resonate.

Fig 3: Ritual at Avebury's south entrance. Druid Greywolf and assembled people ask permission of the spirits to enter the circle.

Avebury

More so than at Stonehenge where 'the stones' have been the main focus, Avebury has been approached as a 'sacred landscape'. The monuments, including Avebury Henge, West Kennet Long Barrow, Silbury Hill and the Sanctuary are prominent, unmissable in the landscape (unlike, say, the Stonehenge Avenue and Cursus which are visible only to the trained eye). Hence, interpretations of the Avebury landscape by pagans, Earth Mysteries enthusiasts and others, are common.

The work of Paul Devereux will be familiar to *3rd Stone* readers. We won't detail it here, though we discuss elsewhere (e.g. Blain and Wallis, 2002; Wallis and Blain, 2002; Wallis forthcoming; and Devereux 2001a) how this work, permeating from 'alternative' into more 'mainstream' archaeology, has introduced concepts that may relate to a 'living landscape'. Others who have publicised – and popularised – 'alternative' interpretations of Avebury include Michael Dames (e.g. 1976, 1977) and Julian Cope (1998; see also website at www.headheritage.co.uk).

Such alternative accounts giving a blend of archaeological and pagan approaches, are on the one hand extremely refreshing, opening up British archaeology and alternative visions of sacred sites to a wider audience (beyond normative Time Team). On the other hand, such work encourages direct engagement with sacred sites in their sacred landscapes, and the intellectual and physical implications of such engagements with ancient sites are disquieting for archaeologists.

Whereas some of Devereux's concepts have made inroads within archaeological interpretations – e.g. 'sightlines' (Devereux, 1991; Tilley, 1994; Bradley, 1997, 1998) and recent work on acoustic properties of rock art (Devereux and Jahn, 1997) and monuments (Devereux, 2001b), other popular/alternative studies rely on outmoded archaeological interpretations, with particularly singular and bounded notions of culture, material culture and goddesses in culture history. Further, direct engagements can be damaging: too many hands on cupmarks may threaten their preservation.

Avebury is a favourite place for such direct engagements, which may (for example, for druids) involve processions around the bank of the henge and ritual at the south entrance and near the Obelisk marker. One druid said, of the Avebury landscape:

> *Many druids like to make ritual at [Avebury and other sacred sites] since there is a strong feeling that they are places where communion with our ancestors may be made more readily than elsewhere... I am drawn to Avebury... because it is my heartland... the place where I feel most spiritually 'at home'... I am not the only person who has experienced the spirit of the place as a great mother with open arms, welcoming all who come.*

Not all engagements are made with good intent. Avebury, the West Kennet Avenue and West Kennet Long Barrow have suffered vandalism ranging from chalked symbols, scorch marks and scratch marks to the painting of stones (in 1996 and 1999) – some the effects of unthinking 'sacred' engagement, some deliberately to seek publicity.

The attraction of monuments and landscapes, and an interaction between unthinking damage and self-publicising, can be seen in developments of the 'Silbury Hole' phenomenon. We have discussed extensively elsewhere pagan responses to the 'hole', and pagan pressure on English Heritage to be seen to be intervening, (Blain and Wallis, 2002; Wallis, 2003). There are, though, other dimensions to this story of people's relationship to landscape. Silbury lies at the centre of 'crop circle' country, and in 2000 and 2001 several people billing themselves as crop circle enthusiasts 'under cover of darkness', abseiled down the 'hole' – taking photographs and making video recordings which they then attempted to sell, via the internet, to the crop circle community. An account – interspersing the abseilers' text with critical editorial comments, and linking to outraged comments from pagans, local people, crop circle followers and archaeologists alike, was also posted on a crop circle website.

But aside from such mindless damage in the cause of self-promotion, or the deliberate damage previously referred to, much engagement with the sites has benevolent intent and may leave few traces aside from the leaving of offerings – of flowers, mead, perhaps some bread or fruit, or even nail clippings, a crystal or coin. These are left with good intentions, to perhaps thank spirits of place, to honour gods and goddesses, to strengthen local land wights. The 'offering' phenomenon is relatively recent – chiefly arising in the last twenty years, and drawing on a number of sources for its inspiration. Local folklore may suggest offerings, or practices may be 'imported' from elsewhere, so new traditions become established – an oak by the path to West Kennet Long Barrow has recently become a 'rag tree', for instance. They might also be left for rather more perplexing reasons, such as the plastic Xmas tree with baubles, tinsel and all which Robert found in West Kennet Long Barrow at Yule 2000! There may be issues of what constitutes suitable practices in such circumstances – in particular arguments about what constitutes 'too many' or inappropriate offerings, and a tension between those who welcome some evidence of living engagement between spirit-people and human-people, and those who consider any trace to be unacceptable. This is not (as it is sometimes presented) a straightforward divide between pagans and heritage management – some pagans may be stricter in their interpretations than some archaeologists or heritage managers (see Blain and Wallis, 2002), and not all making excessive offerings are pagans. Yet some authors of pagan 'how-to' books (e.g. Griffyn, 2000) actively promote these practices, without discussion of effects on site, geology, or wildlife. Clearly, as a matter of concern, archaeologists and other implicated parties should be aware of and respond to these issues.

Stanton Moor

Finally, we return to 'the Peaks' and Stanton Moor. Here controversy over a proposal to reactivate dormant quarrying operations has caused, once again, some alliance between heritage management, pagans, travellers, and local people. Issues are not simple: attempts to quarry based on a 1952 planning permission cannot be easily dismissed, as the Environmental Protection Act, at the time of reapplication in the mid-90s, did not require an Environmental Assessment Study as would now be the case. Stanton Moor is a recognised Area of Natural Beauty, home to various rare plant and animal species, and the site of numerous Bronze Age burials (cairns and cists) and several circles, most notably the Nine Ladies which has become a focus for protest, although it is not directly threatened. A protest website uses the image of an apple 'core' remaining of the moor, holding the Nine Ladies and a single birch tree 'stalk', but with little else remaining, the quarries having taken their 'bites'. A recent announcement indicated that one 'bite' at least will bite less closely – at New Pilhough on the edge of the moor, rather than closer to the circle. Other threats remain present, including those from the 1952 permission.

Fig 4: Ritual at the Nine Ladies, Stanton Moor, begins with people picking up rubbish and attempting to connect with the stones.

In the 'alternative' representation of Stanton Moor by the protest website, the circle becomes a metaphor for the moor, and pagans and others identify with the circle. However, this living landscape means different things to different groups of pagans: many treat the circle as a ritual focus, a place to meet ancestors or spirits of the moor: others engage with spirit-lines or tracks, or ley lines. Some perform ritual at the circle to give energy to stones and land. The Dragon Network has suggested a ritual to awaken earth-energies of moor and stones – this being a ritual that people can perform elsewhere, so that imagining or imaging the landscape is apparently enough. Certainly it is less eroding - and less potentially damaging than some of the ritual manifestations that occur there (involving fires, burned poles, and hundreds of joss-sticks stuck into the eroding turf, for instance). Members of the protest campaign have a reminder and some practical advice for others who would 'help':

> *Try putting your tealights in glass jars. The ones sold with dips for tortilla chips are just right; they're about 9cm. across, and shallow enough that the flame won't run out of air. And there's no danger of leaving molten wax behind. Of course, don't even think about this unless you are prepared to take your jars home with you. We can do without broken glass around the stones, thank you very much.* (Sparky, 18 April 2002).

Parts of the circle and its environs were excavated during 2000–1, to investigate extents of recent erosion. Notably, local archaeologists took pains to explain purposes of the excavation to protestors and visitors – some of whom decorated the site with a pentacle, perhaps to protect the land or bless the excavation. In 19th century illustrations the circle shown encloses a small mound – this area is now flat. People – walkers, ritualists, Neo-shamans, pagans and others – interact directly, leave their mark, sometimes more deliberately: the (broken and mended) 'King Stone' holds 19th century graffiti of 'Bill Stumps'. In 2001, protest rituals by a busload of Birmingham pagans, King Arthur, and a Dorset druid group, included an attempt to 'raise energy' to 'protect the stones', and an effort to pick up the scraps of litter and cigarette ends festooning the site.

The diversity of engagement with the Nine Ladies circle illustrates various challenges and issues we are addressing in our Sacred Sites, Contested Rites/Rights project.

New/Indigenous Landscapes?

To understand the focus on 'archaeological' site, stream or stones, and why people engage with these as they do, we are finding that we need to understand how pagans identify with scene or landscape – how the identification forms part of their daily being, how they may enter into interaction and negotiation with spirits of the landscape, ancestors, and various other-than-human-beings. For some, the land, and particular places within it, matter, not as something to marvel at, somewhere to go on a visit, or even a means to gain a living, but as, one might say, *family* or *kin*: the living landscape. We see people creating/re-creating new-indigenous understandings of a landscape that is to be moved in, through, celebrated actively, and engaged with as part of those ongoing stories of both land and people – not for passive preservation.

There are no clear boundaries here – nor even a continuum, for the same people who clear up ritual litter may accept or deny the existence and activity of land spirits, and some of those who leave non-biodegradable offerings (or degradable ones in places where these do damage) may do so rarely and in places where they feel the local spirits actively call them to do this. There is not one pagan relation to sacred landscapes, but many.

Fig 5: There is not one pagan relation to sacred sites, but many. Stonehenge celebrations after dawn.

For the most part, those who feel 'called' by land and ancestors seek knowledge of how past relates to present, and of how the components of the landscape form a living whole. Our examples include the idea of movement – around a henge, across water, over a moor, through the landscape. In the end, movement represents another point over which pagans and heritage managers conflict: the path around Stonehenge, versus erosion of the grass and people touching 'the stones'; flattening of the mound shown in earlier illustrations of the Nine Ladies; problems with erosion of the Avebury banks. Sebastion (e.g. 2001) and others have pointed to a need to acknowledge movement and its effects, if need be to rebuild the banks of Avebury on an ongoing basis. Such erosion problems are of course recognised, though Baxter and Chippindale (2001, 2002) point out that in the case of the Stonehenge Management Plan, the acknowledgement may be insufficient: in their view, grass within the monument can stand only around 60,000 'visitors' per annum and a 'good Stonehenge experience' (presumably meaning 'majestic silence' unspoiled by too many tourists) would be achievable only if numbers remained below 100,000. To us it seems that with 14,500 attending an all-night solstice celebration where the 'visit' includes not only walking but dancing, processioning, moving all over the area of the stones, this problem is indeed pertinent, but its solution may lie in attempts to draw people into other parts of the area – the earlier experiences of a music festival on the Cursus may be one to reconsider, or reconstructing Avebury's Sanctuary (Sebastion, 2001) to act as a 'new' sacred site and remove the focus from Stonehenge. Negotiations for this year's (2002) event appear to be focussing on plans for a shorter access time, and problematic behaviours, such as drunkenness, rather than multiplicities of meaning[1]. We see a need to emphasise the importance of acknowledging all viewpoints and attempting to understand the engagements – the geographical, social, political, spiritual perceptions of landscape – that generate them.

We see a need to bring together and discuss views and discourses, of archaeologists, pagans, and others who see sacred landscapes as important in diverse ways, informing the present through imaging the past. Can there be a point at which views meet – as a transmission that does not merely inform, but that stimulates and elaborates concepts and mutual understandings? We hope that informed 'alternative' perspectives and voices of *3rd Stone* readers can become a needed, mediating, component of this debate. Therefore, we present for your consideration, our work with narrativised constructions of site, and sacredness, new 'folklores' surrounding sites, and the contested public voices that seek hearing, as part of identity of place and person in this time.

2025 Endnote

The results of the Sacred Sites, Contested Rites/Rights project have since been published in a series of journal articles (e.g. Blain & Wallis, 2009; Wallis, 2015; Wallis & Blain, 2011), chapters in edited volumes (e.g. Letcher, Blain & Wallis, 2009; Wallis, 2012; Wallis & Blain, 2012) and a co-authored book (Blain & Wallis 2007). The topic of pagans, archaeology and landscapes (e.g. Butler, 2020; Rathouse, 2022), particularly around issues of indigeneity/ancestry (e.g. Doyle White, 2016, 2017; Harvey, 2020; Alessio & Wallis, 2025), have attracted considerable interest in recent years.

1 Those few who were deemed to be drunkenly harassing police have since been said to be 'children of the Beanfield' – again, politics and contested narratives of interpretation may need to come more into focus, rather than addressing this problem as one of simply misuse of alcohol.

References

Alessio, D. and R.J. Wallis, 2025, *Faith, Folk and the Far Right: Racist and Anti-Racist Heathenry and Occultism in the UK*. Manchester: Manchester University Press.

Baxter, I and C. Chippindale, K. Fielden, W. Kennet and E. Young, 2001, 'The Stonehenge we don't deserve: responses to Geoffrey Wainwright's report 'The Stonehenge we deserve''.

Baxter, I. and C. Chippindale, 2002, 'A sustainable and green approach to Stonehenge visitation: the 'brownfield' option.' Discussion paper circulated by I. Baxter, February 2002.

Blain, J. and R.J. Wallis, 2002, 'Contemporary Paganism and Archaeology: Irreconcilable?' Paper presented at conference on *Archaeology in the Public Domain*, Sheffield, 9 March 2002.

Blain, J. and R.J. Wallis, 2007, *Sacred Sites, Contested Rites/Rights: Contemporary Pagan Engagements with Archaeological Monuments*. Brighton: Sussex Academic Press.

Blain, J. and R.J. Wallis, 2009, 'Beyond sacred: recent Pagan engagements with archaeological monuments – current findings of the Sacred Sites Project.' *The Pomegranate: The International Journal of Pagan Studies* 11(1): 97–123.

Bradley, R., 1997, *Signing the land: Rock Art and the Prehistory of Atlantic Europe*. London: Routledge.

Bradley, R., 1998, *The Significance of Monuments: On the Shaping of Human Experience in Neolithic and Bronze Age Europe*. London: Routledge.

Butler, J., 2020, 'Contemporary Pagan pilgrimage: ritual and re-storying in the Irish landscape.' *Numen* 67(5–6): 613–636.

Carmichael, D.L., J. Hubert, B. Reeves and A. Schanche, 1994, *Sacred Sites, Sacred Places*. London: Routledge.

Cooney, G., 1994, In Carmichael, D.L., J. Hubert, B. Reeves and A. Schanche, 1994. *Sacred Sites, Sacred Places*. London: Routledge.

Cooney, G., 2000, *Landscapes of Neolithic Ireland*. London: Routledge.

Cope, J., 1998, *The Modern Antiquarian: A Pre-Millennial Odyssey Through Megalithic Britain*. Thorsons.

Dames, M., 1976, *The Silbury Treasure*. London: runes and Hudson.

Dames, M., 1977, *The Avebury Cycle*. London: runes and Hudson.

Devereux, P., 1991, 'Three-Dimensional Aspects of Apparent Relationships Between Selected Natural and Artificial Features Within the Topography of the Avebury Complex.' *Antiquity* 65: 249.

Devereux, P., 2001a, 'Did ancient shamanism leave a monumental record on the land as well as in rock art?' In R.J. Wallis and K. Lymer (eds) *A Permeability of Boundaries? New Approaches to the Archaeology of Art, Religion and Folklore*: 1–7. BAR International Series 936. Oxford: British Archaeological Reports.

Devereux, P., 2001b, *Stone Age Soundtracks; the acoustic archaeology of ancient sites*. Clovis, CA: Vega.

Devereux, P., and R.G. Jahn, 1996, 'Preliminary Investigations and Cognitive Considerations of the Acoustic Resonances of Selected Archaeological Sites.' *Antiquity* 70: 665–666.

Doyle White, E., 2016, 'Old stones, new rites: contemporary Pagan interactions with the Medway megaliths.' *Material Religion* 12(3): 346–372.

Doyle White, E., 2017, 'Northern gods for northern folk: racial identity and right-wing ideology among Britain's folkish Heathens.' *Journal of Religion in Europe* 10(3): 241–273.

Edmonds, M. and Seaborne, T., 2001, *Prehistory in the Peak District.* Stroud: Tempus.

Griffyn, S., 2000, *Sacred Journeys: Stone Circles and Pagan Paths.* London: Kyle Cathie.

Guédon, M.F., 1994, 'Déné ways and the ethnograher's culture', in D.E. Young and J.G. Goulet (eds) *Being Changed by Cross-Cultural Encounters: The Anthropology of Extraordinary Experience*, Peterborough, Ontario: Broadview Press, 39–70.

Harvey, G., 2020, *Indigenizing Movements in Europe.* Sheffield: Equinox.

Letcher, A., Blain, J. and R.J. Wallis., 2009, 'Re-viewing the past: discourse and power in images of prehistory.' In M. Robinson and D. Picard (eds) *The Framed World: Tourism, Tourists and Photography*: 169–183. Farnham, Surrey: Ashgate.

Rathouse, W., 2022, 'Pagans and museums: approaching the ancestors.' *Pomegranate* 23(1–2): 157–165.

Sebastion, T., 2001, 'Alternative Archaeology – Has It Happened?' In R.J. Wallis and K. Lymer (eds) *A Permeability of Boundaries? New Approaches to the Archaeology of Art, Religion and Folklore*: 125–135. BAR International Series 936. Oxford: British Archaeological Reports.

Saunders, N.J., 1994, 'At the mouth of the obsidian cave: deity and place in Aztec religion.' In Carmichael, D.L., J. Hubert, B. Reeves and A. Schanche, 1994. *Sacred Sites, Sacred Places.* London: Routledge.

Tilley, C., 1994, *A Phenomenology of Landscape.* Oxford: Berg.

Wallis, R.J., 2003, *Shamans/neo-Shamans: Ecstasy, Alternative Archaeologies and Contemporary Pagans*. London: Routledge.

Wallis, R.J., 2012, 'Pagans in place, from Stonehenge to Seahenge: 'sacred' archaeological monuments and artefacts in Britain.' In T.A. Heslop, E. Mellings and M. Thøfner (eds) *Art, Faith and Place in East Anglia: From Prehistory to the Present*: 273– 286. Woodbridge, Suffolk: Boydell & Brewer.

Wallis, R.J., 2015, 'Paganism, archaeology and folklore in twenty-first century Britain: the case study of 'The Stonehenge Ancestors''. *Journal for the Academic Study of Religion* (special issue: Religion, Archaeology and Folklore) 28(2): 129 –157.

Wallis, R.J. and J. Blain, 2002, 'Sites, sacredness, and stories: Interactions of archaeology and contemporary Paganism.' Conference paper presented at Folklore Society Conference, *Folklore and Archaeology*, 24 March 2002.

Wallis, R.J. and J. Blain, 2011, 'From respect to reburial: negotiating Pagan interest in prehistoric human remains in Britain, through the Avebury consultation.' *Public Archaeology* 10(1): 23–45.

Wallis, R.J. and J. Blain, 2012, 'Negotiating archaeology/spirituality: Pagan engagements with the prehistoric past in Britain.' In K. Rountree, C. Morris and A. Peatfield (eds) *Archaeology of Spiritualities*: 47–68. One World Archaeology Series. London and New York: Springer.

Fig 1: 'No to Menhirland'; flyer issued by Menhirs Libres. *'5,000 years ago I was a sacred symbol', complains the stone. 'The force of the spirit against the force of cash' reads the caption below.*

No to Menhirland! Conservation and Conflict at Carnac

Andy Worthington

In the second of three articles on 'Contested Landscapes' published in *3rd Stone*, Andy Worthington looks at the issues surrounding access to the megalithic alignments of Brittany.

The article 'A Brief History of the Summer Solstice at Stonehenge' in the last issue of *3rd Stone* [issue 42] looked at how the long-term and the more immediate issues of access to Stonehenge were finally being addressed by English Heritage. In the meantime, in the heart of the most impressive Neolithic landscape in France, some of the monuments at Carnac in Brittany – vast alignments of parallel standing stones at Kermario and Le Menec – have been caged behind 'temporary' fencing since the early 1990s, with all public access denied for most of this time.

The story began in November 1990, when the Ministry of Culture initiated a project called 'Grand Carnac' for the improvement of the Carnac area. The project centred on paid access to certain sites that were to be fenced off, with only prescribed routes allowed around the stones. Land was to be acquired by the state, there were proposals for a large car park and a visitors' centre to replace an existing car park at the end of the Kermario alignments, and there were proposals for compulsory purchase orders or even eviction notices on a number of houses in the vicinity of the stones. The following year, the western alignments at Kermario were fenced off, with Le Menec and Kermario East following in 1993. In total over 10 km of fencing was erected.

Pressures on celebrated monuments and on the land around them are widespread. It is not only Stonehenge where drastic measures have been taken to combat the problems of erosion associated with large visitor numbers. At Newgrange, for example, shuttles and guided tours are obligatory, and in the temperature controlled Hypogeum of Malta only ten visitors an hour are allowed.

Even so, there was something excessive about the French government's attempts to justify the closures by claiming that Carnac was 'A victim of its own fame.' The English version of a leaflet published in 1997 contained this overly dramatic lament: 'Alas, Carnac is suffering damage from vegetation, from being trampled upon by millions of tourists every year, and the progressive erosion of the ground which is exposing the rocky floor. The menhirs are in danger of detaching from their footings and toppling over'[1].

More worryingly, the leaflet suggested that 'the archaeological layers which have not been studied with modern methods are being destroyed beyond recovery. Every 1 cm of soil that disappears is 1 cm of history vanishing forever'. This conclusion was a kind of clinical aversion to the very notion of visitors. Carnac, the Ministry suggested, most emphatically does not belong to you or me.

There have been dissenting voices, of course. Demonstrations against the project have ranged from the casual and short-term – dismantling the fence in the early years, for example – to the more organized, long-term opposition of groups such as *La Confedération Paysanne, Les Amis du Solstice, Le Front de Libération des Menhirs* and *Menhirs Libres* (perhaps best translated as 'Free the Standing Stones'), a local association whose central aim is to restore free access to the stones, to remove the fencing, and to stop the expropriations.

Menhirs Libres suggest that the greatest damage to the monuments was caused by ill-conceived state policies in the 1980s: 'Tractors uprooted the vegetation, and where there was resistance they used herbicides'[2]. For good measure, they add that the government 'had the nerve to blame tourists for the destruction of the vegetation in the first place', and propose that established Breton land management techniques are the solution to the problem.

1 Ministry of Culture leaflet (English version), 1997.

2 This and subsequent translated quotes from: *Association Menhirs Libres, Des Hommes et Des Pierres* ('Of Men and Stones'), 1998.

The association believes that it makes sense to create a number of smaller car parks and reception points throughout the area, avoiding the concentration of vehicles in the one car park at Kermario, which, as they point out, created a disproportionate focus on that particular alignment in the first place. They also oppose the raising of any buildings within 50 m of the alignments. This includes the visitors' centre and two viewing platforms that have been raised at Kermario since the alignments were fenced off. The first viewing platform, subsequently demolished, was described as 'particularly hideous and ugly' by the mayor of Carnac who actually signed the contract for its construction.

Menhirs Libres proposes that the focus on the most prominent alignments of Kermario, Le Menec and Kerlescan to the exclusion of the rest of the Neolithic landscape of Carnac is not only a disproportionate response, but one that also leaves the other sites vulnerable. The 4 km Carnac alignments are just part of a vast landscape running from the river Etel to the river Crac'h, a distance of 19 km, scattered with the remains of 23 alignments and ten cromlechs. Even so, some of these lesser-known sites have been destroyed within living memory. In 1957, around 180 stones were bulldozed in the eight-line alignments of Gueldro à Plouhinec, and in 1991, when the alignments at Kermario were first being fenced off, dozens of stones in the alignments at Erdevan were bulldozed in a tree-planting operation. In 1998, two were even found as a feature on a roundabout in an area controlled by the local council.

Erdevan demonstrates some of the peculiarities of the scheduling of ancient monuments in France. Only 210 out of what was once an estimated 1,100 stones are classified as Historic Monuments, and throughout the Carnac area as a whole only seven out of 23 alignments and five out of ten cromlechs are protected as Historic Monuments. In light of this, the extraordinary focus on security, exclusion and eviction at Kermario and Le Menec seems even less tenable.

When it comes to the evictions, the association's response is scathing. They comment that a government minister 'visited certain residents, particularly those over the age of 80, to tell them they had to move out, because their homes were going to be knocked down'. Of the dozen or so houses that have been expropriated, only one has actually been demolished. Another, which the government said would be immediately destroyed, was used as part of the first viewing platform, and the rest 'are used as offices, warehouses and homes for various state personnel as well as private tenants'. The association notes that, on signing the document approving the initial project, the Minister of Culture, Mr Toubon, declared: 'Carnac will not be made into an enclave from which the people of Brittany will be excluded'. They would like local people to be involved in the management of the site, with the possibility of paid local guides conducting people around the stones.

Over the years, *Menhirs Libres* has organized colourful resistance to the government's proposals, both in Carnac and in Paris. In autumn 1998, a delegation of locals marched on government offices in Paris, their numbers swelled by supporters in and around the capital, many dressed as menhirs in papier mâché costumes. In December 1998 I went over to Brittany to witness a demonstration in Carnac itself, staying at *Menhirs Libres'* headquarters, 'La Petite Métairie', a small farmhouse in the middle of the Kermario alignment, literally hemmed in all round by the perimeter fence.

Fig 2: Supporters of Menhirs Libres *demonstrate in Carnac, December 1998.*

I was treated with extremely generous hospitality – a seemingly endless supply of bottles of the last of the previous year's cider, from apples picked, pressed and bottled on the farm, and a similarly endless supply of fresh crepes, loaded with cheese and ham. My hosts, Mr and Mrs Mary, were small-scale farmers, fighting not only for their land but for the right of all to connect to it. It was no wonder that some of *Menhir Libres'* literature was of a global, ecological tone: 'Is it right to replace gorse with fences, cows with sheep, meadows with car parks and traditional farms with commercial buildings?'

As I was shown around the farm, something of the surreal nature of the conflict was brought home to me. When the fences were first raised, people couldn't even get into their own homes and it was only through the intervention of the police that the fencing was moved to within four metres of the doors to allow the residents access. Even so, the barriers crowded in on every angle of every building like a prison fence, and the track to and from the main road was similarly enclosed, creating a feeling of permanent occupation. Under these circumstances, it seemed to me, resistance was inevitable.

At noon on the Saturday a crowd of hundreds gathered in the town square. There was a carnival atmosphere, with people dressed as menhirs, and rousing speeches from the leaders, after which the microphone seemed to live with whichever local character had the most to say. It was a warm atmosphere of restrained but determined resistance. Clearly, the situation at Carnac was crucial to certain local people, and I had the feeling that these gestures were not only to do with cultural and geographical issues (Celtic issues, the Breton identity, something akin to Cornwall's relationship to central government) but also with issues of class that ran down the centuries, between land owners and small-holders.

Most of all there was the distinct impression, particularly at a few key moments throughout the day, that the demonstration was a way of celebrating an ancient bond with the landscape. The crowd had not been in the square for long when a lorry drove up, filled with models of the stones and lit with torches like a wagon of fire. As the number of protestors grew a few women started singing, a lilting Breton song, full of pride and endurance. They joined hands, dancing in and out in clapping circles, the motion swelled by others joining in – dozens of children, men and women of all ages – circles and song breathing and revolving, creating timeless spaces in the crowded town square.

As dusk fell, the flaming wagon took to the narrow streets at the head of a torch-lit procession. Flags and banners were waved, and there were chants of '*Librons Les Menhirs*!' ('Free the Standing Stones'), a political message laid over what seemed to be the surviving expression of a kind of perennial fire festival of the mind. Folklore and mythology were certainly issues close to those fighting for the stones. Up to the 19th century midsummer bonfires were lit beside the stones and cattle were herded between them for protection and to ensure fertility. There were reports of seasonal festivals at those sites where a living population could keep the observations alive – winter solstice at Kerlescan, summer solstice at Le Menec and the equinoxes at Kermario. The legend that a stone was added to the alignments every summer solstice was told as though it still happened today, but most of all there was a connection to the Breton Saint Cornély that managed to

Fig 3: A bizarre example of the 'enclosing' of a Carnac megalith.

include Christianity, paganism and Breton independence in its wide embrace. It was Cornély who saved the Bretons from Rome, turning the advancing legionaries into avenues of stone, and his feast day is close to the autumn equinox.

At the end of 1998, the government handed over the management of the project to the archaeologist and museum director Jean-Pierre Mohen. It was the fallout from a Public Enquiry in Carnac two years before in which 87 percent of the respondents had rejected the proposals, and even the officials in charge had commented that 'the project had some serious shortcomings' and 'the brief was remarkably imprecise'. Although there was some hope that the project would be overhauled, Mohen's 1999 report mainly endorsed the original proposals. The melodrama of the Ministry's earlier leaflet, with its claims of 'millions of tourists', was modified to a more rational 500,000. Mohen accepted that constraints on visitors were 'necessary in order to conserve the archaeological layers of the soil that still contain numerous clues for the interpretation of the history of the area'[3], and suggested that 'the vegetation should be protected at least during the summer months, with access to this area severely limited'. He also approved the forced eviction of people whose homes were judged to intrude on the alignments, 'either by agreement or by compulsory purchase', as he blandly put it.

So the struggle for Carnac continues. There was a brief flurry of media activity when part of an alignment was reopened in October 1999, but access was to be

3 Translated quotes from: Jean-Pierre Mohen, 1999, *Rapport sur le Projet des 'Alignements de Carnac'* (Report on the 'Carnac Alignments' Project).

restricted to 180 people a day between April and September, and the rest remained closed. The story quietly went away.

Overall though, it was surprising that the struggle at Carnac had gained such little media attention, either at home or abroad. Few noticed, for example, when *Menhirs Libres* delivered a petition signed by over 17,000 people to the European Union in March 2000. It was hard to imagine such a situation in Britain, where hordes of aficionados – archaeologists, new antiquarians, dowsers, pagans – vie with one another, each pressing their claims on the most celebrated monuments like ardent suitors. In France it was as if few cared. Was this a by-product of Republicanism – everything old swept away with the dawning of a new era? In contrast, I wondered why the British Isles contained so many people who looked to the monuments of the ancient past for new ways of seeing. In particular I was left to ponder the apparent indifference of French archaeologists towards Carnac.

In all the arguments about Kermario, what neither side seemed to have noticed was that the car park and buildings alike were built on the remains of a cromlech

Fig 4: 'Free the Stones'. Carnac, December 1998.

that once stood there. It was a truly colossal horseshoe of spaced stones, enclosing an area around 5,000 square metres, the original focus for the alignments of standing stones that still marched uphill towards it. James Miln's 19th century plans showed 'a good southern arc of a much-disturbed semi-circle at the head of the rows'[4], but today's visitor is unlikely to be told what stood there. Three prominent stones remain, but there is nothing to indicate their significance or to mark out the perimeter of the enclosure.

Aubrey Burl commented on the irony that visitors would gaze in wonder at the stone rows but 'overlook the spoiled but significant cromlech at their head'[5], and concluded that cromlechs were 'a form of stone circle which, in respect of planning, listing, study and conservation, remains in much the same state as stone circles in Britain and Ireland thirty years ago, neglected and disregarded'[6]. Fortunately for Carnac, a significant number of local people care enough about the larger ritual landscape of the area to understand not only the importance of its study and conservation, but also its continuing significance as a living environment.

Thanks are due to my good friend Joko for his invaluable assistance with translations and to Dom and Marie for their additional help.

4 Aubrey Burl, 2000, *The Stone Circles of Britain, Ireland and Brittany*, New Haven and London, p.341.

5 Ibid., p.337.

6 Ibid., p.332.

The Devil in Church

Jeremy Harte

Jeremy Harte looks at ways in which Satan manifested himself in the mediaeval mind and church.

It was a hot, still day and few people used the road that led past the lonely Dartmoor inn. So it was welcome news for the landlady when she saw a stranger riding up the dusty track. A gentleman, from the look of him, so he should pay well. And he must be a bit hot, wearing those stiff black clothes and all.

He called out for cider, and she ran forward to serve him. The stranger did not dismount but sat on his tall black horse, draining the full mug at a single draught. Afterwards she remembered two things: the way the liquor hissed as it ran down his throat, and the odd-shaped boot that held his foot in the stirrup. 'I'm bound for Widecombe', said the dark stranger, tossing down a piece of old gold. 'Will you be my guide?'. Wisely, she declined (Bray 1838: 312-3).

They say he found his own way to Widecombe, where Jan the gambler was snoozing through a sermon, his pack of cards at the ready. Down came the Devil, and hauled his prey up through the roof of the church, where the black horse stood tethered to a pinnacle; and so, willing or not, Jan was dragged away through the gathering stormclouds (St. Leger-Gordon 1965: 117-8). That much is legend, but it is pretty clear that something strange happened at Widecombe church that

Fig 1: Widecombe church. The lightning ran up the north aisle, to the left, and flashed across the chancel.

Sunday, 21st October 1638. About 300 people attended the service, when suddenly the church grew dark. The cloud came over, 'the darkness increasing yet more, till they could not see one another': then there was a crack of thunder, and lightning struck the church tower on the north side. The shock forced its way down the stair turret and then, meeting an obstacle, broke through the west window. 'It struck against the north-side wall of the church, as if it were with a great cannon-bullet', and passed up the aisle, killing a man who was leaning against the woodwork. 'The brains fell backward, entire and whole, into the next seat behind him, and two pieces of his skull'. The stream of lightning divided in two: one flash of the electric current broke out of the east wall of the aisle, while the other tore into the chancel. Eight boys, sitting on the communion rail, were thrown off by the shock, but not hurt. Lightning flickered across the chancel, killing another man, and went to earth by the chancel door. Four people had been killed and sixty-two injured (Harley 1809: 1.220-228).

Enough to suggest that the powers of Hell had been at work that day, but in fact the author of the Widecombe tracts does no such thing. In fact he goes out of his way to remind us of 'God's visible judgements, and terrible remonstrances', instead of pointing the finger at the traditional culprit. His motives were probably spiritual ones; everyone thought that the Devil came to carry off the most notorious sinners and blasphemers, while those who died in the church at Widecombe were just ordinary people. But we were all sinners, we all deserved to be cooked by lightning, and what was really surprising about the incident was not that four people were killed, but that 296 were saved. Truly, the mercies of the Lord were past understanding.

They showed themselves again, two years later, at St Anthony in Cornwall. On 24th May 1640, the people were gathered for a service when lightning struck twice – once on the tower and once beside the chancel, with 'a noise, as though divers Cannons had been shot off at once, to make one single and terrible report; the noise did not descend from above, but was heard, and seemed to begin close at the Northside of the *Communion Table*' (Hone 1826: 2.664).

This was caused by lightning blowing apart the walls of the building. Stone is a poor conductor of electricity, so the charge tends to short-circuit along the lines of mortar and wooden beams, especially if they are damp (Morris 1989: 330). The expansion of super-heated water then hurls the stones out of their bedding: at Widecombe 'there were also stones thrown from the tower, and carried about, a great distance from the church, as thick as if a hundred men had been there throwing'.

No-one was killed at St Anthony, although several of the people kneeling at the communion rail were burnt. This was at the moment when 'the minister... saw (to his thinking) a flaming fire about his body, and withall, heard a terrible and unspeakable sound'. There was more in the way of spectacle – 'divers balls of fire came into the *Church*... a great fire, far redder then any lightning'. This sounds rather like the 'purplish nubecula' seen in the church at Loughton in Staffordshire when a storm broke out at the time of divine service in 1649. It broke in like lightning 'and did kill and hurt many, with spotts and holes' (Aubrey 1881: 259). At Widecombe, too, the minster saw 'as it were, a great ball of fire, and most terrible lightning, come in at the window'.

At first this sounds like ball lightning, and this would be plausible if there were only one reference: but it seems unlikely that the same rare effect would have recurred in three successive storms. Besides, ball lightning takes the form of luminous spheres, about a foot across, which bounce or float along the ground during storms. They come into buildings, but do not rip along the walls; and they are usually harmless (Devereux 1982: 98-104). Then there are fireballs, which are much more destructive, and smash into buildings during storms – but they occur instead of a lightning strike, not in addition to it. Widecombe and St Anthony were clearly struck by lightning. When people saw a ball of fire, they must have been looking at the lightning flash itself. Lightning strikes quicker than the eye can see. The line of conductivity between tower and chancel would already have been established when the return stroke took place, the one that makes the flash and the explosion. The lightning is less than an inch wide, but it blazes so fiercely that it leaves an afterglow on the retina that suggests something much larger. In the tumult of the moment, it was natural to experience this as a kind of object invading the building, and not as the path of an invisible energy.

The idea of a lightning entity comes over very clearly in accounts of the storm at Great Chart in Kent. It was on 27th December 1612 and, once again, people had assembled for Sunday worship when the sky grew dark, 'and a thing in the middle aisle of the church burned, as one might perceive it, but yet it was like unto a black cloud and smoked, and the preacher seeing the people dismayed came down out of the pulpit, and came near to the thing and desired the people to pray with him, and presently the thing rose up and gave 2 or 3 flashes of fire and killed one man dead and hurt 20 more, very sore, that they are not recovered as yet and it broke down the chancel stone wall and went out' (Hinds 1940: 19).

Here the black fire may have been produced by a first strike, while more of the damage was done by the flashes which followed it. Otherwise the story seems almost interchangeable with the other three, although this in itself doesn't cast any doubt on the individual reports. They are similar because the phenomenon itself was similar, and not that uncommon. In the days before lightning conductors, an enormous number of churches must have been struck by lightning: one eighteenth-century study counted 386 during 33 years (Simons 1996: 124). The tower (always a 'steeple' in the original reports) was the natural point of contact, and then the electric current ran along joists and the mortar in the walls. Where churches were laid out in the conventional plan, this meant that the shock would take the longest line that it could through the building, before earthing itself in the more resistant ground. This path would run down the nave or aisles and into the chancel. Behaviour like this is fully compatible with ordinary lightning, so it seems unnecessary to involve other causes – though some researchers have done just that. Widecombe, for instance, is supposed to have been assailed by a thunderstorm, tornado and ball lightning all at once, with hailstones thrown in for good measure (McEwan 1991: 172-6). It's more likely that these diverse effects are conventions of seventeenth-century disaster reporting, and not some freak conjunction in the weather itself.

A lot depended on the reporter. Adrian Saravia, the minister of Great Chart, wrote a straightforward and moving account of the calamity at his church, but this was nothing to what the pamphlet press made of it. Saravia's 'thing... like unto a black cloud' became 'a most ugly shape out of the ayer like unto a broadeyd bul', and it is this bull which dashes the minister's book out of his hand and terrifies the crowd, including one man 'slaine by the fright of this mishapen spirit'. And

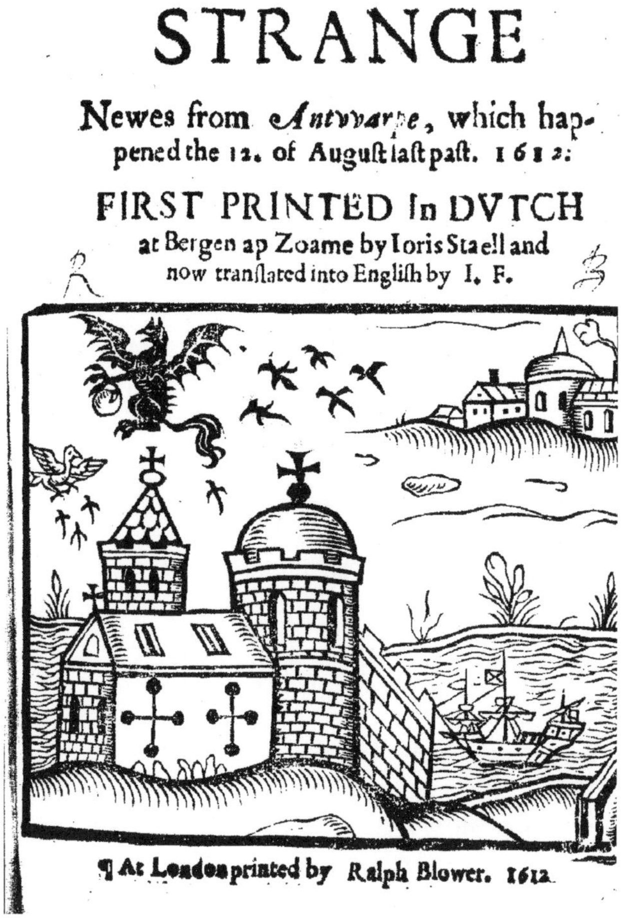
STRANGE

Newes from Antvvarpe, which happened the 12. of Auguſt laſt paſt. 1612.

FIRST PRINTED In DVTCH at Bergen ap Zoame by Ioris Staell and now tranſlated into Engliſh by I. F.

¶ At London printed by Ralph Blower. 1612.

Fig 2: The Devil shows his disapproval of Catholics by dive-bombing Antwerp church, 1612.

why? Because the parishioners were accustomed to get together, four or five at a time, and discuss worldly business during service time. No wonder Hell was unleashed (Briggs 1962: 161).

The worse the storm, and the further it was from the publishing house, the more exciting the appearance of the Devil could be. Four months before Great Chart, on 12th August 1612, lightning struck a church at Antwerp. In the English translation of the original report, it is Satan who appears in bodily form over the tower and causes fire to rain on the church. There he is on the pamphlet cover, hovering in dragonish form with his claws poised to throw a sort of infernal bowling ball, which must be the lightning bolt itself. Then he rages through the church, contemptuous

Fig 3: The black dog of Bungay appears on a weather vane in the marketplace. Further proposals to commemorate him in a Millennium statue were blocked by the vicar.

alike of holy water and sacred images: in fact he stops in his progress to rip down an 'idolatrous picture' over one of the altars, which he 'spoyld & defaced... with his wicked nayles and clawes'. A good Protestant could hardly have done more, which leaves the moral of the story rather confused (Oldridge 2000: 76). The first of the storm pamphlets, Abraham Fleming's *A Straunge and Terrible Wunder*, is also the most dramatic. When lightning struck the church of Bungay in Suffolk (4th August 1577) the current broke apart the metalwork of the bell-frame, killed two ringers in the tower, and passed through the body of the church (Holinshed 1808: 4.344). But the details of its passage were of little interest to Fleming. He was concerned not with the 'fearful flashes of fire' but with something much more unusual: 'a dog as they might disceme it, of a black colour... This black dog, or the divil in such a likeness (God hee knoweth all who worketh all) running along down the body of the church with great swiftenesse'. Two people were killed by the stroke and a third 'shrunk up, as it were a piece of lether scorched in a hot fire' (Westwood 1985: 178-9; McEwan 1986: 123-4).

Fleming's black dog is Holinshed's lightning discharge – given shape partly by the retinal afterglow scorched on the eyes of those who had seen the flash, and partly by the cloud of smoke and steam released as it ripped apart the woodwork.

A few details of the actual damage are included in the pamphlet – the masonry and church door were 'merveleously renten and torn, ye marks as it were of his clawes or talans' – but this kind of detail is subordinated to the image of a sudden black, evil presence in the church.

It is the same with Fleming's report on Blythburgh, twelve miles from Bungay. The same storm passed over and lightning struck the woodwork of the tower and passed through the church to the vestry, where it discharged a yard deep into the ground (Holinshed 1808: 4.344). As Fleming perceived it, the black dog hurled himself through the church to perch on the roodloft and then swung down among the crowd, killing two of them. In pre-Reformation accounts, there was no ambiguity about what was going on. Lightning came as the intervention of a physical demon. At Shrewsbury, on 6th January 1533 'the dyvyll apearyd in Sainct Alkmonde churche there when the preest was at highe masse wth tempest and darknes so that as he passyd throughe the churche he mountyd up the steeple in the sayde churche teringe the wyer of the sayde clocke and put the prynt of his clawes uppon the iiijth bell and toocke one of the pynnacles awaye wth hym and for the tyme stayed all the bells in the churches wthin the sayd towne that they could neyther toll nor rynge' (Leighton 1880: 255).

Fig 4: The church at Danbury, where lightning took on the form of a grey friar, 'behaving himself verie outrageouslie'.

This was written a generation after the event, but it is not too exaggerated. Bells were liable to be silenced when lightning fused the metal of the clapper to the bell itself, and this was all the more frightening since it was by ringing these bells that people had hoped to drive away the demons of the storm in the first place. In England, the use of bells as a daemonifuge came to an end in 1547, along with many other customs of the old religion, but it continued in the Catholic countries. Bells were still regularly rung during storms in nineteenth-century France. The authorities viewed this with concern, not least because the ringers were placing themselves near conductive metal at the most exposed point of the building. Lightning took a fearful toll of bell-ringers: one abbé had seen five such accidents in his own career, and knew of a further twenty (Corbin 1998: 101-110).

Fig 5: The Tower Struck by Lightning, from a fifteenth-century Italian Tarot.

Under the circumstances, the ringers of St Michael's Cornhill got off lightly when 'an vglie shapen sight' appeared in the London church during a storm. 'They all fell downe, and lay as dead for the time, letting the Bells ring and cease of their own accord', but suffered no further harm. The discharge came in through the south window of the tower and passed through the north window on its passage to the ground, ripping out stones 'as if they had been so much butter' and leaving holes, three or four inches deep, that looked as if they had been made by a lion's claws (Stow 1908: 1.196).

Or take the events of 24th June 1402, when a thunderstorm broke over the home counties. So frightful were the flashes of lightning that people thought the Last Day was at hand. Mind you, chroniclers always said this about any impressive storm; either mediaeval people had very short memories, or else it was a rhetorical commonplace. The old enemy was unleashed at Hertford, where lightning was an evil spirit which came into the church of All Saints and tore up the steps to the tower, scratching the treads on the stairs with great gashes like the claw marks of a lion or bear. It twisted the wheels from which the bells were hung, and broke the joist above them. A luckless bell-ringer was struck by the discharge, but survived with severe burns. Meanwhile at Danbury in Essex, the lightning demon was yet more plainly visible: in fact he took on the form of a Franciscan friar, although as this detail comes from the pen of a monk at St Albans it may not be altogether reliable. There was no love lost between the monks and the friars.

At all events this fiend, or friar, or whatever it was, entered the church, where its hideous appearance struck fear into the hearts of the people. It damaged the roof and they saw it run up to the altar and leap onto it, not once but three times. There was a crucifix behind the altar, and the infernal force broke this effigy apart, blackening the wood. Then it passed through the legs of a bystander and smashed its way out of the church, breaking up the chancel wall and leaving an intolerable stink behind. The unfortunate bystander was badly burnt in his feet and legs, which turned black as pitch (Riley 1866: 340, 342; Collins 1985: 17).

It seems that Catholic lightning behaved in much the same way as its Protestant counterpart, coming in through the roof or tower, and discharging to earth outside the chancel. The diabolical stench came partly from the vapourising of superheated wood and stone, but mostly from ozone released in the suddenly electrified air. Described, even by a modern observer, as 'a suffocating, sulphurous odour' (Lane 1966: 53), this gave an unmistakable whiff of Hell to the whole business. We have records from the great abbeys and cathedrals where monks advanced in procession after a lightning strike, sprinkling holy water in large quantities, and breathing with relief as the sulphurous air dissipated around them (William of Malmesbury 1847: 342; Morris 1989: 330).

Mediaeval churches differed in one respect from their successors; they had a stone altar in place of a wooden communion table. The altar slab was set on stone walls bedded into the earth, which meant that a lightning flash, if it followed the usual path from tower to chancel, would discharge near the altar and anyone standing close to it. This would account for the leaping behaviour of the grey shape at Danbury, and it also explains the greater frequency with which priests were killed by the lightning. At High Mass there would be no-one but the priest and a server near the altar, or in the chancel at all. Hence the scene of horror on Christmas Eve 1171 at Andover: 'at midnight, with everybody looking on, a priest was suddenly struck by lightning within the church and no-one else was hurt. But a shape like a pig was seen between his feet, and it ran hither and thither' (*Eulogium Historiarum* 1863: 3.80).

The black pig is an unusual touch, but not a completely unexpected one. Gregory the Great has an exemplary tale of a church taken over by the Catholic party from the wicked Arians, and reconsecrated. As they celebrated Mass for the first time, 'some of them that stood without the chancel heard an hog running up and down through their legs, and... the hog made towards the church door to go forth'. The story was well-known in the Middle Ages – Mirk uses it in his *Festial* as an example of how unclean spirits are evicted from a church – and the account from Andover shows enough similarity to suggest that the author of the *Eulogium* was showing off his acquaintance with the literature.

The earliest accounts of storm demons certainly betray a fondness for fine writing. Gunthar, the Bishop of Cologne, wrote a letter to a colleague about what happened in his cathedral on 15th September 857. Darkness fell on the church, and as it shook with the sound of thunder, lightning flashed in through the gutters of the roof and grounded itself within the church, killing a priest at one altar and a deacon at another. In a more lively version, it was not just lightning but 'a thunderbolt in the form of a long dragon'. Not to be outdone, Theodgaud the Bishop of Trier said that he too had been celebrating Mass during this storm, and yes, there was a dense black cloud and fearful thunder, and lightning smashed into the bell tower. The church grew dark, so dark that people could scarcely see one another – much as it would at Widecombe, eight centuries later. But they could still see something else. This was a huge black dog, tearing past the altar, until suddenly he disappeared into the ground (*Annales Fuldenses* 1891: 48; *Annales de Saint-Bertin* 1871: 91).

Just like the black dog of Bungay, in fact. Stories of the storm demon show a remarkable similarity, though they were written hundreds of years apart, and this comes from their basis in physical reality. To be sure, the stories which made it into pamphlet or chronicle had been screened to make sure that they fitted the traditional template. There must be a crowd attending service on a major feast day, sudden darkness should precede the flash through the church, the priest or minister should show exemplary bravery, and so on. This is not to say that these things didn't happen, simply that other occasions which did not fit the template so well were quietly forgotten. And a certain latitude was permitted in bodying forth the lightning flash itself. But it wasn't a demon dog, pig, dragon or bull: it was lightning, not even ball lightning or some other faintly mysterious phenomenon, but honest to goodness lightning of the sort we have all seen from a window on a stormy night.

Physically, at least. Intellectually it was a different matter. People saw a different lightning when it flashed across the skies of 856 or 1638, because they did not see it with the understanding that it was a random discharge of electricity. Mediaeval lightning was not necessarily attributed to spirits, and anyone who could read their Aristotle would find it treated as a natural phenomenon. But faced by lightning

Fig 6: For these seventeenth-century bell-ringers, the day began like any other day...

which seemed purposeful, which tore into God's house and killed his ministers and left an unholy stench, people felt compelled to take a different kind of interpretation. Suddenly, natural violence became the arm of the demons who had descended from their ancient kingdom of the air and were waging war on humanity.

That's the difference between then and now: our ancestors had perfectly well-developed ideas of natural law, but they suspended these ideas when the relationship between people and nature seemed to be a purposeful one. Lightning in church was not a random discharge of energy, into which people might choose to read some meaning: it was a sign from God, or the Devil. Given half a chance, that's what we would like to believe today (Michell 1985): remember the fuss when lightning struck York Minster? In the eighth century, a thunderstorm descended on the village of Tauberbischofsheim, so frightening that the inhabitants took refuge in the parish church. There, they pleaded with Abbess Leoba for help. 'As if she had been called to a contest' she strode to the door, threw it open and made the sign of the cross in the face of the lightning and the thunder... which sank away, like a naughty child after a rebuke (Fletcher 1997: 243). There is something heroic about a lone woman, armed only with faith, defying a hundred million volts of raw energy. But you get better results with a lightning conductor.

References

Annales de Saint-Bertin et de Saint-Vaast, 1871, ed. C. Dehaisnes, Renouard.

Annales Fuldenses, 1891, ed. Friedrich Kurze, Scriptores Rerum Germanicarum.

Aubrey, John, 1881, *Remaines of Gentilisme and Judaisme*, James Britten, Folk-Lore Society.

Bray, Anna, 1838, *Traditions, Legends, Superstitions and Sketches of Devonshire*, London.

Briggs, Katharine, 1962, *Pale Hecate's Team*, Routledge & Kegan Paul.

Collins, Andrew, 1985, *The Knights of Danbury*, Earthquest.

Corbin, Alain, 1998, *Village Bells: Sound and Meaning in the 19th-Century French Countryside*, tr. Martin Thom, Columbia University Press.

Devereux, Paul, 1982, *Earth Lights: Towards an Understanding of the UFO Enigma*, Turnstone.

Eulogium Historiarum, 1863, ed. Frank Scott Haydon, Rolls Series 9.

Fletcher, Richard, 1997, *The Conversion of Europe: From Paganism to Christianity 371–1386 AD*, Harper Collins.

Harley, Edward, 1809, *The Harleian Miscellany*, White & Murray.

Hinds, A.B, ed, 1940, *Report on the Manuscripts of the Marquess of Downshire 4: Papers of William Trumbull the Elder*, Historical MSS Commission 75.

Holinshed, Ralph, 1808, *Chronicles of England, Ireland and Scotland*, London.

Hone, William, 1826, *The Every-Day Book*, William Tegg.

Lane, Frank, 1966, *The Elements Rage*, David & Charles.

Leighton, W.A., 1880, 'Early chronicles of Shrewsbury 1372-1603', *Tr. of the Shropshire Antiquarian & Natural History Society* 3, 239–352.

McEwan, Graham, 1986, *Mystery Animals of Britain and Ireland*, Robert Hale.

McEwan, Graham, 1991, *Freak Weather*, Robert Hale.

Michell, John, 1985, 'God's mysterious way: or did he spell it out at York Minster?', *Fortean Times* 43, 54–7.

Morris, Richard, 1989, *Churches in the Landscape*, Dent.

Oldridge, Darren, 2000, *The Devil in Early Modern England*, Sutton.

Riley, Henry Thomas, ed, 1866, *Johannis de Trokelowe et Henrici de Blaneforde necnon Quorundam Anonymorum Chronica*, Rolls Series 28iii.

Simons, Paul, 1996, *Weird Weather*, Little Brown & Co.

St. Leger-Gordon, Ruth, 1965, *The Witchcraft and Folklore of Dartmoor*, Robert Hale.

Stow, John, 1908, *A Survey of London*, ed. Charles Lethbridge Kingsford, Clarendon.

Westwood, Jennifer, 1985, *Albion: A Guide to Legendary Britain*, Granada.

William of Malmesbury, 1847, *Chronicle of the Kings of England*, tr. J.A. Giles, Bohn.

Acknowledgements

I am most grateful to Ian Currie for meteorological advice on what lightning can and cannot do. Ian is the editor of *Weather Eye*, a lively magazine on the subject.

Re-evaluating Monumentality: Arthur's Stone, Dorstone, Herefordshire

Dr George Nash

Dr George Nash[1] looks again at the monumentality of Arthur's Stone, a famous example of the Black Mountains Group of chambered long cairns, which he first wrote about in *3rd Stone* 45, Autumn 2002.

In this article, I will re-evaluate a Neolithic chambered long cairn and highlight some of the misunderstandings and misconceptions that have accompanied its interpretation. The monument is Arthur's Stone, in West Herefordshire (Fig 1). I will argue that re-evaluation is important not only for Arthur's Stone but also for other enigmatic monuments with questionable architecture within the Black Mountains Group in southeastern Wales and elsewhere.

This impressive barrow is one of the most notable of all prehistoric monuments along the Welsh Marches. However, it is also a monument that has received only superficial investigation and discussion, and was up until 2006, never excavated. Despite the lack of excavation in or around the stonework, the site had been a focus for discussion (Castleden 1992; Daniel 1950; Darvill 1982; Grimes 1936a, 1936b; Hemp 1935; HWCC 1981; Stanford 1990; Children & Nash 1994; Nash 1997; Olding 2000; Sant 2000; Watkins 1928). An account by members of the Woolhope

1 Department of Archaeology, Classics and Egyptology, University of Liverpool, UK.

Fig 1: The main chamber components of Arthur's Stone, looking northwest.

Naturalists' Field Club on 25th May 1882 gives important and detailed observations of the site[2].

Within the recent past, the monument's guardian, English Heritage (now referred to as Historic England), has erected a fence around Arthur's Stone to protect the mound. Information boards provide a brief narrative regarding who may have used the monument, when and why. An artist's impression shows Arthur's Stone as the scene of Neolithic burial-ritual activity. The same reconstruction depicts the monument as a small mound with an enclosed entrance – nothing of the chamber or passage architecture is shown. Visitors therefore leave with the impression that, although Arthur's Stone is an impressive monument, the site, when in use, amounted to nothing more than a small oval mound with internal stone architecture used by a community to bury their dead. This visual interpretation, along with limited archaeological investigation, creates an interesting contradiction that requires re-addressing.

2 See Woolhope Naturalists' Field Club transcript (1882, pp. 175–77 [https://www.woolhopeclub.org.uk/document/transaction/transactions-1882]).

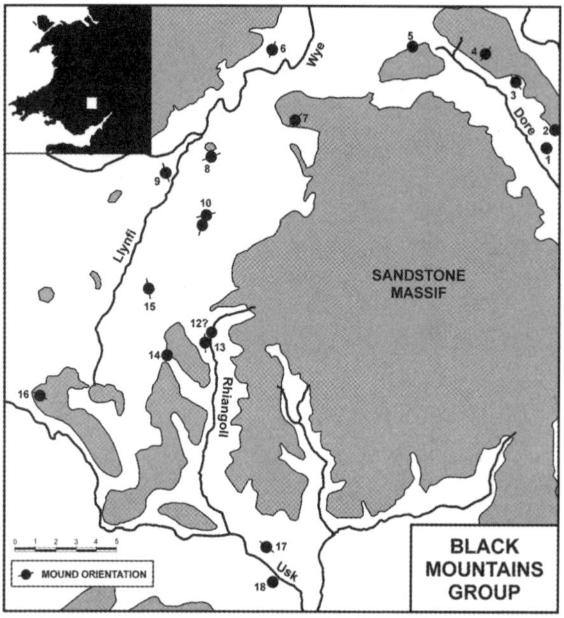

Fig 2: Distribution of monuments of the Black Mountains Group. Monuments: 1. Parkwood; 2. Dunseal; 3. Cross Lodge Barrow; 4. Arthur's Stone; 5. Little Mountain; 6. Clyro Court Tomb; 7. Pen yr Wyrlod; 8. Little Lodge Barrow; 9. Pipton Long Cairn; 10. Ffostyll North; 11. Ffostyll South; 12. Croesllechau; 13. Ty Isaf; 14. Mynydd Troed; 15. Penywyrlod; 16. Ty Illtyd; 17. Gwernvale; 18. Garn Coch.

Facts and Figures

The monument, once referred to as *Artil's Stone*, is first described by Nathaniel Salmon in his *A New Survey of England* (1728–9).

Comments by Salmon suggest the monument has changed little in appearance over the past 200 years. Although never excavated during the 19th and 20th centuries, Arthur's Stone appears to have captured the imagination of antiquarians and archaeologists alike (Figs 2 & 3). According to Crawford (1925, 147), the northern edge of Arthur's Stone Lane (which runs past the monument) formed part of the parish boundary between Dorstone and Bredwardine. The lane, which runs along the spine of Arthur's Stone ridge – from Merbach Hill to Dorstone Hill – is believed to be of ancient origin. During the recent past, the monument was conveniently used to delineate this recognised parish boundary.

The monument, dating from about 3500 BCE, is one of the most northerly chambered tombs of the Cotswold-Severn Group and is one of five tombs that dominate the Neolithic landscape of the northern reaches of the Golden Valley in West Herefordshire (Children & Nash 1994). Other monuments within the group lie further west and occupy the hinterlands of the eastern slopes of the Black

Fig 3: A romantic interpretation of the site made by John Berwick in John Duncomb's unfinished Collections towards the History and Antiquities of the County of Hereford (1804).

Mountains (Fig 2). The high concentration of Neolithic burial-ritual monuments within the Black Mountains Group (the only inland group in Wales) suggests that the hinterlands and valleys would have been attractive to the first agriculturists. Fowler (1983) argues that, annually, at least 240 potential growing days were available. This figure is relatively low compared with coastal areas such as the Gower, Southwest Wales, and Anglesey, which annually have 365 potential growing seasonal days.

Located between nearby Cross Lodge Barrow (SO 3325 4168) and Arthur's Stone is the Dorstone Hill settlement (SO 326 423). Excavated between 1965 and 1972 by Christopher Houlder and Roger Pye, this rare example of a Neolithic settlement yielded 4,000 pieces of flint, including more than 30 arrowheads and 60 polished stone axe fragments (HWCC 1981; Children & Nash 1994, 17)[3]. The settlement is thought to cover up to eighteen acres and may have been enclosed by an earthen bank with a wooden stockade. A continuous line of post-holes from the top of the stockade, each measuring up to 0.13 m in diameter, suggests that the Dorstone Hill settlement was strategically important. Trial excavations within the area of the settlement exposed a series of post-holes, a hut occupation floor, along with associated domestic debris (Pye *pers comm.*). The site appears to have been in use from the Neolithic to the Iron Age/Roman periods and would have had

3 Note, this site has been re-investigated by archaeologists between 2011 and 2019.

*Fig 4: Late 19th century engraving by E.L. Barnwell (*Archaeologica Cambrensis *1873).*

associations with Arthur's Stone and nearby Cross Lodge Barrow. Another possible settlement site may be present on nearby Cefn Hill at Abbey Farm, northwest of the ruins of Craswall Priory (SO 2715 3816).

Arthur's Stone and other Neolithic burial-ritual monuments in the area appear to represent continuous human activity since at least the Late Mesolithic (c.6000–3800 BCE). Diagnostic lithics, in particular microliths, have been found beneath and around Arthur's Stone (Brown 1963:76–91; Gavin-Robinson 1934; Tilley 1994, 118). So, even during the Neolithic, Arthur's Stone and other monuments within this group would have possessed a history and, more importantly, an affinity with its ancestors. In addition to a pre-cairn history, it should also be noted that diagnostic lithics dating to the Bronze Age have also been found along the west-facing slopes of Arthur's Stone ridge, including several barbed and tanged arrowheads (Brown 1963, 80). The continuous use of later prehistoric sites is not uncommon. During the excavation at Gwernvale (one of the Black Mountains Group), 1.5 km north of Crickhowell, Upper Palaeolithic and Mesolithic flints were found beneath the southern section of the facade (entrance), which suggests that this site was in use (albeit periodically) for up to 7,000 years prior to the construction of the monument (Britnell & Savory 1984)[4]. This Cotswold-

4 The majority of Late Upper Palaeolithic flint discovered at Gwernvale was found within an ancient buried palaeosol and comprised an array of chalcedonic chert and backed blades (Healey & Green 1984, 130). Tools included a penknife point, blades, a microlith and microburin. Also present were diagnostic Mesolithic tools, including 56 microliths (23 of these were broad-backed industries dating to the Early Mesolithic), 10 microburins, two notched blades and 10 truncated blades. Similar tool kits have also been found on Merbach Hill. However, these clearly date to the Mesolithic.

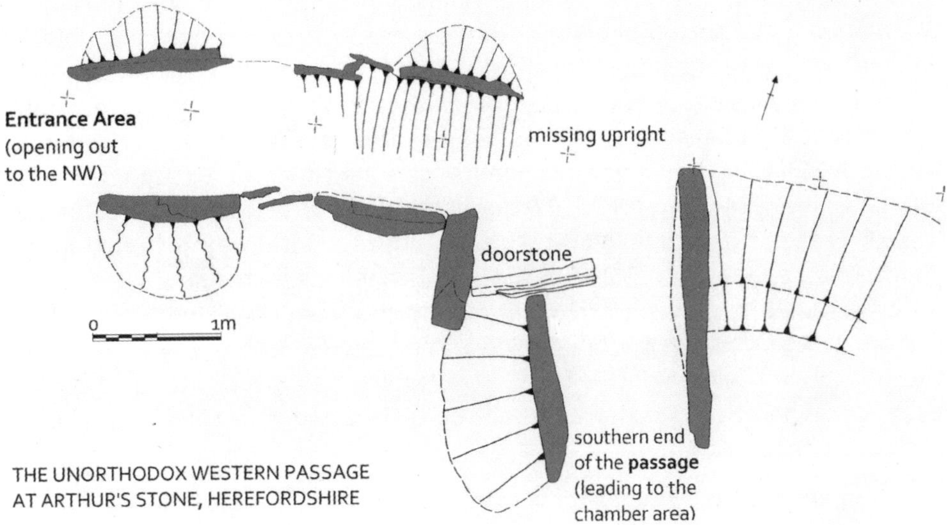

Fig 5: Plan of the unorthodox western passage (drawing: *G.H. Nash).*

Severn monument may represent only a fraction of the total number of open sites (as distinct from caves) that once existed in the lower Usk Valley. Likewise, along the western reaches of Merbach Hill to Vowchurch Common, to include Arthur's Stone ridge, substantial lithic scatters have been dated to the Late Mesolithic (Brown 1963; Gavin-Robinson 1934).

Prior to the excavation of the monument, it was considered that the chamber and passage alignment of Arthur's Stone was set within an oval mound (approximately 26 m x 17 m). The chamber has nine upright stones that support an enormous capstone that is estimated to weigh more than 25 tonnes (Corcoran 1969, 23)[5]. The capstone covers a polygonal chamber that is constructed from nine stone uprights. At its western end is an unorthodox right-angled passage that is delineated by eight uprights (Fig 5). The passage does not possess any of its capstones; however, based on the height of the uprights, during use, visitors to the chamber areas would have had to crawl along the passage in order to gain access.

Seasoned archaeologist Wilfred James Hemp (1935, 288) describes the chamber as kite-shaped, approximating the plan of the capstone. The chamber is regarded by Daniel (1950, 74) as being laterally sited. Several metres south of

5 Based on documentary evidence, the capstone appears to have been one block of stone, however, a legend that featured an altercation between two giants claims that the stone was in at least two pieces, the result of one giant hitting another so hard causing the capstone to break into two [three] pieces.

the capstone and chamber is a large upright sandstone slab which, allegedly, has as many as twelve large finger-dint cupmarks on the inner face, probably dating from the Bronze Age (Crawford 1925, 147; Daniel 1950, 118). Also present and extremely visible on the upper part of the stone is graffiti with clear dates, one of 1912. It is believed that this stone represents part of an anti-chamber (Daniel 1950). Lying between the chamber and the sandstone upright is a single stone setting. Crawford (1925, 47) suggests this stone is actually recumbent. It is likely that this stone, along with the cupmarked upright, form part of a southern axis chamber entered by a separate passage on the south or west side of the mound (Children & Nash 1994) or part of a false portal arrangement that mirrors other monument architecture within the Black Mountains group (e.g., Gwernvale, Penywyrlod and Ty Isaf). This strategically-placed stone would have been accompanied by two horns (constructed of earth or cairn) that would have enclosed a façade area.

The capstone, measuring approximately 5.8 m x 3.0 m, is split into three pieces as a result of weathering processes, and is oriented northeast/southwest with the south/west end pointing towards the southern section of the Golden Valley. A large section of the capstone has also split horizontally, with an enormous fragment collapsing into the central chamber[6]. The geology of the capstone is Old Red Sandstone (originating from the Pedolli Series of sandstones).

The chamber has at its western end, a false portal stone, partly blocking the doorway to the main chamber, and an inner passage that is oriented north. However, the passage changes direction to the northwest, pointing towards the impressive Hay Bluff and the northern extent of the Black Mountains (Children & Nash 1994, 26; Tilley 1994, 140). Crawford (1925, 147) has suggested the chambers of Arthur's Stone and Gwernvale (near Crickhowell) are similar, although the former is much larger. The unorthodox redirection of the passage and the orientation of the capstone suggest that Arthur's Stone may have been positioned deliberately so as to completely encompass the visual aspect of the Black Mountains. The tomb also incorporates views from both the southern and northern extents of the Golden Valley (Nash 1997, 20). Many other tombs within the upper Wye, Lynfi and Usk valleys (in Powys) appear to be similarly positioned (Children & Nash 1994; Olding 2000) (see Fig 2).

Members of the Woolhope Naturalists' Field Club, visiting the site in July 1882, remarked that a series of stones laid out in a circular fashion surrounded the monument. According to members, these may have represented the outer kerbing, or what 18th and 19th-century antiquarians termed as *peristaliths*, enclosing the

6 What Crawford (1925) terms the vertical fracture as false-bedded stratification.

mound[7]. However, there was no sign of any kerbing by 1928 (Watkins 1928, 150)[8]. An alternative view, and one that I support, suggests Arthur's Stone may have been trapezoidal in form[9], or at least elongated, and that the monument extended across the lane, with the present passage on the side of the monument. The actual façade area (with false portal) would have been located in the southeast and is represented by the upright which is recognised as being part of an ante-chamber (Fig 6).

Within fields east of the lane are a number of stones which cannot be considered as naturally occurring rock-outcropping. It is possible that these stones, along with smaller stone debris, represent the terminal end of the Arthur's Stone monument[10]. The destruction of this part of the monument must have occurred prior to the early 18th century; accounts by Nathaniel Salmon suggest Arthur's Stone was as it is today, although later witnesses remark that the site was being robbed of its stone for building (cf. Crawford 1925). Furthermore, monuments such as Arthur's Stone, with its folklore and local superstitions, may have suffered destruction in the past, especially during the 16th and 17th centuries[11]. In support of this, it would seem unlikely that Arthur's Stone was the only distinct oval mound within this group (except for the first architectural phase at Ty Isaf, near Talgarth). The other seventeen monuments within the Black Mountains Group appear to use the long (or at least oval) mound as an architectural blueprint, similar in design to other Cotswold-Severn Group monuments. Those adopting a hybrid trapezoidal plan, including Gwernvale, Penywrlod, Pipton and Ty Isaf are probably later monuments which were designed and built as a development of the long/oval mound principle.

---

7 Within the recent past, the remains of the oval mound has been damaged by the erection of fencing around its perimeter by English Heritage. Photographs taken in 1928 and 1935 show the site enclosed by a wrought iron fence (Hemp 1935, 291, Watkins 1928, 149). Hemp refers to 'a cart track [which] has cut away part of the north-eastern side, and the whole of the upper part has been removed' (1935, 288).

8 It was probably the Woolhope Naturalists' Field Club's description, plus the present shape of the mound, that prompted the artist's reconstruction of the site to be used on the then English Heritage information board.

9 As suggested by Ruth Richardson, Hereford Sixth Form College (pers. comm.).

10 See the Endnote, this article, which briefly discusses the evaluation of this area between 2005–6 (Nash 2008).

11 Although there is no documentary account of any destruction of Arthur's Stone during this period, many other more prominent monuments were either partially or completely destroyed (e.g. Skinner 1802).

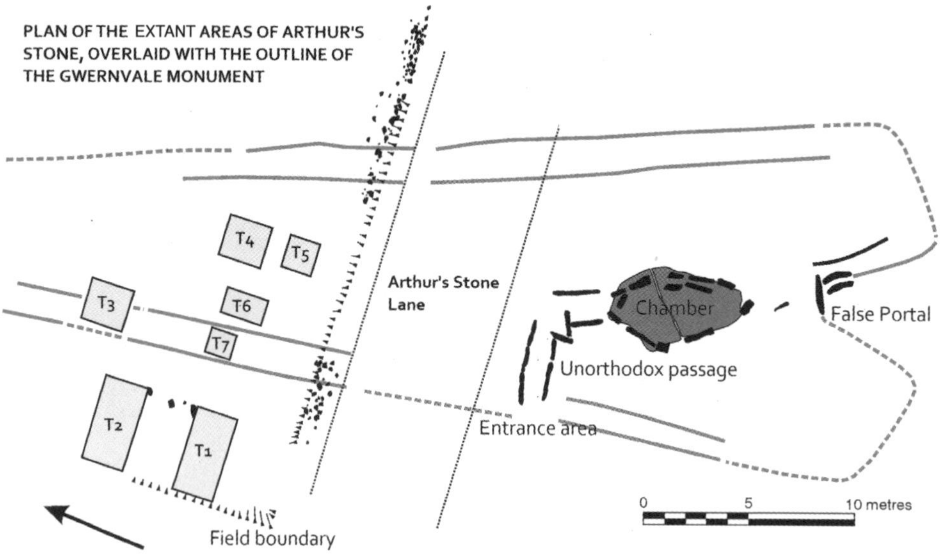

Fig 6: The possible original shape of the Arthur's Stone monument and the location of evaluation trenching, undertaken by a University of Bristol team in 2005–6.

Arthur's Stone in an Architectural-Landscape Context

Arthur's Stone shares a landscape affinity with many other Neolithic monuments, both within the Black Mountains Group and elsewhere. The monument stands on the western ridge of Dorstone Hill and has clear, uninterrupted views across the northern, western and southern extents of the Golden Valley, Cefn Hill and the eastern slopes of the Black Mountains beyond, from Hay-on-Wye to Abergavenny, a distance of c.40 km. To the east of the site, views are restricted to the nearby eastern ridge of Merbach Hill, some 300 m away. No other landscape features are visible beyond this ridge. Interestingly, there is no further Neolithic activity, in the form of lithic scatters and monuments, beyond this point (Children & Nash 1994). This would suggest that all Neolithic (and Early Bronze Age) burial-ritual activity is focussed on the visual draw of the Black Mountains. A similar distribution of lithic scatters and monuments is also present along the lower Usk and Upper Wye valleys, suggesting an affinity between monuments, the hinterlands in which they stand and the mountains.

Fig 7: View of the inner section of the unorthodox passage with its door stone (photograph: G.H. Nash).

The relationship between Arthur's Stone and its immediate landscape, together with the spatial organisation of the tomb, suggest that its builders clearly understood how certain parts of the monument should be constructed and sited, using various aspects of the landscape (Tilley 1994). Standing at around 274 m AOD, views from outside the small façade area into the entrance and outer passage are uninterrupted. However, views into the inner passage and chamber are restricted due to the 90° bend that lies halfway along the passage (Fig 7). Likewise, restricted visuality is in operation when viewing the outer passage and entrance from the chamber. It is as if, by a simple visual device, a conscious attempt is being made to separate human space – the realm of order and control – from the outside world – from nature, what Christopher Tilley (1991, 1994) would term *liminal space*. The transition between the two is achieved precisely at that point, equidistant between chamber and entrance, where the passage abruptly changes direction. It is here that social order merges with nature.

However, this is only part of the potential meaning behind the monument's construction. The redirection of the passage and the orientation of the capstone suggest Arthur's Stone may have played a key role in the socio-symbolic process of territory formation (see Renfrew 1976). The monument was probably constructed so as to visually encompass the entire length of the Black Mountains. In this way, the mountains were incorporated into the social and symbolic identity of Neolithic settlers, helping to create a sense of belonging using monument building in a strategic way. Other tombs in the upper Wye and Usk valleys interact with the landscape in the same way. Similar to many other chambered burial monuments of the Neolithic period, Arthur's Stone is not on the highest point within the immediate landscape, but slightly away from Merbach Hill's summit (Nash 1997, 20). It could be argued that there is a clear attempt to control the surrounding landscape from the monument. However, the monument cannot be seen from any part of the Golden Valley. I would suggest that a form of restricted visual access was in operation, where only certain members of the community could see the monument, and then perhaps only periodically. If this was the case, then Neolithic communities were stratified on at least three levels. Those occupying the first level would have had no visual access to the monument. The second tier may have been allowed visual access, but only to the outside. Finally, the third level was able to access the inside of the monument, to bury the dead and to perform ritual activities, possibly associated with death, fertility and political and social consolidation. This could have been further complicated by the way in which the monument is constructed (i.e., the access into the narrow passage and the right-angled kink around the doorway – see Fig 6).

The arrangement of the monument's passage may also suggest a degree of social complexity. Of the twelve sandstone slabs that form the passage and were recently recorded by the author (and previously by Grimes 1936a), eight construct the walls of the passage (see Fig 5). The doorstone, similar to others found at Parc-le-Breos-Cwm on the Gower Coast (SS 537 898) and Ty Isaf, near Talgarth (SO 182 291) appears to have been deliberately set in order to limit the view from the entrance to the chamber. Likewise, when inside the chamber, the light from the entrance would have forced mourners to use an artificial light source. The upright stones would have supported a series of small capstones, thus enclosing the passage. What has been noticed within this arrangement is that the passage appears to be constructed in order to restrict visual access. Here, the door-stone blocks the visual access from the entrance/facade to the chamber and vice-versa. Further restricted access is also present in the way in which the passage stones are arranged. Between the entrance and the chamber, each of the stones appears to gain height. Between the door-stone and the chamber, an individual can crouch through the upper section of the passage into the chamber; however, initial access into the monument from the entrance, individuals would have to crawl! As well as witnessing a gradual rise within the passage roofing, the uprights appear to widen as one moves through the passage. A similar architectural trait occurs with the passage grave traditions of North Wales, Ireland, central southern Sweden and Denmark (Tilley 1993). It could be the case that the passage acts as a boundary between life (outside the monument) and death (inside the chamber), similar to the spatial divisions inside a Christian church, whereby the congregation and the ritual performances of the priest are strictly divided.

The socio-political division within Neolithic communities would have been stratified, creating a boundary between those who know and those who do not; here ritual and symbolic knowledge is power.

Concluding Remarks

I have suggested in previous research (Nash 1997) that Arthur's Stone, and other monuments within the Black Mountains Group, utilise both organic and inorganic architecture in their construction. Recently, the siting of monuments has been interpreted fundamentally as a form of statementing the landscape: turning a space into a place (e.g., Bradley 1993, 1998; Tilley 1994). Both ritual and socio-political knowledge make *this* place special. However, I would stress that Arthur's Stone, with its covering mound, was hidden away within its immediate landscape. Certainly, Berwick's interpretation of the monument in 1804 would suggest this, albeit by then, a ruinous monument and missing much of its covering mound (see Fig 3).

When one looks at tomb architecture, one is faced with only part of the monument, usually a few uprights and a fragmented capstone: what may be referred to as the frame or skeleton. Thomas and Tilley (1994) use the term rib-cage for the design plan of certain monuments in Brittany when discussing the tomb architecture. Here, chambers, along with passages physically and metaphorically represent the human torso; they are visible within the immediate landscape. Gone, from Arthur's Stone and other monuments within the Black Mountains Group is the drystone walling, cairn decoration, from some sites, the mound, the façade and small internal and external features, such as doorways, thresholds, cairn curbing, roofing slabs etc. The rigidity of the frame (uprights and capstone) becomes structurally and visually opposed to the organic nature of the landscape. Representing an angular and somewhat recognisable structure, it clashes immediately with the irregularity and disorder of the surrounding landscape. However, during the Neolithic, the frame (or skeleton) would have possessed *flesh* (i.e., a covering mound or cairn). Each capstone, each upright, would have been hidden beneath a mound, causing the shape and design to merge into a homogeneous whole, thereby becoming part of the landscape rather than opposing it. Within the tomb, nature is in part rejected. Here, the social and symbolic order dominates. Space becomes legitimised, humanised and clinical. Although the raw materials (i.e. stone and earth) are arguably organic, the way these materials are used in the construction of the monument is not.

This would have created an interesting dichotomy: the monument could be seen by those who built and used it. However, it was also unseen; by those whose visual access to the monument was controlled, including those looking at the monument from high points within the surrounding landscape. This restriction on visual access outside the monument, as well as the concealment of the inner passage and chamber inside its forecourt area, established visual control inside and outside the monument, and is suggestive of the social complexities of the people who created Arthur's Stone. For some members of the community using this monument 5,500 years ago, Arthur's Stone is a symbol of power and prestige, as indicated by the surviving architecture. Not surprisingly, this architecture is repeated in at least 18 locations around the hinterlands of the Black Mountains; here landscape vistas, tomb location and their architecture would have played an essential role in how the elites controlled and manipulated society.

2024 Endnote

Recent newspaper articles and social media accounts have claimed that the current excavation in and around Arthur's Stone is the first to be undertaken. On the contrary, two previous excavations were undertaken in 2005–6 and 2011: each revealing new sections of what is a fragmentary archaeological site belonging to the Cotswold-Severn group of monuments (Crawford 1925; Darvill 1982), and as proved through excavation by Nash (2008).

The 2005–6 archaeological excavation programme was undertaken by students and staff from the Department of Archaeology, University of Bristol. The rationale for this project was to prove through geophysics and targeted excavation that Arthur's Stone possessed similar architectural traits as with other monuments within the Black Mountains Group, in particular, the presence of a [buried] mound that extended into a field north of Arthur's Stone Lane (see Fig 6). The excavation comprised seven test pits of varying size and depth that were targeted over rubble spreads that were interpreted as belonging to the rear northern section of the monument. The initial survey undertaken by the author in 2005 revealed a surface rubble spread, the result of historic ploughing. Of the seven trenches excavated, five yielded substantial cairn rubble spreads, along with a meagre assemblage of later prehistoric worked and diagnostic flint (Nash 2008). Those trenches with rubble present allowed the team to calculate the trajectory of the eastern and west line of the rear section of the monument, thus proving beyond doubt that Arthur's Stone was a Cotswold-Severn monument with an in-use date range of c.3600 to 2800 BCE. Despite the estimated date range, samples taken for radiocarbon dating proved to be either contaminated or, more likely, the result of bioturbation.

By far, the most revealing insight into understanding the architecture of the monument was made in 2011 by a team from Headland Archaeology [report by Boucher & Rouse]. This investigation, commissioned by English Heritage included the excavation of test pits around the circumference of the mound. The test pits were in advance of the construction of a timber fence that would surround the earthwork of the mound. The test pit programme exposed disturbed and undisturbed sections of drystone walling and cairn that formed the north and western sides of the monument. Of particular interest was Post Hole No. 32 which revealed a clear drystone wall section that extended to a depth of 0.50 m below the existing ground level. Prior to excavation, the Headland Archaeology team undertook a detailed earthworks and geophysical survey of the monument area, south of Arthur's Stone Lane.

Excavations undertaken between 2022 and 2024 by the Universities of Cardiff and Manchester and Herefordshire Archaeology were concentrated in the south and west sections of the monument. The interim reports suggest that an avenue was present at the southern end and would have terminated within or around the façade area where the false portal is present. At the time of the publication of this paper, Keith Ray and Julian Thomas had turned their attention to excavating an area around the side entrance area that leads to the chamber, where Boucher and Rouse undertook fruitful excavations in 2011 and, around the rear section of the monument, where I conducted excavations in 2005/6. The full results of this recent work will be probably published in due course.

References

Bradley, R., 1993, *Altering the Earth*, The 1992 Rhind Lectures, *Soc. of Antiquaries of Scotland* Monograph Series No. 8.

Bradley, R., 1998, *The Significance of Monuments: On the shaping of human experience in Neolithic and Bronze Age Europe*. London: Routledge.

Britnell, W. & Savory, H., 1984, *Gwernvale and Penywyrlod: Two Neolithic Long Cairns in the Black Mountains of Breconshire*, Cambrian Archaeological Monographs, 2.

Brown, A.E., 1963, 'Records of surface finds made in Herefordshire', 1951–60, *Transactions of the Woolhope Naturalists' Field Club*, XXXVII, 76–91.

Castleden, R., 1992, *Neolithic Britain: New Stone Age Sites of England, Scotland and Wales.* London: Routledge.

Children, G. & Nash, G.H., 1994, *The Prehistory of Herefordshire.* Hereford: Logaston Press.

Children, G. & Nash, G.H., 1997, *The Neolithic of Cardiganshire, Carmarthenshire and Pembrokeshire.* Hereford: Logaston Press.

Corcoran, J. X.W.P., 1969, 'The Cotswold-Severn Group'. In Powell, T.G.E., Corcoran, J.X.W.P., Lynch, F. and Scott, J.G., *Megalithic Enquiries in the West of Britain.* Liverpool: Liverpool University Press.

Crawford, O.G.S., 1925, *The Long Barrows of the Cotswolds.* Gloucester: John Bellows.

Daniel, G., 1950, *The Prehistoric Chambered Tombs of England and Wales*, Cambridge: Cambridge University Press.

Darvill, T.C., 1982, *The Megalithic Chambered Tombs of the Cotswold-Severn Region.* Varda Research Series No.5.

Fowler, P., 1983, *Prehistoric Farming.* Cambridge: Cambridge University Press.

Gavin Robinson, R.S., 1934, 'Flint workers and flint users of the Golden Valley', *Transactions of the Woolhope Naturalists' Field Club*, XX, 54–63.

Grimes, W.F., 1936a, 'The Megalithic Monuments of Wales', *The Proceedings of the Prehistoric Society* II, 106–39.

Grimes, W.F., 1936b, 'The Long Cairns of Breconshire Black Mountains', *Archaeologia Cambrensis*, 259–82.

Healey, E., & Green, S., 1984, 'The Lithic Industries'. In W. Britnell & H. Savory (eds.) *Gwernvale and Penywyrlod: Two Neolithic Long Cairns in the Black Mountains of Breconshire*, Cambrian Archaeological Monographs No.2.

Hemp, W.J., 1935, 'Arthur's Stone, Dorstone, Herefordshire', *Archaeologia Cambrensis*, XC, 288–92.

Hereford & Worcester County Council 1981, *Countryside Treasures of Herefordshire,* H&WCC Planning Department.

Nash, G.H., 1997, 'Monumentality and the Landscape: The Possible Symbolic and Political Distribution of Long Chambered Tombs around the Black Mountains, Central Wales'. In G.H. Nash (ed.) *Semiotics of Landscape: Archaeology of Mind.* Oxford: BAR International Series 661, 1–30.

Olding, F., 2000, *The Prehistoric Landscape of the Black Mountains*. Oxford: BAR 271.

Pipier, G.H., 1881, 'President's Address', *Transactions of the Woolhope Naturalists' Field Club*, 175–80.

Powell, T.G.E., Corcoran, J.X.W.P., Lynch, F. & Scott, J.G., 1969, *Megalithic Enquiries in the West of Britain*. Liverpool: Liverpool University Press.

RCHAM(W), 1997, *An Inventory of the Ancient Monuments in Breconshire (Brycheiniog): The Prehistoric and Roman Monuments*, (Part II).

Renfrew, C., 1976, 'Megaliths, territories and populations. In S. de Laet (ed.)', *Acculturation and continuity in Atlantic Europe*, Bruges: de Tempel, pp. 98–220.

Salmon, N., 1728–9, *A New Survey of England, wherein the defects of Camden are supplied and the errors of his followers remarked*.

Sant, J., 2000, *Stone Spotting in Herefordshire*. Moondial.

Stanford, S.C., 1990, *The Archaeology of The Welsh Marches*. Hereford: Harper.

Thomas, J.S. & Tilley, C., 1994, 'The axe and the torso, symbolic structures in the Neolithic of Brittany', in C. Tilley (ed.), *Interpretative Archaeology*, London: Routledge, pp. 225–324.

Tilley, C., 1993, 'Art, architecture and the landscape in Neolithic Sweden'. In B. Bender (ed.) *Landscape, Politics and Perspectives*. Oxford: Berg.

Tilley, C., 1994, *A Phenomenology of Landscape: Places, Paths and Monuments*. London: Berg.

Watkins, A., 1928, 'Arthur's Stone', *Transactions of the Woolhope Naturalists' Field Club*, XIV, 149–51.

SOUTHERN EVENING ECHO

Stonehenge, Druids: What of the future?

By AUSTIN UNDERWOOD

THE present-day Druids have always had a special place in the hearts of Wiltshiremen, and whatever might have been their connection with Stonehenge in prehistoric times, they have become indissolubly linked with the monument in the minds of those who live on Salisbury Plain today.

Veteran Druid

EXPLOSIONS AND SMOKE AT STONEHENGE RITES

"Echo" Correspondent
AMESBURY, Thursday.

THUNDER flashes and smoke bombs were thrown at Stonehenge, early this morning, as crowds gathered to watch the Druids' mid-summer solstice ceremony at the ancient monument at dawn.

NO REPORTS OF INJURIES

AT THE MIDNIGHT SERVICE

WARNED ABOUT THE BOYS

LIKE BEACH-HEAD, SAID TEACHER

ARRESTED, AND RELEASED

Fig 1: Southern Evening Echo *press reports from 1962 (top) and 1956 (bottom).*

The World Turned Upside Down: Stonehenge Summer Solstice Before the Hippies

Adam Stout

Notorious as it was, the Stonehenge Free Festival wasn't the first time people had assembled at Stonehenge in modern times. Adam Stout revisits earlier midsummer gatherings at the stones.

> *Military Police were everywhere. Both civilian and military police dog-handlers patrolled the five-foot Dannert wire perimeter... the whole of the monument and its concentration-camp barbed-wire entanglements were floodlit throughout the night*[1].

A flesh-creepingly familiar description, to the many thousands of folk who had the pleasure of trying to visit the Stones at Solstice-time during the reign of Margaret Thatcher, evocatively chronicled by Andy Worthington in *3rd Stone* 43[2].

However, this *Salisbury Journal* account dates from 1966, not 1986. It's a much-forgotten fact, but for most of the Swinging Sixties the mighty edifice was just as firmly out-of-bounds at the Solstice as it was to be in the Awful Eighties.

1 *Salisbury Journal* 23 June 1966.

2 Andy Worthington, 2002, 'A Brief History of the Summer Solstice at Stonehenge', *3rd Stone* 42 (Spring 2002): 41–47.

The reasons Harold Wilson's officials gave in 1966 were much the same as those of Thatcher's in the 1980s. The 'concentration camp atmosphere' was necessary if the crowds – 'organised parties of hooligans' – were to be successfully controlled[3]. Already Stonehenge was a magnet for the counter-culture.

Solar Cyclists

No-one knows just when people began to congregate at Stonehenge at midsummer. It is possible that people have been meeting there continuously ever since the place was built (although, as Kate Prendergast has suggested, it's a more natural midwinter Solstice observatory[4]). In 1680 royal approval was granted for a two-day annual Fair, to be held at Stonehenge in late September. The date was later switched to the Solstice[5], perhaps as a result of Stukeley's well-publicised claims for the midsummer sunrise: if sizeable crowds were gathering at midsummer anyway, what better day to hold a fair?

By the late nineteenth century, the Solstice was attracting visitors in their thousands. 'They journeyed from far and near – some in brakes, waggonettes, and traps, while the majority travelled on bicycles. The roads leading to the place presented a very animated appearance', wrote the *Devizes Gazette* journalist in 1896. 'People... kept coming in hundreds until nearly sunrise. They heralded their approach by bugle and horn blowing and bell ringing. It was estimated that between two and three thousand were present, including nearly a thousand cyclists, and the sight of the innumerable lamps converging upon the stones from different directions was one that impressed the spectators by its novelty and beauty'[6].

Numbers dipped in the early 1900s, largely because the landlord had fenced the Stones off and was now charging admission. They picked up again between the wars, when for the first time a generation of city-dwellers had both leisure and inclination to rediscover the countryside in pursuit of fresh air and exercise, nature and wonderment, and a touch of ancient mystery. Railway companies ran very popular 'mystery trains' that whisked ramblers away to the ancient places;

---

3 Wilts Record Office 2860/21 *Report of meeting to discuss summer solstice arrangements at Stonehenge* 6 January [1966].

4 Kate Prendergast, 'Neolithic Solar Ritual at Stonehenge: Mad Midsummer or Bleak Midwinter?' *3rd Stone* 45 (Winter 2003): 38–43.

5 Christopher Chippindale, 1983, *Stonehenge Complete*, London: Thames & Hudson: 43.

6 *Devizes Gazette* 25 June 1896.

Fig 2: A 1920s postcard of the summer Solstice sunrise at Stonehenge.

in 1932, 1,400 people took advantage of the Southern Railway Moonlight Ramble to see the sunrise at Chanctonbury Ring[7].

But Stonehenge was a fair distance from any railway. In 1931, when as many as 3,000 people turned up to see the 'Glorious Sunrise', there were 300 cars and 200 motorcyclists, but the majority arrived in 'motor coach parties'. 'Some erected portable tents by the roadside. Music was provided by several gramophones at various points outside the enclosure and minstrels enlivened the vigil with mandolin selections'[8].

7 Helen Walker, *1900–1939, The Outdoor Movement in England & Wales*, Sussex Dphil thesis 1987, p.315 and *passim*

8 *Salisbury Journal* 26 June 1931

Fig 3 The early 1960s: 'So long as there were druids about, there would be a substantial body of weirdies making a thundering nuisance of themselves.'

Nothing More than a Popular Festival

Ah yes, the music. There was generally something of a party atmosphere. People got drunk: a phenomenon much abetted by local licensees who took advantage of a loophole in the law that allowed them to sell alcohol to 'bona fide travellers' at any hour of the day or night[9]. The right was abolished in 1921, but people still flocked to the Stones, bringing their own alcohol – and their own entertainment. Jazz – the rebel music of the Twenties – was a regular feature, and the sound system made an early debut at Stonehenge: in 1929, the large crowd 'passed the hours listening to gramophone selections which were "broadcast" from a motor van through an amplifier'[10].

9 *Salisbury Journal* 23 June 1939 cf *Wilts County Mirror* 22 June 1894.

10 *Salisbury Journal* 23 June 1929.

There were critics. 'It was eerie, absolutely still, until the silence was broken by an electric gramophone wailing "The Song of the Nile"', lamented an *Evening Times* reporter the following year. 'An atmosphere reminiscent of Blackpool beach spread over the roadways leading to the ruin. Girls and boys danced by the lights of motor-cars which lined the roads to the music of gramophones and a complete jazz band'[11].

John o'Wiltshire, in the *Wiltshire Times*, dismissed the 1932 throng as 'a twittering multitude', remembering how in his day a handful of people turned up on foot, having 'toiled through the night in ones and twos'. These days, they came in droves. 'They make it a joyous, laughing, almost ribald thing. They spoil it'[12]. The *Salisbury Journal* agreed, sniffily observing that 'Midsummer morning at Stonehenge has become nothing more than a popular festival'[13].

For 'popular' read 'lower class'. There was a smattering of scientists and other cranks amongst the Solstice-goers, and well-heeled tourists from Bristol, Portsmouth or America; but mostly they came from the lower orders. '[P]rincipally from the poorer classes' (1875); 'of a mixed description' (1896). In 1932 the crowd had 'a strong cockney accent'[14].

Fencing out the Hoi Polloi

Big gatherings of oiks have always tended to make the middle classes go all twitchy. Already by 1885 a letter-writer to the *Salisbury Journal* was complaining that: 'For some years past the gathering at the grand ruin has been degenerating and... [t]his year it has reached a pass which calls for interference to preserve the peace, and apparently interference of an energetic character'[15].

At that point, there was little anyone could do to prevent people assembling at the monument, unfenced and isolated, because the landowner, a crusty old baronet called Sir Edmund Antrobus, refused to countenance any form of cooperation with the authorities. Sir Edmund died in 1899, however, and his heir – another Edmund – tried to blackmail the government into buying the Stones for the colossal sum of £125,000[16]. When he failed to get his way, Antrobus put a fence

11 *Evening Times* 21 June 1930.

12 *Wiltshire Times* 25 June 1932.

13 *Salisbury Journal* 24 June 1932.

14 *Notes & Queries* 31 July 1875; *Salisbury Journal* 27 June 1896; *Wiltshire Times* 2 July 1932.

15 *Salisbury Journal* 4 July 1885.

16 Chippindale, *op cit*, p.162.

up and began to charge admission – not a lot, but enough, it was felt, to deter the poorer classes. Charles Hercules Read, Secretary of the Society of Antiquaries, wrote to the *Times* in support of the fence. He invoked the threat posed by various proposed developments in the area, and the large numbers of undesirables that they would attract: 'The establishment of a huge camp in the neighbourhood, with the inevitable band of followers of various kinds, and the importation of gangs of workers for the new railways, increase the possibility of damage to the stones a hundredfold'[17]. There was an outcry from the Conservation movement, who took the landlord to court. The case failed; the judge, according to Lord Eversley of the Commons Preservation Society, being 'evidently under the impression that the vulgar population had, by their destructive propensities, disqualified themselves as visitors to a place of antiquarian interest'[18].

When the Government finally acquired Stonehenge in 1918, they decided to retain the fence, the admission charge – and the right to decide who could or could not enter the circle.

The most effective resistance to enclosure was mounted by the Universal Bond, a body of fractious druids who led many protests over paying admission fees to what they considered to be the peoples' temple. They were led by the redoubtable Dr Macgregor Reid, Chief druid until his death in 1946 (a gentleman blessed with 'a godlike mentality verging upon genius' according to a follower – they were a loyal bunch) and claimed connection with just about every radical in English history.

After the war, the Government imposed restrictions on the druids' rights to hold their ceremonies – 'some limit must be set to this absurd and degrading nonsense'[19] – and a long and acrimonious correspondence ensued. In 1925 they rushed the turnstiles, urging others to follow them ('Come on, People!') and a 'disorderly crowd' of about 1,000 people got in for free[20].

Briefly banned as a result, the druids took to holding their services at the 'Double Circle', a prehistoric earthwork a mile or so's trudge across the Plain from the Stones; here, in 1926, the Chief druid addressed an audience of 600 people and spoke up in favour of the miners, still holding out after the collapse of the General Strike[21].

They were allowed to return to Stonehenge a couple of years later, and continued to stir things up. In 1930, a retired Army major wrote to the authorities to complain

17 *Times*, n.d. [1901?] in WANHS Cuttings Book C/8/5.

18 Quoted in Walker, *op cit*, p.71–3.

19 Public Record Office (PRO), WORK 14/2135, endorsement on letter from Thomas Ireland 27 May 1920.

20 PRO *op cit*, Custodian's Report 21 June 1925.

21 *Salisbury Journal* 2 July 1926.

Fig 4: Early 1960s: the barriers go up...

that the Chief druid had been inciting visitors to pull down the fence and that he 'spoke against the Church and religion and upheld the Soviet Government... His general speaking was Communistic and anti-Government'[22].

The druids retired from the fray after 1932, largely because Reid was by now well over 80. Numbers celebrating the Solstice dropped steadily as the 1930s wore on, perhaps, as the *Salisbury Journal* suggested in 1939, because the druids no longer came: in that year, only 400 people made the Solstice, where they encountered the Wiltshire Folk Dancers, 'who performed traditional dances to the music of an accordion'[23].

22 PRO *op cit*, letter from Major Wheatley 23 June 1930.

23 *Salisbury Journal* 23 June 1939.

Skiffle and Weirdies

The druids returned after the war, now led by Reid's son Robert, and numbers attending rose steadily during the 1950s, rising to almost 3,000 in 1960[24]. Visitors came from all over the world, but there were large numbers of people in uniform from the many military bases on Salisbury Plain, who were often very lairy. 1952's Morris dancers were 'frustrated by the disgusting carryings-on of some 20 Air Force officers who were completely drunk and a disgrace to all around them', wrote an indignant Salisbury resident to the *Journal*[25].

The druids, by now an accepted part of the Stonehenge Solstice ritual, now found themselves the butt of anti-establishment feeling. Things really kicked off at the 1956 Solstice (a symbolic year indeed since that was the year in which rock and roll first hit Britain). People in the 2,000-strong crowd started lobbing thunderflashes at the druids, as they marched to the Stones. 'The crowd became a rabble', claimed the *Salisbury Journal*. 'They closed in on the procession, and there were scornful remarks and cries'. 'It looked like the Battle of Alamein', declared a military policeman as he sent for reinforcements.

Press post-mortems pinned the blame variously on a group of Young Conservatives, a suspected undergraduate in a duffle coat (duffle coats were *de rigeur* for students in the 1950s, or at least that's what the papers thought), but mostly on a group of young soldiers from one of the camps on the Plain, much the worse for wear[26]. These three very different categories of people had one thing clearly in common: their youth, and a sense of being in a very different world to their parents.

Next year saw less trouble but more people, more druid-cheeking – and the arrival of skiffle, with 'two rival skiffle groups, each with its own band of supporters, trying to drown each others' efforts from opposite sides of the circle'[27]. Skiffle drove a despairing Mrs Prideaux-Brune of Gosport to write to the *Telegraph* about her experience at the '59 Solstice: 'we suffered from "skiffle groups" yelling vulgar songs with vulgar voices (about four songs which they repeated over and over again with ghastly monotony)'[28].

24 *Salisbury Journal* 24 June 1960.

25 *Salisbury Journal* 27 June 1952.

26 *Salisbury Journal* 22 June 1956; *Daily Telegraph* 22 June 1956.

27 *Salisbury Journal* 28 June 1957.

28 *Daily Telegraph* 14 July 1959.

1961 saw the first intimations of hippy chic. The 'trouble-hunting teddy-boys and their girlfriends in bizarre dress' mostly left early, according to the *Salisbury Journal*, but many of the rest were 'weirdly garbed... slightly embarrassed spectators eyed each others' clothes – many of which bore silent tribute to their wearers' imagination. One youthful Beau Brummel wore a long, bright blue blanket over his head, decorated with a pheasant tail-feather. The rest of his outfit consisted of dark corduroy trousers, no socks, 'peep-toe' sandals, and sunglasses'[29].

Was such sartorial deviance the last straw? Analysing the '61 Solstice, the civil servants involved claimed that the Chief Constable of Wiltshire was convinced that: 'so long as there were druids about, there would be a substantial body of weirdies making a thundering nuisance of themselves. It was clear that he did not hold the druids responsible... but he was quite sure that the mere presence of druids would attract undesirables to the neighbourhood and that the latter would then proceed to make the night hideous'[30].

Prominent archaeologists such as Glyn Daniel sought to get 'those horrid, bogus druids' removed altogether[31]. They didn't succeed, but they did convince the Government to close the monument to everyone else. From 1964, only a handful of locals and press photographers were allowed to join the druids inside the circle, although hundreds watched from beyond the barbed wire. The numbers crept up again until in 1969 an unexpected 2,000 people turned up for the Solstice. The crowd-control barriers broke down, and the Government resolved on 'reinforcing the defences' the next year. The suggestion that the crowd might respond to loud-speaker remonstrations was pooh-poohed by officials: 'It is our view that appeal to a crowd consisting largely of drunks and hippies (as was the case this year) are likely to be entirely wasted, and would not justify the expense of a PA system. The small minority of normal individuals are not in need about [sic] exhortations about their behaviour'[32].

Numbers increased steadily during the early Seventies; and in 1974 some of them decided not to rush back home again once the sun had come up. This was the nucleus of the Stonehenge Free Festival, ably chronicled in these pages by Andy Worthington. It became the hub of a counter-culture that grew so audacious and successful that by the 1980s it had come to rank alongside the miners and the GLC on Mrs Thatcher's hit-list of internal dissident movements. The Festival was duly crushed, violently and shamefully, and the counter-culture was dispersed.

---

29 *Salisbury Journal* 23 June 1961.

30 PRO WORK/14/2789, letter from Gilpin to Cunliffe dated 2 February 1962.

31 See my 'Making the Past: The Politics of Prehistory' in *3rd Stone* 40 (Summer/ Autumn 2001): 34–42.

32 Wilts Record Office 2860/20, copy of letter from J M Melhuish to J B Score.

They couldn't keep the Solstice-goers out for ever, however; and in 2000 English Heritage let the people back to Stonehenge for the first time in 15 years, to cavort beneath the arc lights (and then to be moved swiftly out of the way so that they can open up for the tourist trade at 0900. Every generation gets the Stonehenge it deserves, observed Jacquetta Hawkes; our Stonehenge, our Number One tourist attraction, is a nice little earner...). 14,000 turned up in 2001; 21,000 last year: how many this year?

The Subversive Solstice

Why Stonehenge? What is it that's so appealing about this pile of stones far out on a windswept plain? Before the 1960s, celebrating the Solstice at Stonehenge meant a naughty night out. It was a once-a-year subversion of norms, the World Turned Upside Down, an element of licensed carnival in a society that found it difficult to let its hair down. 'There is no doubt we permit behaviour at Stonehenge on these occasions which we would not tolerate even on a much smaller scale at other monuments in our care', wrote one civil servant to another in 1957[33].

From jazzed-up twenties revellers to 50s skifflers, the Solstice challenged social uptightness; and then, with the expression of more far-reaching opposition to Western values in the 1960s and 1970s, it became the icon of 'another way to be'.

There is something so provocative about Stonehenge. It is forever beyond absolute explanation, yet it is clearly functional and very well-made: it is proof of prehistoric sophistication. It's a monumental mockery of modern pretension, and all those comforting notions of 'progress' that support the status quo. Stonehenge is a good place for rebels.

The photographs and press cuttings in this article form a small part of the Austin Underwood Collection held at the Wiltshire Record Office, Trowbridge. Permission to reprint these materials was granted by Ms Ruth Underwood and Steve Hobbs (of the WRO), both of whom 3rd Stone *would like to thank.*

33 PRO WORK 14/2136, memo dated 25 July 1957.

Forever Changing Avebury

Brian Edwards

Brian Edwards' 'Changing Avebury' (*3rd Stone* 47, 2003) looked at what change had brought to Avebury in the past. Expanding on the material from that article, 'Forever Changing Avebury' brings the rich threads of the story up to date. All images are courtesy of Wiltshire Museum.

Introduction – Avebury in 2003

Change to facilitate tourism was increasingly in evidence in 2003. On being converted into the Tourist Information office, Avebury's Five Mile chapel had recently undergone major building work, and with modern facilities being installed, roads and paths were dug up to lay pipes and cables. Around the same time double yellow lines were painted along the West Kennet Avenue and other roadside borders, newly installed wooden posts lined the northern approach, parking was restricted and increased charges introduced. Furthermore, the intense activity of the police and landowners in advance of the annual surge of visitors for summer solstices posed stark reminders to Avebury villagers, that no such tradition had existed in Avebury before the decision to withdraw access to Stonehenge during the late 1980s summer solstices.

These activities were also a reminder that even a small percentage increase in visitor numbers could alter the character of Avebury considerably, and not a little reminiscent of when state-enforced change induced an influx of 'Five Milers' that had built Avebury's sarsen built chapel.

Fig 1: Signs erected recently around Avebury greet visitors to the World Heritage Site, 2003. But will plans for Stonehenge lead to many more visitors?

Changing Avebury

After John Aubrey introduced Charles II to Avebury in 1663, the monarch was keen that the site was recorded and protected. Which is rather ironic as only two years later Charles II gave assent to the Five Mile Act (1665) that instigated a five-mile exclusion zone around towns precluding those non-conformists dispossessed by the Act of Uniformity (1662), and Avebury just happened to be a little over five miles from Marlborough, Pewsey, Devizes, Calne, Wootton Bassett, Wroughton, Chiseldon and the Ogbournes.

Highlighted as an official haven for 'Five Mile' refugees, Avebury presented such an oasis that Noah Webb travelled each week from Hampshire to preach and, having been dispossessed of Barford St Martin, Thomas Rashley relocated. Dispossessed of Chiseldon in 1662, John Baker started a chapel at Avebury with Thomas Mills of Calne in 1670, and other dissenters followed. In 1670 there were 25 non-conformists and 181 Anglicans in Avebury, but by 1715 the non-conformist congregation had swelled to 130. As the Act of Indulgence was introduced in 1672, the increase was perhaps not all due to incomers, but if it was not an influx of Puritanism that sought to destroy the Avebury stones, then the expansion in population and focus saw sarsens removed to create plots and pasture with the stones broken up for building material. Based around the chapel built in Samuel Morris's centre circle garden, a geographical community grew in focus to form a chapel enclave. Housing a quite separate and distinct satellite community,

Figs 2 and 3: Avebury Five Mile Chapel, and scorch marks on the chapel sarsens.

nucleated throughout a centre circle farm, walls, paths, and buildings were constructed of sarsen, as was the 'Five Mile' chapel. The Five Mile Act saw the internal boundaries of Avebury redrawn a century prior to being redrawn again under the enclosure movement. Stones that remained part of boundaries tended to survive unless they fell, in which case they were broken up and removed (see

Figs 4 and 5). A pocket of stones survived on ground petrified between the chapel's west boundary and the pre-existing common pound that bordered the road from the south (see Figs 6 and 7). In contrast, those stones that remained on the corner

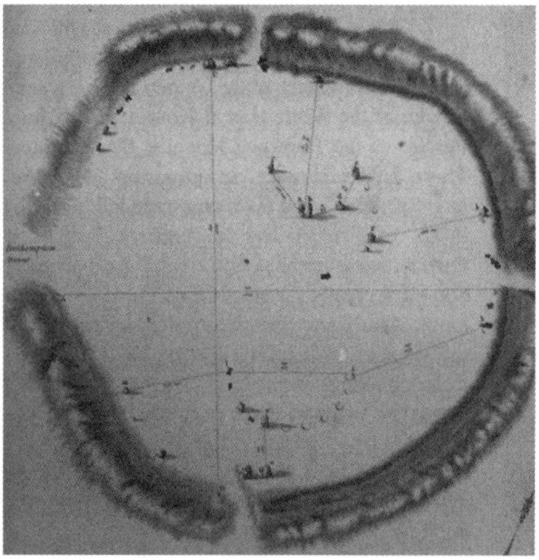

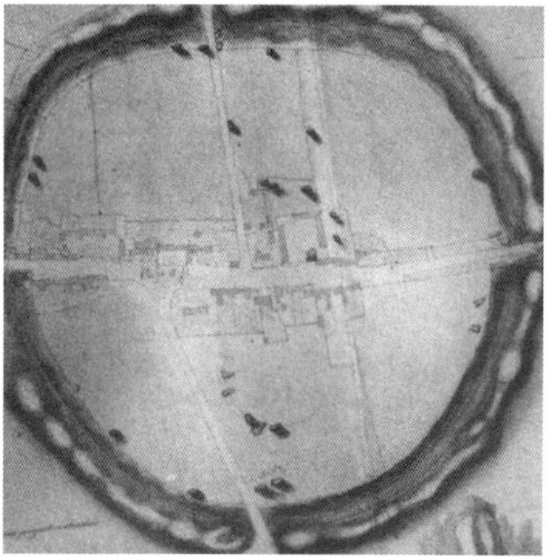

Figs 4 and 5: Avebury: the inclusion of boundary lines explains sarsen survivals.

of the Kennett Road and Green Street fell prey to the convenience and increased speed of wheeled transport entering and leaving the Five Mile village. Change begets change, and in 1694 Avebury's Great Bank was to accommodate a large threshing barn titled the 'Parsonage Barn', with a base made of broken sarsen

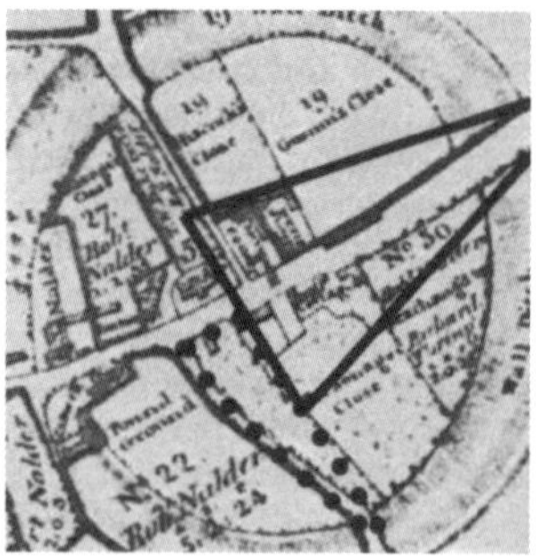

Figs 6 and 7: map detail: Large sarsen survivors, notably all to the west of the chapel boundary on a strip of land within dotted line (see above right detail from the Enclosure Map of 1794) between the common pound and the chapel take-over of the eastern sector of the circle (inside solid line).

stones. In 1697 Joseph Howard of Beckhampton cleared some fields of stones and opened a local shop, and in 1706 Avebury had a market. Many of the buildings the 18th century antiquary William Stukeley was to draw were new or newly extended, and albeit hardly noticed, the Revd. James Mayo gave the vicarage and its garden a make-over when he took over from John White (d.1712).

The traditional impression of Avebury's non-conformist community at the turn of the century, has been shaped by the antiquary William Stukeley, who paid repeat visits between 1719 and 1724. Stukeley punctuated his account of contemporary Avebury with characters such as 'stone-breaker' Thomas Griffin, whose father was a founder member of the chapel, and Stukeley's arch-villain Thomas Robinson (through stone clearances of individual pasture plots and sarsen-breaking for infill housing, Robinson was accommodating and speculatively encouraging colonisation of the Avebury circle by immigrant dissenters). Their characterisations reflect the hostile attitudes demonstrated towards non-conformist settlers by the Anglican local establishment of squire, vicar and parish clerk: a denominational bias that the soon to be ordained Stukeley wilfully interpreted as their individual fondness for sarsens.

Changing Ways

Passing through Avebury in a coach in June 1668, when travelling between Bath and Marlborough, Samuel Pepys mentions some 'menders of the highway' when crossing the Marlborough Downs. The geographical misfortunes of the Five Mile Act were compounded by Avebury's position on an adopted route betwixt London and the port at Bristol, and the draw created by dissenters regularly travelling to Avebury was an incitement to those piloting haulage and coaching routes on what frequently were no more than droves. Littered as the Downs are with sarsens, the stones were destined to feed the at first sporadic and local, then later systematic and national road repairs.

With the carriage of goods to and from the port at Bristol compounded by Bath's popularity attracting increasing numbers from London, William Stukeley's sketch of the remains of the Beckhampton Avenue shows the state of the river crossing (see Fig 8), which is surely why Avebury's 'New Bridge' was built south of this crossing in 1701. The old western approach, while still in use, was becoming increasingly impassable to developing travel, and a by-pass would have avoided both the hazardous river crossing and corners difficult for horse teams, noted by James Waylen as increasingly great in length and number. In 1724 Avebury's south

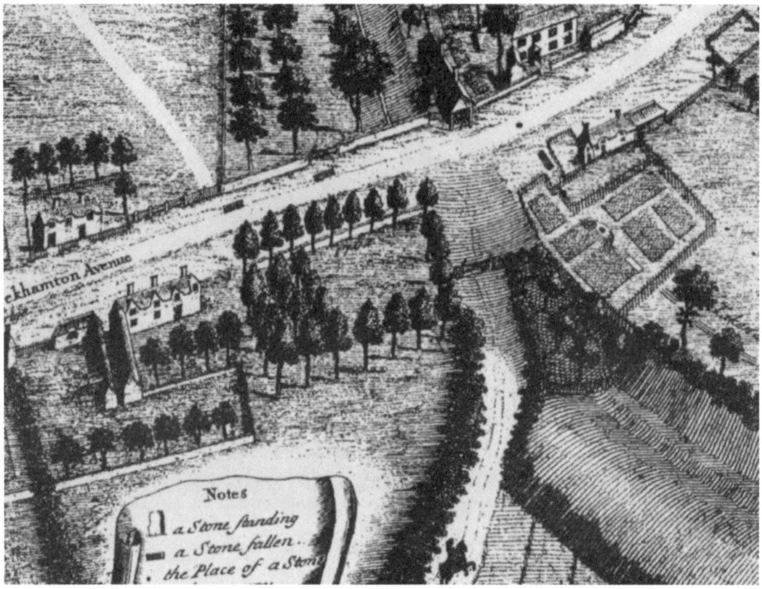

Fig 8: Stukeley's Engraving of 1724 showing an equestrian using the west ditch entrance.

bank was cut back to facilitate the faster passage of coaches, and the danger posed by further main road improvements was to linger for some time. Such was the enforced change that the old boundaries, routes and paths, were superseded through wheeled transport demanding easy convenient speedier access, and by 1794 the Avebury witnessed by Aubrey a century before was unrecognisable (see Fig 9). The Waggon and Horses opened near Beckhampton Crossroads in 1669 as the Bear, and was also known in this period as the Folly, and the Hare and Hounds. Existing premises also attempted to appeal to a wider range of passing trade: the

Fig 9: Stukeley's sketch of the remains of the Beckhampton Avenue in 1724 (redrawn from the original).

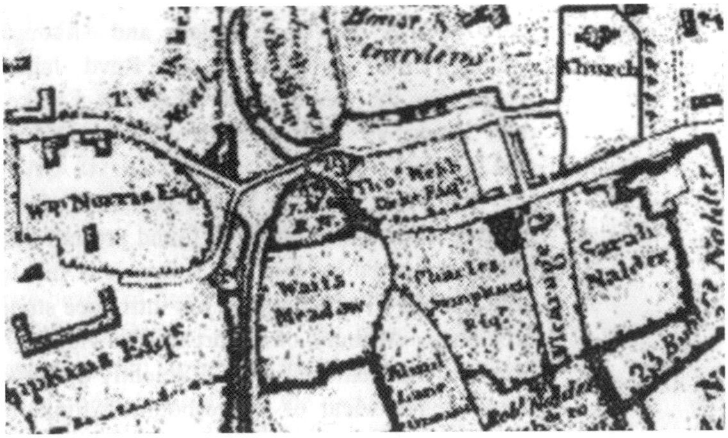

Fig 10: Detail from the 1794 Enclosure Map, by which time the old boundaries, routes and paths to west Avebury were almost unrecognisable.

extension and refurbishment of wayside taverns and inns was both a reaction to increased custom arising from travel, and proactive in attracting travellers. The enlargement and improvement of facilities could encourage carriers and coaches to patronise routes served by refurbished inns over routes that could prove more direct for freight and passengers. Entrepreneurial landlords thus helped shape England's road tapestry and aesthetics, for after churches, monasteries and manor houses, the buildings most notably utilising stone were inns.

It is then instructive that those most criticised by William Stukeley, if not separatists, were entrepreneurial landlords, such as John Fowler of the White Hart at Kennet and Richard Fowler of the Hare and Hounds at Beckhampton. Of Walter Stretch, the landlord of the Catherine Wheel in Avebury, Stukeley reported that 'around 1694' Stretch initiated the destruction of Avebury by discovering 'the way of demolishing these stones by fire':

> *He [Stretch] exercis'd this at first on one of the stones standing in the street before the inn, belonging to the outer circle of the southern temple. That one stone, containing 20 loads, built the dining-room end of the inn.*

Walter Stretch had not of course introduced stone breaking by burning to Avebury. The vicar of Winterbourne Monkton, Parson Brinsden, informed the antiquary John Aubrey how the stones were being heated up to be broken more than thirty years before Stretch added his sarsen built extension to the Catherine Wheel Inn.

Figs 11 and 12: The northern (top) and southern (bottom) approaches to Avebury during recent roadworks, 2003.

Until the seventeenth century there were few stone buildings in the vicinity, restricted perhaps to church, manor, and priory. The process of using natural landscape materials to construct simple vernacular buildings was mostly restricted to timber, chalk, wattle and daub. Simple structures had no foundations, and prior to the discovery of the fire and water method for breaking megaliths, whole sarsens of a manageable size were introduced at the base of vernacular structures. Surviving buildings that deploy sarsens in this fashion remain evidence of both the simple early uses of sarsen, and an indication of the period when they were first used.

The Forge demolished at West Overton in 1986 had whole uncut sarsens in its make-up, and dated from a coin in the base of the structure, was of early 17th century origin. Slightly later buildings featuring cut sarsens conveniently support the supposition that while Aubrey started recording Avebury after stone breaking had begun, it was perhaps not very long after cut sarsens began to be put to wider use. Indeed, it was in 1644, more than twenty years before the Five Mile Act, that Richard Symonds noted stones being broken on Fyfield Down. The period between the outbreak of the Civil War and the Restoration seems an ironic starting point for the wholesale destruction of sarsens, albeit primarily for roads, but had it started very much earlier it seems likely that John Aubrey would not have found so many stones remaining *in situ* when first encountering Avebury in 1648.

Taking Tea with Thomas Free

Travelling from near and far to take tea at a special service of welcome for their new minister on Wednesday 15 October 1902, the stormy weather failed to daunt the gathering at Avebury Chapel, which was surprisingly reported as 80 in number. Presiding over this welcome for the fifty year old Revd. Charles Edward Elford, on his transferring to Avebury from Bulford, near Stonehenge, Thomas Free, mayor of Marlborough, was well known to many of those present. It was customary during these special services, which marked the appointment of a new minister, or when the chapel reopened following building work much as it had ten years earlier, that those presiding would offer something of their background in addition to an account of the history of the building.

Having risen to his feet in the sarsen built Avebury Chapel to remind those present of the 'circumstances that led to the building of that place of worship in 1670,' we are left to wonder what Thomas Free might have to say.

Having settled at nearby Fyfield within living memory, the Free family had introduced up-to-date sarsen splitting technology in the middle of the previous century. Between 1847 and 1939 the new technique was used to turn locally sourced sarsens into road scalpings and kerbstones, cobbles and walls for buildings and courtyards, and cartloads were also famously dispatched to repair Windsor Castle. The surface spread of sarsens, once in evidence from Fyfield Down through Piggledene to Lockeridge Dene, was harvested until a fundraising appeal was launched in 1907 to acquire much of this land for the National Trust. The charity took possession of 22 acres in total in December 1908, and it is perhaps sobering to consider that the Frees arrived 150 years before the additional strip on the north side of Lockeridge was purchased on 27 March 1997.

Whilst many sarsens were disappearing from Wiltshire, a select few were singled out for concreting by archaeologist Maud Cunnington backed by the Wiltshire

Figs 13 and 14: Having fallen, Adam Longstone was 'restored' in concrete in August 1912: the before and after images reveal the result.

Fig 15: The second failed attempt to raise Adam, 1912.

Fig 16: Devil's Den being concreted by A.D. Passmore in 1921. The work cost £56.00, which WANHS launched an appeal to cover.

Archaeological and Natural History Society (WANHS). Despite the landowner having agreed not to cultivate the ground immediately around it in future, an attempt to raise one of the Avebury Longstones that had fallen in December 1911, was undertaken the following year on the grounds 'that a standing stone is more likely to be respected and safeguarded than one fallen.' The first attempt to lift this stone known as Adam, involved both mechanical jacks and traction engines, but merely resulted in each of the latter being dragged backwards towards the stone. The second attempt saw a hawser break. When finally raised, Adam was left slumped in a position this stone had never been in history.

The lifting equipment being at hand, Maud Cunnington transferred her attention from raising Adam to the restoration of a stone (33a) in the West Kennet Avenue. It was said this stone had fallen in February 1889, although the date remained uncertain and the exercise lacked forethought, discussion and research. Mrs Cunnington's re-erection of this stone was later controverted in the 1930s, taken down and re-erected by Alexander Keiller, six foot away and the opposite way up. This sarsen became known as the 'Upside Down Stone' but a tide mark at the upper tip, first noticed by photographer Pete Glastonbury in the 1990s, suggested the previous restoration may have positioned this stone as it had been originally.

Fig 17: Alderman J. Beard and H.J. Vaisey pictured on 30 July 1921.
'Mr. Beard, after referring to the pleasure of attending a fete amid druidical stones, said he wished to draw their attention to the serious things in life.'

Entertaining Avebury

Whilst drinking tea in the Inn in 1925, the writer and society hostess Edith Olivier recalled a dream-like sequence of events in October 1916. Having apparently travelled by car along the Beckhampton Avenue (the course of which lay unidentified until 1999), Edith had witnessed a village fair taking place at Avebury within the stone circle, complete with swing-boats and visitors milling around booths and stalls. Edith then gleaned from an unnamed guidebook, that Avebury's village fair had been abolished in 1850. That was not the case, and it has hitherto remained unmentioned that a fair fitting that description had been held relatively recently. Featuring swing-boats and booths within the henge, the Workers' Union demonstration and fete held opposite the Red Lion on Saturday 30 July 1921, included all manner of athletic events and tug of war in revisiting an influentially popular tradition.

Avebury witnessed a particularly important Victorian rural village festival in 1876, after the newly formed National Farm Labourers' Union Co-operative Land Company had purchased several acres of farmland. This small estate purchased at Avebury, was the first acquired anywhere in the world by a trade union. Forty more acres were added on a lease, and the whole area was divided into allotments which were let to local union members at a time when unions were not permitted to hold land. In celebration, a tea meeting and demonstration was held on Monday 6 March 1876, which was launched by a procession through Avebury accompanied by a brass band. With a remarkable 21 baptisms the following year and only seven funerals in the same period, it is not perhaps unreasonable to link the expanding population with the food security of homegrown produce and the family sustainability represented by Avebury's trade union allotment produce.

In 1892 the Avebury Friendly Society (AFS) announced a celebratory 75th annual festival on Whit Monday, at which the Swindon Gorse Hill Band would play. If correct, the organisation of rural village celebrations may have been an initiative of the Kemm family, that arrived at Avebury Manor in 1816. The format during the 1860s surrounded a brass band leading an AFS banner procession from the Red Lion to the parish church for a service, then returning to the Red Lion for dinner. Later the church bells would peal (one of the Kemms was a churchwarden), to signal an evening of rustic sports and dancing. Something not that dissimilar would coincide with Avebury's annual flower and produce show, organised and hosted by the Kemms under various names, but without the involvement of the Red Lion or any procession taking place. The AFS's loyal banner would decorate the outside of the judging tent, and a blessing by the vicar could be expected to launch the show. The judging would be executed whilst those present watched some cricket, on at least one occasion ginger beer was mentioned, and what followed was usually games (and/or football) and dancing.

The pageantry continued with the founding of an Avebury branch of the Ancient Order of Foresters, established in 1878 and named the 'Court of the Druid's Rest.' This Court's meeting place was the Red Lion, the overall membership climbed to 300 with a youth section of 130, and the Grand Fete and Gala in 1880 attracted 1,000 visitors to 'Rural Sports and Old English Pastimes' set up within the stone circle. Four mounted outriders in Lincoln green flanked the band and members marching with banners aloft, as the procession wound its way to the parish church where at an especially arranged service the sermon was based on St John 15:13 – 'Greater love hath no man than this, that a man lay down his life for his friends.' After leaving St James's, the parade paid visits to the landowners of several farms then finally arrived at the front door of farmer George Brown. Bearing a gift of a volume about forestry delivered with an address by the District Chief Ranger, the Foresters wished Brown a happy 86th birthday. Brown had signalled the end of an era the previous year, in resigning from the position of churchwarden that he had held for 49 years. An address remarked on Brown's 'conscientious manner' and the 'great influence which he has ever exerted in the promotion of the best and highest interests of the parishioners.' He died shortly after his 87th birthday, but his legacy was Avebury's broad church.

Fig 18: Ancient Order of Foresters Court of the Druid's Rest in 1911.

George Brown had proved a tremendously calming presence when Avebury's wider reputation and identity had been notoriously overwritten by the controlling behaviour of two disruptive vicars during the 1850s and 1860s: John Lockhart Ross and Bryan King. Since the 1850s Ross was renowned for his campaign against dissent. In 1863 he swapped parishes with King, who was famous for the extraordinary riots that disrupted his services and followed him around the streets of St George's in London. In 1867, King faced unsettling shouts as he walked about Avebury too, after he stopped Avebury's bellringers celebrating a wedding in the Free Church. King had faced far greater intimidation than hearing calls of 'Three cheers for the Pope!' and 'Go back to St George's!' in Avebury; but this harassment would hardly encourage visitors. King eventually surrendered the belfry key to one of the churchwardens, George Brown, whose influence facilitated further positive change during the 1870s.

On 21 August 1877 Sir John Lubbock MP (the future Lord Avebury and a future patron of the Court of the Druid's Rest), visited Avebury with his wife Ellen and his 17 year old daughter Conny. To protect what areas of this ancient landscape he could, Sir John had recently purchased Silbury Hill along with parcels of land within the henge. Sir John would also introduce the Ancient Monuments Protection Act in 1882, and would place monuments he had purchased in Guardianship. It was the vicar of Avebury, the Revd. Bryan King, that had contacted Lubbock when part of the henge came up for sale at the beginning of the decade, and the churchwardens had intervened by approaching tenants and other local people to smooth the course of the transaction. One of those churchwardens was the farmer George Brown, who owned the local cricket ground, and in 1874 the Avebury Cricket Club adopted the name the Avebury Druid's Cricket Club.

In addition to the Avebury Druid's Cricket Club, this was also the decade in which Avebury raised a football side and a rugby team. In March 1878 the latter beat Winterbourne Bassett in Avebury's Vicarage Meadow by four goals and six tries to one (today that would be 58 points to just 5), and 'The day being lovely a great number of visitors witnessed the game.' Of those players that represented Avebury in all three sports, two were named Kemm. Alongside the vicar's son Gilbert King, the Kemm family of Avebury Manor were also the driving force behind an annual triune entertainment of a concert, a sketch and a farce, that proved so popular it was usually repeated a few weeks later. Typically, in January 1878, Gilbert King played Mrs Browne in the John Templeton Lucas farce 'Browne the Martyr,' then dispensed Mrs Winslow's Soothing Syrup to historical figures when playing the lead in 'Mrs Jarley's Waxworks,' to leave the audience in 'roars of laughter.'

In addition to the village cricket club and a branch of the Foresters cheerfully identifying with Avebury's Druidical remains, late Victorian postcards and souvenirs further advanced the enthusiasm. Parties travelling from much busier places were by now increasingly arriving by bicycle, and with visiting groups arranging for an area within the henge to be at their exclusive disposal through booking an afternoon tea at the Red Lion, Sunday Schools and other groups made such bookings as a treat. Guides were always on hand, as was Lewin Henry Chivers, who ran his photography business from his cottage on the Monkton Road. In 1899 photographs were taken of the Cyclists' Touring Club after visiting the henge and 'the old barn,' and they were given an open air talk on the summit of Silbury Hill.

By the time Edith Olivier drank tea in the Red Lion in 1925, visitors were travelling to Avebury to attend Remembrance Day church parades and British Legion fetes, Workers' Educational Association outings and village charabanc trips, and dances and pantomimes. To hear an open air lecture at Avebury on Sunday 12 June 1927, cyclists from Bath, Bristol, Cheltenham, Swindon, and Frome joined cyclists from Trowbridge and Melksham and places nearer to hand. The lecturer on this occasion was George Basil Bareham and the arrangements for the event centred on a GWR rendezvous by train at Devizes. As strange as it may seem, given the distance from train stations, Avebury featured in a GWR poster series and another much later by British Railways.

Fig 19: Avebury's Red Lion as the Stag and Hunt Inn in A Cuckoo in the Nest*, 1933.*

A Cuckoo in the Nest

When *A Cuckoo in the Nest* went on general release in 1933, unsuspecting cinema audiences were confronted with a stage set that was familiar to Avebury residents: this first ever silver screen version of the popular Aldwych farce deployed a very convincing mock-up of Avebury's Red Lion Inn as the main stage. Having previously enjoyed regular exposure in photoshoots, as the base for the British Falconry Club in the 1930s media; Avebury's Red Lion was perhaps then at the height of pre-BBC television fame. And yet within three years, the Red Lion was included on an Avebury wish list of buildings for demolition. With Avebury undergoing its biggest transformation in centuries, two 1930s Avebury residents captured film footage whilst dramatic change was taking place. One of these film enthusiasts was 34 year old Percy Lawes, a pianoforte tuner and lifelong Avebury resident. In 1936, Lawes launched Saturday morning film shows in the Red Lion that were a firm favourite with children and adults alike. The other local camera enthusiast was Alexander Keiller, the millionaire marmalade heir and archaeologist, born in Dundee in 1889. Renting then purchasing Avebury Manor, Keiller bought up as much of Avebury as he could, then excavated and raised so many of Avebury's ancient stones upright in concrete that his attempt at restoration was dubbed 'megalithic landscape gardening.' In addition to featuring Keiller and his labourers executing this work, Lawes' film clips were strung together to make 'Avebury Bits and Pieces,' a compilation which also captured the comings and goings of Avebury's residents against a background of the then familiar homely cottages and other buildings within the henge. It was an Avebury that made way for visitors, as Keiller started demolishing houses and other buildings with the aim of removing all traces of the village from the vicinity of the henge.

To house those villagers displaced by Keiller's reconstruction of prehistoric Avebury, a new municipal housing development was to be built at Little Avebury (Avebury Trusloe). The completion of this housing scheme was delayed until the end Second World War, but meanwhile a truly remarkable new building was added on the other side of Avebury for John Rawlins. Built in 1937 at the northern entrance of the henge, the art deco 'New Garage' replaced 'The Garage' repair workshops and filling station which had for a decade been dispensing petrol from cans and pumps close to the Cove. Erected on land given by Keiller, around the time the marmalade millionaire donated land for a cricket pitch at the opposite end of the henge, this unique building was later renamed the 'Rawlins Roadhouse.' With alterations, the building continued to operate as a vehicle workshop and filling station after John Rawlings died in 1979. Renamed Bond's Garage, it was demolished when planning permission was granted for new housing in 2008.

Identified in the middle of the 1920s, as being home to the largest tin bathtub ever seen, the Red Lion was also to be the scene of change. Picture postcards reveal the Victorian 'Club House' sometimes called the Assembly Rooms, the interwar Pratt's petrol pump on the forecourt which changed to Esso in 1934, and the repair workshop known as the 'Red Lion Hotel Garage' which was demolished in 1956. The most imperceptible change was perhaps the splendid redesign of the Red Lion's porch. This saw the disappearance of the convenient nook that had once accommodated the rolled up banners for village parades, and now it appears as if the entrance was always thatched.

Fig 20: Demolition of Fowler's Cottage and Forge, south west quadrant.

In the new century the 'Avebury Bits and Pieces' film compilation, that Percy Lawes primarily filmed between 1937 and 1939 but including clips of wartime refugees at play, was discovered in a biscuit tin in the bottom of a wardrobe. Safely transferred to video, some of the adults that were children that appeared in the original film, were invited to watch it once again in the Red Lion where they last saw it in wartime. The resulting interviews and some of the original and other footage were broadcast at 7.30pm on BBC2 on 6 December 2001, in Available Light's *Homeground*: 'The Village in the Stones' (it can be found online).

Silbury Hill and the BBC

Spectacular aerial footage of Avebury was screened in July 1966 in the first of Anglia Television's regionally broadcast series *Who were the British?* It was remarked that it may have been more widely viewed, had it not been screened at 22.40 on a Monday during the school term. It was also broadcast during the football World Cup tournament, held in England and won by the host nation. The following December the series was repeated on Sunday afternoons, but as a repeat the weekly broadcasts remained unpromoted in the press. In contrast, the showmanship of a televised press conference at Silbury Hill on Wednesday

13 September 1967, was at that time unsurpassed in attracting the public's attention and echoed something of the outside broadcasts from the previous year's World Cup.

From Silbury Hill the BBC announced sponsorship of a two-year archaeological excavation into the enormous mound, at considerable but undeclared financial cost to license fee payers. Fieldwork was to begin the following Easter, and was to be covered both live and in recorded episodes by outside broadcast units, which were more familiar to the public through sporting competitions of national interest. Amid discussions of a life-size equestrian statue made of gold at the heart of Silbury Hill, the public were informed the project 'is not a treasure hunt,' and yet, were Silbury Hill found to be a Bronze Age burial mound, 'it should contain a burial of quite exceptional interest – a Royal tomb.'

In addition to a memorable replica model of Silbury Hill, BBC2's *Chronicle* programme advanced what at the time were largely unfamiliar names: the television presenter Magnus Magnusson, who was recalled for being born in Iceland, and the archaeological leader of the project, Professor Richard Atkinson, who was memorable for a plummy voice and having written the official guidebook to Stonehenge and Avebury in 1959. The public turned up in significant numbers to visit the BBC's outside broadcast unit, the cheaply available BBC guide to *Silbury Hill* proved popular, and the takings in Charles Perry's shop increased by a quarter during the summer of 1968.

Concurrent with the opening of the M4 in 1971, Silbury Hill was recharged with popular interest when the archaeological storyline of Season 8 of *Dr Who* proved more than a little reminiscent of Atkinson's excavation being filmed live by the BBC. Set in a quintessential English village, the cast and crew stayed in Marlborough whilst filming took place at nearby Aldbourne: where the parish church and an inn on the Green provided the fictional 'Devil's End' with archetypal village stages within the story, and a bridleway leads to the barrows featuring as the fictional Devil's Hump, an archaeological site from which a BBC film crew were broadcasting the excavation live. When the five episodes of Season 8's *Dr Who and the Daemons* were first broadcast, between May and June 1971, the public soon recognised the locations and the archaeological parallels. It was then inevitable that enthusiastic *Dr Who* fans would be visiting both Aldbourne and Silbury Hill.

In addition to being Europe's largest mound of irreplaceable prehistoric archaeology, Silbury Hill was classified as a SSSI (Site of Special Scientific Interest), because of a record of its flora and fauna extending back to the Victorian period, and repairs had twice been carried out on the enigmatic chalk path in evidence since John Aubrey first sketched Silbury Hill's outline in the 17th century. It was

Fig 21: Front cover of the Radio Times *18 April 1968. Television has played a unique role in attracting late 20th century visitors to the Avebury monuments.*

Fig 22: The TARDIS litter bin, Aldbourne, with thanks to Jo Hutchings. With the built environment punctuating the landscape with so many architecturally stepped reminders of time travel, the TARDIS was not required in Dr Who and the Daemons. *Matt Baker noted that Aldbourne had subsequently acquired a rubbish bin in the form of a Police Box and another shaped as a Dalek.*

then probably inevitable that concerns over erosion and other impacts of footfall, when combined with the hazards of climbing, would see public access being restricted. Access to Silbury Hill had been permanently withdrawn by 1976, yet still the climbers came.

Tourists climbing Silbury Hill on 29 May 2000 discovered a ragged hole in the centre of the summit, that had been created by a massive internal collapse. Unbeknown to the public, but brought to Atkinson's attention more than thirty years beforehand, a reoccurring dip in the summit of Silbury Hill indicated the gradual collapse of an 18th century shaft at the very centre of the giant mound. This dip had a history of being occasionally topped up and ignored, until further collapses at the summit between May and November 2000 revealed a hole with even vertical sides that resembled a lift shaft – this was the shaft cut by miners in 1776.

When the cameras stopped rolling in 1969, Silbury Hill was left 'an eyesore' and Wiltshire Councillor Archie Kidd accused the BBC of 'licensed vandalism'. The response from a BBC public relations officer featured in the *Bristol Evening Post*:

> *We gave an undertaking that we would restore the hill to its original condition and this we will do. We are filling in the tunnel, and will reseed where necessary with the exact variety of grass.*

Had the tunnels been adequately backfilled, the upper contents of the 18th century shaft would not have emptied by material surging into the void created by Atkinson in 1968–9. It was reported that contractors were to complete the backfilling, on behalf of the BBC, which would surely require someone from the Ministry to check the work was carried out to the required specification. The official records that could be traced do not include this information. In 2010 English Heritage initiated restorative works which made Silbury safe, but at an enormous financial cost.

A Complex Avebury

When the opening of the M4 motorway in 1971 significantly reduced traffic on the A4 between Marlborough and Beckhampton, there was fond talk of seeing a local dairy herd once again crossing the Bath Road at Fyfield for milking. A bucolic revival was something of an invitation it would seem, to the increasing number of sightseers and visitors that were unexpectedly noticeable in Avebury. Whilst unable to visit the Avebury recognised as an early planned landscape by William Stukeley in the early eighteenth century, visitors were drawn to a series of megalithic monuments the 20th century had partially restored and set in concrete.

Some sense of the contemporary fascination for archaeology was captured in *A Journey to Avebury*, which Derek Jarman filmed in 1971. Jarman's eerie silent sequences offer up recently installed fingerposts and far more resident sheep and cows than exploring tourists, which were barely noticeable as they wandered along a distant ridge. Jarman and others exploring Avebury's surroundings on foot could trek out to the Longstones or to Windmill Hill, or Silbury Hill. The West Kennet palisaded enclosures were about to be unearthed, and by the end of the decade more and more visitors were seeking out Swallowhead Springs. Facilitated by signposts and published walks, the imagination joined scholarly research in

Fig 23: Avebury c.1948, by Edward Stephen Billin (1911–1995).

conjuring up a series of open air views and field sites that were to be discovered and visited by late 20th century archaeology tourists, prehistory enthusiasts, and spiritual harmonists. The more remote, out of the way or less visited, the more enticing and the opportunity to sense something that was 'hidden' or supposedly secret.

As Avebury's hinterlands became increasingly visited on foot, the mysterious sounding 'Avebury complex' fostered interests in spiritual elements as a visitor attraction. The revived fascination with the Avebury complex and its manifold spirituality in the late 1970s, is rightly attributed to benchmark publications by Michael Dames that includes *The Silbury Treasure* and *The Avebury Cycle*. An undercurrent introducing a Goddess deity runs back to the previous century and interwar archaeologists such as Stuart Piggott and O.G.S. Crawford were drawn towards it. This scholarly enthusiasm formulated an orthodoxy and though there was no convincing consensus, there is always a groundswell by a wider public prompted by highlights in newspapers and the media to explore ideas for themselves.

In March 1923, O.G.S. Crawford explained in a talk to the Royal Geographic Society, that air photography 'provided a new instrument of research', that revealed 'earthworks on ploughed land which were invisible' or confusing to those on the ground. The following year Alexander Keiller joined Crawford on a survey from the air, which eventually led to aerial photography's significant contribution to popularising Avebury. In the same year, however, before the public had heard of an 'Avebury complex;' Ordnance Survey maps highlighted Avebury as 'a centre of prehistoric monuments' to the bicycling Charles S. Brooks. From the ground Brooks reported 'names which betray this fact – Sarsen Stones, the Temple, Long Barrow, Stone Circle, Earth Works, Three Barrows, Tumuli.' Brooks even asked a police officer on a motorbike the way, and received a uniformed escort to the foot of Silbury Hill. Many visitors were following in Brooks's path by the time Crawford and Keiller published their aerial photographs of Avebury, Avebury Trusloe and Beckhampton in *Wessex from the Air* in 1928. The interwar generations were searching for the beginnings of England, and something to believe in.

'Powerful religious impulses' were cited, when an Avebury complex had first been promoted as an official government vision in an article published in *The Times* and repeated in other newspapers in 1935. With an eye on Keiller's re-erection of megaliths in the West Kennet Avenue, the First Commissioner of Works, Conservative MP and banker William Ormsby-Gore, underlined the importance of protecting Avebury's monuments, and cited the Guardianship of a few sporadically located Neolithic monuments alongside barrows and unspecified archaeological sites on private land and in the ownership of several landowners. Irrespective of an ongoing intention that the Avebury complex was shorthand for a landscape that embraced officially designated satellite monuments, it is unsurprising given statements made by Ormsby-Gore, that relatively unexplored sites joined restored monuments when this mysterious Avebury complex developed independent meanings:

> *There is probably not a field in the whole area which does not contain hidden below the surface the evidence of the successive occupation of our Neolithic ancestors.*

The Avebury of 1956

It was in 1956 that Avebury starred in John Betjeman's Shell sponsored 'Discovering Britain' television advertisements, which were undoubtedly popular. In the accompanying leaflet – available at all Shell filling stations 'in a 56 mile radius' – Betjeman opined:

> *Avebury is a haunting place at all times and in all weathers, but most impressive of all on a moonlit night, when it seems to be peopled with*

> *ghosts and the old church and cottages of the village seem quite new and insignificant beside the ancientness of the vast stones of a pagan people who existed 2,000 years before Christ.*

It was also in 1956, following the death of the millionaire archaeologist Alexander Keiller the previous October, that Avebury was noticeably developing into a postwar tourist mecca.

Complementing the spine of monuments in State Guardianship that the National Trust had purchased from Keiller during wartime, which included Windmill Hill, the henge and the nearby section of the West Kennet Avenue; the flagship marking Avebury's transition from Keiller's prewar enterprise to a State controlled heritage empire was the West Kennet Long Barrow. Having been transformed into a cave like structure that proved a magnet for tourists, West Kennet Long Barrow was officially opened in 1956. Visiting motorists needed little encouragement to create extended pull-ins on the Bath Road, which would eventually be enshrined as three kerb lined laybys serving the Sanctuary and Silbury Hill as well as West Kennet Long Barrow. The unveiling coincided with Fyfield Down being declared a Nature Reserve by the Nature Conservancy, and the privately owned Avebury Manor being launched as a visitor attraction for the first time. The adjacent building housing the Morvern Museum was meanwhile undergoing improvements, including plans for a car park, and receiving parties of schoolchildren sparked by schools radio broadcasts of 'A Trip to Avebury' by Jacquetta Hawkes in the BBC series *How Things Began.*

Nurturing this new impetus in Avebury sightseeing between 1956 and 1961, and in agreement with local councils and the Ministry of Works, the National Trust took an active lead in demonstrating a commitment to Keiller's imaginative prehistoric rebuild, by sweeping away even more village homes and sarsen built walls that had uniquely characterised the village since the 17th century. In addition to various farm buildings, the purge of Avebury's characterful roadside buildings expunged the extraordinary Gothic cottage fondly remembered as the 'Toll House' at the southern entrance to Avebury henge, the cottages opposite the entrance to the Red Lion, and the charming row of homes adjacent to the Cove stones, known as Monkton Road Cottages.

It was during this phase of collaborative demolition that the views dramatically altered for those travelling through Avebury, with the roadside setting of the staggered crossroads predominantly transformed. Twenty years on only long term residents would notice the absence of the Red Lion Hotel Garage or any of the cottages in what proved a cult television series. Primarily for an audience of

Fig 24: Monkton Road Cottages before demolition.

children and set in the fictional village of Milbury, named after Silbury Hill, HTV's *Children of the Stones* was filmed in Avebury in 1976 and the series of seven episodes were broadcast by ITV the following year. The setting was essentially a henge-centric Avebury, and a scene of a mysterious occurrence in the first episode features those views from the crossroads created twenty years earlier.

When fencing off the surviving Cove stones from visitors between 1997 and 2003 (having feared the enormous megaliths might fall), it was discovered that one of these stones had not moved at all but the Trust's building purge had caused the instability of the other when the charity demolished the adjacent row of houses. A further irony perhaps being that when the Red Lion starred on the cinema screen once again, this time in the 1998 comedy *Still Crazy*; the film makers ordered up realistic giant polystyrene megaliths to supplement the prehistoric setting opposite the pub.

Forever Changing Avebury

At the dawn of the 20th century some of the Avebury born and bred descendants of 17th and 18th century nonconformists and 'stonebreakers,' that built and gathered

Fig 25: The late Terry Dobney provides some scale alongside one of Still Crazy's fake megaliths when on display in the Alexander Keiller Museum's 70th anniversary celebration in 2008.

in the Five Mile chapel, were still living in the village. They and the communities that shaped their family's lives across the generations are largely forgotten, as is the Avebury they were familiar with.

Until the present century, the Five Mile chapel communities had promoted independent thinking in Avebury for over 300 years. The once vibrant worshipping community had ebbed away, and after Wiltshire Council had withdrawn funding the Tourist Information office had closed in 2011. A concerned Avebury Parish Council rightly encouraged extensive discussions about future use of the chapel before the United Reform Church put the building up for sale. It stands only a short stroll from the site of the Providence Chapel which stood in Avebury High Street and was purchased by the National Trust in 1953. Having opened 2 October

1873 with a 'spacious marquee' accommodating some of the estimated 1,000 worshippers, this chapel represented a religious community stretching back to the Strict Baptists of the 1820s. Demolished by the National Trust purge of 1956, along with adjacent farm buildings, the plot was converted into a car park.

The press first referred to Avebury as a 'National Trust village' in 1981, and in 1989 a former curator of the Alexander Keiller Museum suggested: 'It would be sad if the once rural and mysterious peace of Avebury were to be shattered by excessive tourist facilities.' This was before the National Trust had acquired the extensive portfolio of properties in and around Avebury that it has now, including hundreds of acres of farmland and West Kennett Farm. It was before the National Trust was handed day to day running of Avebury's Guardianship sites by the State in 1994, before the charity became Avebury's largest employer, and before the charity's catering outlets in Avebury included the Circles restaurant, the Manor Tea Room and the Coach House Café.

It was suggested in 1995 that there was no intention the visitor experience should be defined by the National Trust; but in addition to buying and opening Avebury Manor to the public, the charity directly controls both the Museum and the Great Barn that had previously offered visitors independent interpretations. In 2017 the National Trust purchased then renovated the Avebury Five Mile chapel: a notice mounted at the entrance gate states: 'The Trust now provides this space to the local community for interpretation and engagement with the living landscape in which it is located'. Since 2019, the Five Mile chapel has been run by a rota of community volunteers and used for events and an exhibition space. After the charity cancelled this arrangement in 2025, It remains to be seen whether the chapel's long tradition in independent representation will continue under the National Trust. The only certainty is that Avebury is forever changing.

Fig 26: Avebury's Five Mile Chapel when home of the Tourist Information Centre in 2010.

Acknowledgements

Many thanks once again to Pete Glastonbury for the early 21st century photographs of signs, lines and posts. Thanks also to Jo Hutchings for the TARDIS litter bin. All other images courtesy of Wiltshire Museum. Thanks also to Kat Petersen, Archivist at the Society of Antiquaries of London for tracking down the date of Trepplin's election on 1 June 1893 – the year before he directed the excavation at Avebury. Many thanks in addition to all my ASAHRG colleagues, especially those that read and commented on draft passages, including Ros Cleal and Katie Whittaker, Steve Marshall and Amanda Chadburn. This extended account is extracted from a work in slow progress.

Some Additional Currency

In addition to newspaper archives and the other usual sources see: *Compton Census* (Canterbury, 1676): William Salt Library Salt MSS. 33. D.A. Crowley (ed), 1983, V.C.H. *Wilts*. XII, p.103. Hilary Dunscombe, *Avebury: A Five Mile Chapel* (Avebury, n.d.). David Boyd Haycock, 2002, *William Stukeley: Science, Religion and Archaeology in Eighteenth-Century England*, Woodbridge, especially pp. 109–133. B. Haynes, 1794, 'Plan of Allotments and Exchanged Lands in the Parish of Avebury', Salisbury. W.H. Hyatt, 1820, 'Avebury Wilts'. R.B. Pugh and E. Crowley, eds., 1956, V.C.H. *Wilts*. III, pp.104–7. Donald A. Spaeth, 2000, *The Church in an Age of Danger: Parsons and Parishioners 1660–1740*, Cambridge, pp. 150–1. 'Marden 19 August 1776': WSRO, 510/11, and Ordnance Survey 1886, as illustrated in John Chandler, *The Vale of Pewsey*, Bradford on Avon, 2000 edition.

Michael McGarvie, 1973, *Silbury Hill and Wansdyke*, Essays in local history series, Frome Society for Local Study. J.P.D. Dunbabin, 1974, *Rural Discontent in Nineteenth-century Britain*, Faber and Faber. Lucy R. Lippard, 1983, *Overlay: Contemporary Art and the Art of Prehistory*, New York: Pantheon Books. Kay Gardner, May 1989, 'Freestyle: Visiting Women's Sacred Mystery Sites', *Hot Wire*, Vol. 5, Issue 2, p.54. Adam Stout, 2008, *Creating Prehistory: Druids, Ley Hunters and Archaeologists in Pre-war Britain*, Oxford: Blackwell. Andy Worthington, 2009, 'Mystics and Mavericks: The Pagan Reinvention of Avebury', in Joanne Parker (ed.), *Written on Stone: The Cultural Reception of British Prehistoric Monuments*, Newcastle upon Tyne: Cambridge Scholars Publishing, pp. 100–110. M.L. Crook and I.E.T. Free, 2011, *Grey Wethers. The Free Family in Marlborough and the Upper*

Kennet Valley c1847–1998, Wiltshire: Crook and Free. Mark Gillings and Joshua Pollard, 2015, 'Authenticity, artifice and the Druidical temple of Avebury', in J. Kolen, R. Hermans, and H. Renes, eds., *Landscape Biographies: Geographical, Historical and Archaeological Perspectives on the Production and Transmission of Landscapes*. Landscape and Heritage Studies. Amsterdam: Amsterdam University Press, pp. 117–142. Avebury Parish Council, 30 August 2015, *Minutes of the Extra Ordinary Meeting* held at the Red Lion 24 August 2015. Bill Bryson, 2015, *The Road to Little Dribbling*, London: Transworld. Ronald Hutton, 2016, 'Modern Avebury', in Matt Leivers and Andrew Powell, eds., *The Avebury Resource Assessment, Wessex Archaeology Monograph 38*, Part I, pp. 136–142. Matt Barber, 2018, *Black Archive 26: The Daemons*, Edinburgh: Obverse Books, esp. 76–9, 94–6, 106–8. Roger Day and Tim Green, 2021, *A Motoring History of the Kennet Valley*, Reading: Countryside Books. David Matless, 2024, *England's Green: Nature and Culture since the 1960s*, London: Reaktion Books. Stuart Raymond, 2024, 'The Inns of Avebury, c.1600–1800, *WANHSM* 117, pp. 159–167.

Fig 1: Spooked by the skull on Green Hill...

A Minilithic Marathon

Neil Mortimer heads to southeast Dartmoor to go wandering through the Erme Valley.

Earlier this year I set off for southeast Dartmoor to walk the length of the world's longest stone row, situated in the Upper Erme Valley on Stall Moor. Sites on Dartmoor are notoriously difficult to date because so few dateable artefacts are found associated with them. What is certain however, is that there was an explosion of monument building began in the ill-defined period between the later Neolithic and Early Bronze Age. Despite a long history of tinning, mining and clay extraction, particularly in the south of the moor, there are still hundreds, and perhaps thousands, of sites existing in a relatively unspoilt state. Dartmoor's very long stone rows are among the most enigmatic.

The Erme Valley can be joined from various points of access along the fringes of the southeast moor. I headed out from above Torr, at SX 625 611, close to the reservoir at New Waste[1]. From here Stalldown stone row, one of the most impressive of Dartmoor's many megalithic sites, is just visible below the crest of the hill called Stalldown Barrow. The most southerly stones of the 500 m row, around SX 632 621, are only a 15 minute stroll around the eastern flank of Stalldown Barrow.

Despite most of the stones being flat prior to the Revd. Sabine Baring-Gould's

1 Since this article was published in 2003, this part of Dartmoor has become even more difficult to access. New Waste is now privately owned and all access has been shut off, meanwhile the nearby parking area at Harford Moor Gate has also been closed. There is plenty online about these unfortunate changes – which are needless to say entirely motivated by greed – and the ongoing campaign to restore access to this part of the Moor.

Fig 2: Stall Moor stone circle, from the north.

speculative reconstruction of the site in 1897, Stalldown stone row is nonetheless a spectacular monument. Typical of the Dartmoor rows, the monument is aligned more-or-less north-south. The row races towards the crest of Stalldown Barrow, passing by the kerb of a ruinous cairn, and on through a line of cairns which run along the crest of the hill. Just as the land begins to fall away down the northern slope of the hill, the stones increase in size dramatically. Between six and nine feet tall, the last six stones, two of which have fallen, are truly megalithic. From here, at SX 633 626, the mighty vista of the Erme Plains high moor opens up, dropping down into the Erme Valley and rising again into the potentially agoraphobia-inducing upland plateau of Stall Moor.

A handful of interesting cairns stand on the lower slopes of the north side of Stalldown Barrow. One, at SX 633 632, is particularly impressive; a low cairn with a megalithic kerb enclosing a sturdy open kist. Crossing Bledge Brook, or dropping lower into the marshy valley bottom, there are signs of prehistoric activity all around. Ancient settlements line the slopes of the valley, each facing out onto the River Erme below.

Heading uphill, and passing through a complex of prehistoric walls, the land opens out onto the flat plateau, on which stands the Stall Moor stone circle, at SX 635 644. Known as The Dancer or the Kiss-In-The-Ring, the circle has 26 stones and encloses a low cairn. A little over 16 m across, most of the stones are below waist height; one 1.6 m tall stone in the north-northwest of the circle is much larger than the others. The circle is the southern terminal of the longest prehistoric stone row in the world, the Upper Erme or Stall Moor stone row. This is a great place to be.

Few of the 1,000 or so remaining stones that form this astonishing monument are large, and many are hidden in the rough Dartmoor grass. Perhaps half of the stones have been removed, or more likely, have fallen and been covered by the always-encroaching turf. The size of the stones is of no consequence when the length of this stone row is an incredible 3,320 m long. To put this into context, the second longest row of single standing stones in Britain, on Butterdon Hill, only seven or eight kilometres southeast of Erme, runs for a measly 1950 m, only 150 m shorter than the longest row in Brittany. The Erme row is not only the longest row anywhere, it wipes the floor with the competition. The prehistoric builders of this row may have been using small stones, but they were certainly thinking big.

From the Stall Moor stone circle the four large stones at the northern end of Stalldown row are visible approximately 2 km away as tiny dots breaking the southern horizon, formed by the ridge of Stalldown Barrow. This visual alignment is unlikely to be down to good fortune.

And so a minilithic marathon begins. The first kilometre of the row is in good condition. The evenly spaced stones march north-south across the western slope of the valley, paying no attention to a tributary feeding into the Erme. Any thoughts of archaeoastronomy must be put aside when faced with an alignment that follows the lie of the land in the way that this stone row does. Across the valley on the eastern slopes, the later Hook Lake settlements look magnificent, even if a double stone row was wrecked in antiquity during the construction of the southern enclosure. One of the most outstanding Dartmoor monuments soon comes into view: Erme Pound. From afar this massive prehistoric enclosure looks as if it has been abandoned only recently. The stone row drops down into the lower valley bottom, and all but disappears. Crossing the River Erme at a shallow point in the water – perhaps a factor in the siting of Erme Pound – the stones of the row have either sunk in the marshy ground or were robbed in prehistory. Making guesses as to where the stone row may actually be at this point, a three feet tall upright stone sets the row back on track. Twisting out of the valley bottom, the row suddenly reappears with an impressive stretch of small stones running sharply uphill, before giving up the ghost around Red Lake. From this point on followers of the stone row are on their own. The remainder of the row is marked only by occasional standing stones lying deep in the long grass. Finally, the row

Fig 3: Looking south towards the section of the row that has largely disappeared.

comes to an end at a lonely wrecked cairn, at SX 637 678, high on Green Hill. On clear days the stone circle at the southern end of the row 3.2 km away is just visible far below the horizon.

An earlier visitor has propped the skull and lower jawbone of a fallen Dartmoor pony on a stone on Green Hill, perhaps a knowing nod to the funerary associations of stone rows. I'm not sure that the skull wants my company; the weather on Green Hill has closed in and I realise that I haven't seen a soul since setting out some eight kilometres earlier. I turn tail and head south back down the row...

The Erme Valley certainly isn't the easiest place on Dartmoor to get out to, but the going is fairly easy and the remoteness of the area means that it is one of the most well-preserved prehistoric landscapes in Britain. There is nothing quite like the Erme Valley stone row, and every megalithomaniac should walk it at least once[2].

References

Aubrey Burl, 1995, *A Guide to the Stone Circles of Britain, Ireland and Brittany*, Yale University Press.

Aubrey Burl, 1993, *From Carnac to Callanish: The prehistoric Stone Rows and Avenues of Britain, Ireland and Brittany*, Yale University Press.

Jeremy Butler, 1993, *Dartmoor Atlas of Antiquities: Volume Four - The South-East,* Devon Books.

R. Hansford Worth, 1967, *Worth's Dartmoor*, David and Charles.

2 Sandy Gerrard's fantastic stone row website (https://stonerows.wordpress.com) has more details about this site, including Sandy's (and some of my own) fieldwork since this article was published.

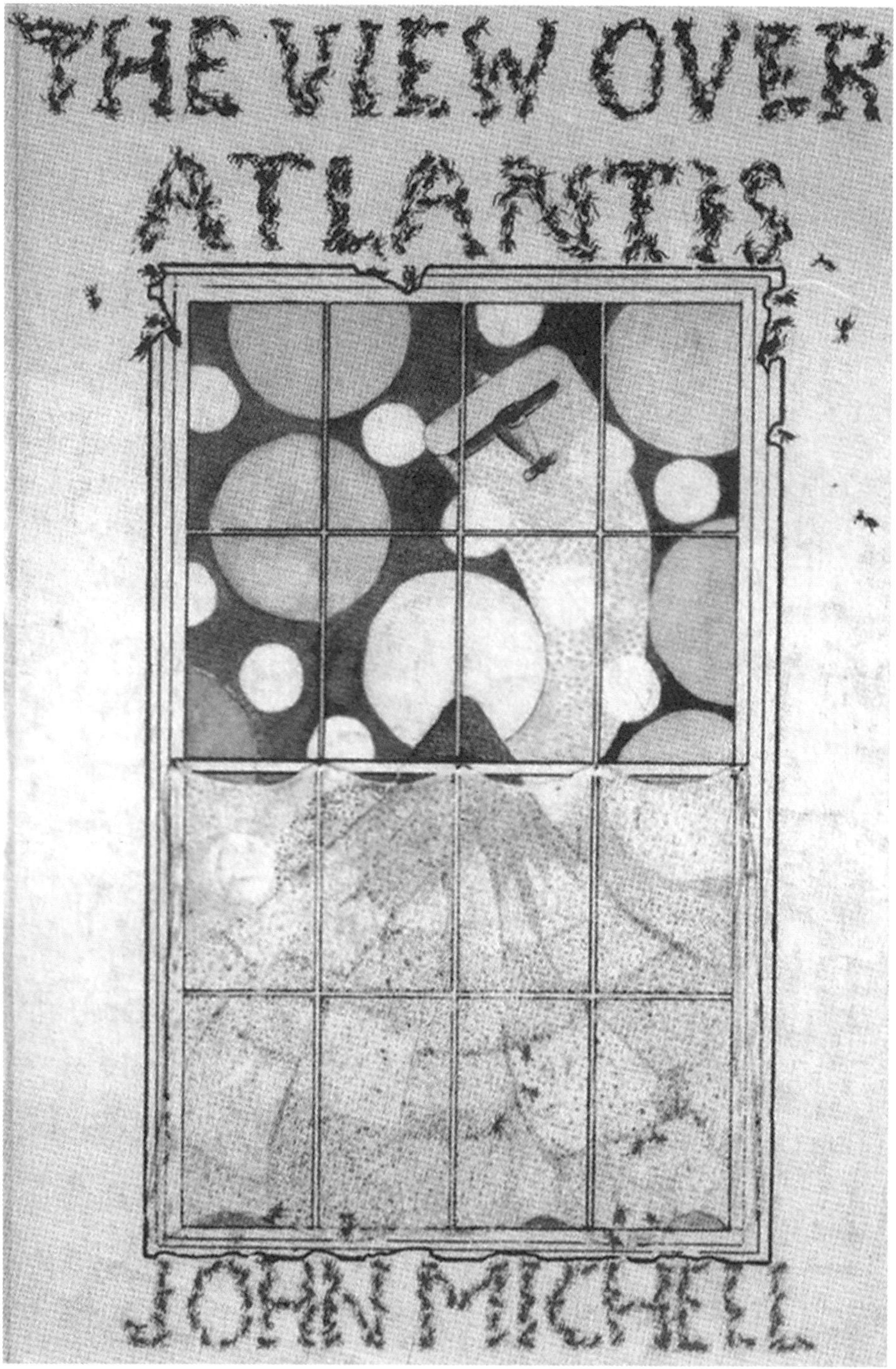
THE VIEW OVER
ATLANTIS
JOHN MICHELL

Tome Raider

This 'retrospective review of seminal or heretical works that have influenced modern alternative thinking about past and place' was intended to be a regular feature, but it turned out to run for just three issues, from issues 38 to 40.

Tome Raider 1
John Michell's The View Over Atlantis
by Danny Sullivan

In these modern days of pluralist approaches to the interpretation of the ancient past it is difficult to imagine the effect this book had when it first appeared in print over thirty years ago. Through the gun barrel of hindsight it would be an easy task to shoot down this eclectic mish-mash of folklore, archaeology, anthropology and numerology. But I believe that would be a mistake. *The View Over Atlantis* played a significant part in the moulding of today's liberal approaches in a number of 'ologies'. It was a pioneering work that boldly reflected the cultural changes of the time.

Many current beliefs and convictions can be readily traced back to the boiling pot of the 1960s. Popular culture underwent a massive overhaul, morality and social behaviour were reconstructed and the academic world fought amongst itself as tenets of establishment thinking were rent apart. Writers and commentators seized the opportunity to meddle with institutions under threat from a wave of change. In the mid-Sixties the enclosed and stuffy world of archaeology had come under attack from academics of other persuasions in the form of the populist Gerald Hawkins, whose startling claims about Britain's most celebrated prehistoric monument captured the popular imagination, and the almost impenetrable Alexander Thom, whose surveys of megalithic monuments from the Hebrides to northern France suggested a prehistoric knowledge of astronomy and universal use of standard measures. Almost overnight the prehistoric landscape had changed and controversy raged. To top it all off Hans Suess announced that recent radiocarbon dating methods were woefully inadequate and the entire chronology of prehistory would have to be reassessed. The effects of this invasion of archaeological privacy can still be felt in modern archaeological attitudes today.

Popular interest in our cultural identity and history were high on the agenda in the late 1960s, and Michell captured the mood of a generation with his observations on the supposed lost knowledge of our ancestors in his writings in *International Times*, the leading alternative publication of the day. Michell was, and is, a romantic. His contention was that an ancient wisdom was once in the possession of our forebears, and traces of it can be found in the landscape, its ancient monuments and fragmented folklore. Ancient earthworks and monuments built for an unknown purpose seemed to share certain features that suggested that they were built as part of a worldwide system. These enigmatic monuments he suggests played a part in the elemental science of an archaic civilisation which Plato refers to as Atlantis.

The View Over Atlantis, published in 1969, is an inspirational synthesis of alternative views of prehistory interlaced with selected anthropological data and wrapped up in numerology and sacred geometry. In the same year Alfred Watkins' *Old Straight Track* had been republished for the first time in twenty years, and laid down the blueprint for *The View Over Atlantis.* Michell was a great apologist for Watkins' ideas and sought out parallel examples of the ley, straight track and astronomical alignment in other cultures. Indeed the first section of the book deals almost exclusively with leys and the theories about them. He went further than any of his contemporaries in introducing to mainstream audiences the Australian Aboriginal 'Dreamtime' and what later came to be known as 'songlines', and the complex Chinese pseudo-science of feng shui – now a household word and subject of fashionable media attention.

The second part of *The View Over Atlantis* deals with the mythical code of numbers, the root of all ancient arts and sciences. Armed with the dry writings of Alexander Thom, Michell extended the argument about the megalithic yard into the question of all ancient units of measure, dissecting the measurements and the proportions of the prehistoric temples and monuments to reveal a common purpose and method in their construction, and that the builders had knowledge of the size and shape of the spheroidal Earth. He explains the art of Gematria – a code in which the letters of ancient Hebrew and Greek alphabets were given numerical values in a way that allowed sacred numbers and mathematical ratios to be hidden within names and phrases. Thus, he maintains, the sacred knowledge of mathematics and temple building were safely stored in ancient texts for unlocking by future generations.

Read today, there are gaping holes in Michell's argument. But so what? He alerted a huge number of people to the possibility of an alternative view of prehistory, set the ball rolling for *The Ley Hunter* and a plethora of alternative small press publications and seeded the invention of geomantic studies, now gradually filtering down into mainstream academic thinking. On the downside, *The View Over Atlantis* also paved the way for the Graham Hancock School of Prehistory, whose adherents, whilst re-treading much of the same ground first trod in *The View Over Atlantis*, manage to do so with an ignorance of the facts, sometimes a phenomenal arrogance and a frequently a determined lack of grace and style.

In The View Over Atlantis Michell pines for a lost Albion where our weights and measures are based on simple and symbolic fractions of the Earth's dimensions, where the earth spirit still flows through the landscape and where poetic inspiration is as important in our understanding and experience of the universe as scientific deduction.

> Michell: *The important discoveries about the past have been made not so much through the present refined techniques of treasure hunting and grave robbery, but through the intuition of those whose faith in poetry led them to a scientific truth. The gradual accumulation within each succeeding generation of the total knowledge of the past through the hereditary medium, known to biologists as DNA, is a phenomenon of which we have again become conscious, and this realisation ensures the ultimate re-establishment of the former belief in revelation on which the science of the ancient world was founded.*

The View Over Atlantis influenced a generation that is now shaping the study of our ancient past. Attitudes have definitely changed and the not-so-lunatic fringe has been quietly absorbed into the mainstream, due in no small part to this book and the pioneering work of the eager amateurs that it inspired.

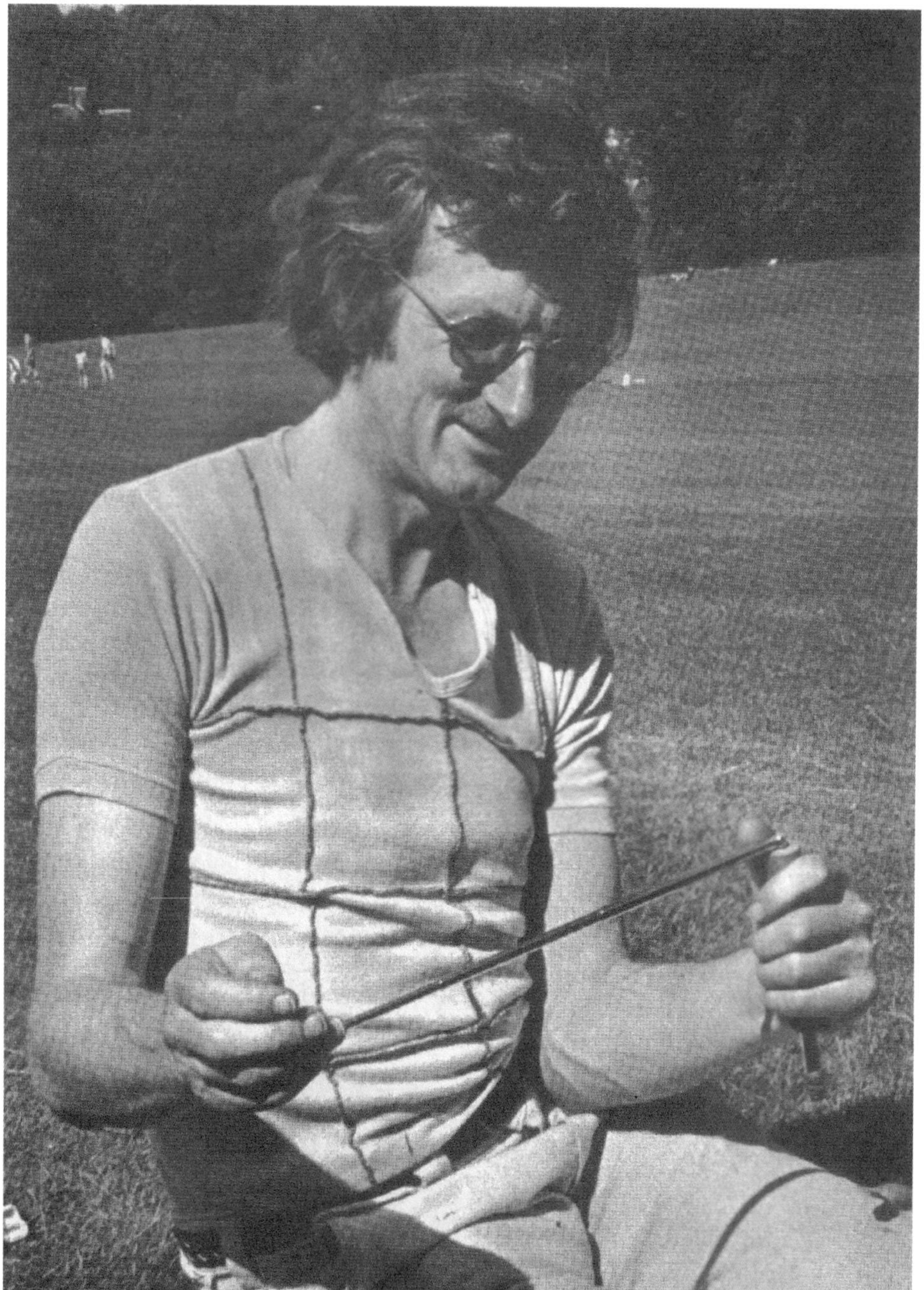

John Michell at the Ley Hunter Moot, Hampstead Heath, London, 2 July 1977
© Fortean Picture Library.

Tome Raider 2

Alexander Thom's Megalithic Sites in Britain

John Michell reappraises Alexander Thom's seminal yet widely misunderstood book, which destroyed the view of prehistoric people as 'simple primitives' and recast them in the role of early scientists.

In 1967 the Oxford University Press published an academic thesis by a retired Oxford professor of engineering, Alexander Thom. Prosaically titled *Megalithic Sites in Britain*, it contained surveys he had made of stone circles, mostly in his native Scotland, with statistical analyses of their dimensions and observations on their astronomical functions. OUP did not expect many sales, for they printed few copies and priced them high, but Thom's book suddenly exploded and archaeology has never been the same since.

The common presumption among archaeologists at that time was that stone circles had been erected by primitive barbarians in connection with local rites and superstitions. That view had been challenged earlier in the century by the astronomer Norman Lockyer, founder of the 'astroarchaeology' movement that led, among other things, to Watkins's ley theory. There was also the problem of ancient

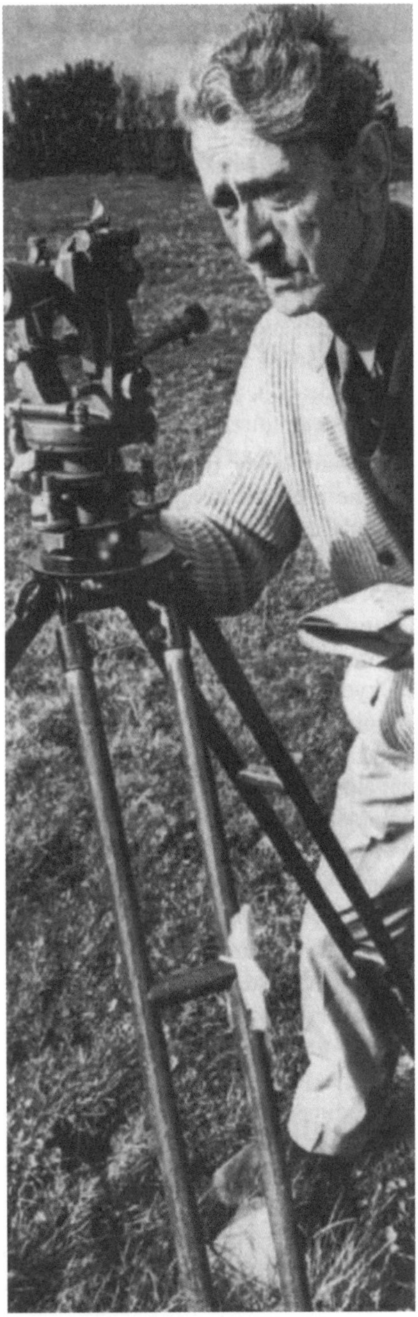

Thom in the field, from John Michell's A Little History of Astro-Archaeology.

MEGALITHIC
SITES
IN BRITAIN
A. THOM

astronomy at Stonehenge, a subject made popular by Gerald Hawkins in his book of 1965, *Stonehenge Decoded*. But before Thom came along, archaeologists seemed to have restored order. Lockyer, Watkins and their ideas were forgotten, Hawkins's sight-lines were found to be imprecise, and the view of megalith builders as simple primitives remained dominant.

Thom's view, derived objectively from his surveys, graphs and statistics, was completely different. The evidence of stone circles told him that their builders were expert astronomers and surveyors, with a unified, synthetic code of science based on number and geometry. In the dimensions of their monuments throughout Britain he found a common unit of measure, the 'megalithic yard' of about 2.72 feet, the use of which produced certain integral numbers evidently of symbolic significance. Geometric construction lines in the groundplans of circles were sometimes extended as sighting lines to seasonal positions of the Sun, Moon and certain stars, and these positions were indicated on the horizon by natural or artificial markers. Thom was impressed by the surveying skills with which the circle builders located sites with the conditions required by their peculiar code of science, in which astronomy, topography, the measurement of time and other forms of knowledge were somehow combined. These people were certainly not savages. By Thom's reckoning the quality of their science was at least equal to that of medieval Europe. And there are features of it which have no correspondence in modern science.

Published in the same year as Thom's *Megalithic Sites* was my own first book, re-introducing the then moribund subject of leys. The main objections to ley theory had always been that the ancient Britons were too primitive and concerned with mundane survival to range long-distance straight lines across the country. Nor was there any good reason for them to do so. Thom's discoveries seemed to remove those objections. In high excitement I wrote to him, we corresponded and, having enthused about his book and its relevance to ley theory in articles for the 'underground' mag, *International Times*, I visited him in Ayrshire. My main interest was in hearing his views on the meaning of the strange prehistoric science he had identified. Was it really science in the modern sense? Or a kind of ceremonial magic? Where had it come from? How had it been lost? – and so on. Thom was a careful Scotsman, not a speculator, but on one point he was firm. The megalith builders, he insisted, were men like himself, highly qualified scientists. In the subsequent loss of their civilized code of knowledge, he said, was a warning to the present – that our civilization too could vanish, leaving barely a trace.

A letter I had from him, responding to questions I had asked about the nature and origin of his megalithomania, gives a good idea of his sensitivity and the sort of man he was. Its date is 23 Dec. 1967. Here is the inside of it:

> *I first saw Callanish from the deck of a small sailing vessel I had taken thro' the Sound of Harris and up that very exposed coast outside Lewis. As we stowed sail the Moon rose behind the stones. I went ashore in the moonlight & got to the rock at the South end of the N.-S. alignment & saw how perfectly the thing orientated on the pole. But there was no pole star in Meg. times. How was it done?*
>
> *From that minute I knew I had to deal with a highly developed culture and everything I have uncovered since lends support.*
>
> *Since I wrote my book I have gone far. I now know that they had a geometry worked out in small units & so they had something they could use as dividers (& scales). This I shall prove if I am allowed to publish.*
>
> *As you think, much of their work goes beyond the utilitarian & I have never liked the ritualistic explanation. Artistic yes. Look at Moel ty Ucha [stone circle in Denbighshire, Wales], or look at the spirals on the cup & ring marks – beautiful things yet based on integral Pythagorean triangles. A computer could help but could not originate such designs.*
>
> *Yes this work has taken me into some of the most beautiful bits of Britain.*
>
> *I am so glad to have my work really appreciated. Most of the reviewers had read only the 'handout' & did not begin to understand what I was saying.*

Thom need not have worried about the reception of his book. *Megalithic Sites* found an unexpected readership among mystics and ley enthusiasts of the Sixties and, as if in response to their interest, the archaeological press began to take notice. Reviewing the book in 1969, Richard Atkinson, the Stonehenge authority and leading prehistorian of his time, confessed to being partly converted by Thom's thesis. He called the book 'a well-constructed parcel-bomb... capable of damaging severely a number of received theories about the prehistory of Britain'. That was not quite accurate, because Thom did not dispute any particular theory. The damage he did was to the official, overall picture of megalithic life and culture. The sort of picture he himself had in mind was of orderly, educated societies, led by Stone Age professors of science who dedicated themselves to the pursuit of abstract knowledge. That seems a rather personal image, not wholly convincing. Megalithic science, as John North [*Stonehenge: Neolithic Man and the Cosmos*, 1996] has recently concluded, was surely practised in connection with the myths, rituals, festivals and magical beliefs of its time, and was integrated in the rhythms of tribal life. Astronomy in all traditional societies is not speculative in the modern manner, but ritualized, bound up with astrology, geomancy and other forms of divination whose ultimate purpose is to maintain contact with the gods, spirits and the dead. That is not science but magic. And magic is a subject that Thom, for all his natural sensitivity, could never acknowledge. Neither can his followers, the archaeo-astronomers, experts on ancient sighting lines but with no idea of necromancy and thus completely missing the object of their studies.

But enough! To wind up on Thom and his legacy, I would say that he left us with a mystery, diverse, many-headed and approachable from many different angles. It is a stimulating mystery and a great improvement on the archaeological pseudo-certainties that stifled megalithic studies until blown away by Thom and his parcel-bomb.

Tome Raider 3
Theo Brown's The Fate of the Dead

Jeremy Harte reappraises a book about supernatural belief which kick-started a new genre of historical folklore.

If you like collecting old things, then folklore makes a very attractive field of study. You can carry it home without getting your pockets muddy, and it takes up much less room in the garage than veteran lawnmowers or a set of disused phone boxes. And this means that there is something of the squirrel about every folklorist, happiest when arranging the collections into dictionaries, surveys, handbooks and the like.

But against this modest background there are books that achieve much more, and one of the classics is Theo Brown's *The Fate of the Dead* (D.S. Brewer for the Folklore Society, 1979). Subtitled 'a study in folk eschatology in the West Country after the Reformation', it was published in 1979 – a time when the supernatural had barely begun to attract scholarly interest. There was *Religion and the Decline of Magic* but Keith Thomas left off at the eighteenth century, which was when Theo Brown really got going. In any case she was not an academic: her roots were in her own community, the old Devon whose topographical sketches and provincial glossaries rest in leatherbound obscurity on the upper shelves of local libraries. And out of these scattered materials she virtually created a genre of folklore history.

True, historians had begun to draw on the resources of folklore. But what interested Bob Bushaway and E.P. Thompson were the things that people did, especially if they were radical things – rioting, rough music and rick-burning. Theo

The Fate of the Dead

A Study in Folk Eschatology in the West Country after the Reformation

THEO BROWN

FOLKLORE SOCIETY
Mistletoe Series

Brown was trying to find out what they thought, which is a much more difficult enterprise. They order these things much better in France, where the study of *mentalités* was under way at the same time, but Brown had the great advantage of being an amateur, and she struck out on her own track.

The Fate of the Dead is about the spiritual vacuum which existed for most people after the Reformation, and before the Victorian evangelising of the working class. From an old Catholic world richly populated with supernatural beings, ordinary parishioners found themselves lost in the bleak individualism of a severe Protestantism. The community was robbed of the social presence of the dead and the saints, who had made sense of life for so many generations. And the folklore of ghosts, conjuring and exorcism was one way in which they tried (without much help from the elite) to put order back into their universe.

This is, as Brown makes clear, a sub-Christian world. In the years immediately after the Reformation, people struggled to dispense among themselves some of the comforts which had been provided by the old church – raising their own cuttings, so to speak, from the wreckage of monastery gardens. This process, recently reviewed by Ronald Hutton, often co-existed with anti-Catholicism of the most vituperative political brand. In fact religious faith hardly seemed to matter: the parson does not appear in these stories as a spiritual comforter, but as a superior kind of witchdoctor, and the more Latin he uses in his conjurations, the more everyone is impressed.

Modernity, as in Peter Burke's analysis, was made when the ruling classes came to have a culture quite separate from that of the folk: not a more refined, more reflective version of common beliefs, as seems to have been the case in antiquity and the middle ages, but a completely different mental world. Only women and children, those oddly marginal figures, were able to move hesitantly between the social levels. This was how things were until the last century – and Brown herself came from the last generation, and grew up among warnings (thankfully disregarded) that she should not pick up stories from the servants' hall.

Born in 1914, she was one of that clan of resourceful ladies who steered the Folklore Society through the post-war years – Katharine Briggs, Hilda Ellis Davidson, Violet Alford, Venetia Newall. She was also one of the few members of the Society since Andrew Lang to keep up an interest in parapsychology. The *Fate of The Dead* is alive to the possible existence of ghosts, as well as ghost stories, and in that respect is preferable to Ronald Finucane's bright but shallow scepticism on the same topic.

Cunning folk, who feature in Owen Davies' exhaustive surveys as fortune-tellers and witchbusters, appear here as ghostlayers: a different string to their bow, and one less likely to appear in newspaper condemnations, as ghosts (unlike, say, people falsely accused of being witches) were not going to bring actions for libel or assault. Certainly they were libelled, or at least stereotyped as mad parsons, wicked squires and the like. Individuals are viewed with unease in this tradition. Those who rest unquiet in their graves are the people who stood outside a community – the murderers and suicides and plain eccentrics, the unjust and the plunderers of the poor – while the great mass of folk went quietly to their long home in the village churchyard.

Brown looks at the afterlife through Anglican eyes: there is not much said about dissent. But before the nineteenth century purged the magic out of Methodism, it had shown signs (especially in upland areas) of developing into a folk-Christianity of almost African proportions, with spirits, ecstasies and exorcisms. Baring-Gould famously thought that Cornish Methodism was simply Celtic animism come back to haunt us. But then a man whose great-grandmother still visited the parish as a white owl was in no position to dismiss other people's superstitions.

There is certainly something animist about the eerie landscape of Brown's ghost stories, through which the shadowy figures move a cockstride each year on their endless journeys. They weep by the rivers as they weave ropes of sand, or howl devil-pursued round the icy tors. Left to their own devices, the folk were reinventing an Iron Age world of numinous caves and pools. But these eighteenth-century ghosts are also looking forward, to the landscapes of the Romantic movement. Anna Bray – another resourceful lady, collecting folklore on the banks of the Tamar and the Tavy – was a correspondent of Southey, although she reserved her romantic enthusiasm for the scenery, and could be sharply realistic about its inhabitants.

Rural folklorists of the old school were often suspected of being soft on Merrie England. Theo Brown was quite immune to this. As might be expected from someone reared mentally on the harshness of Dartmoor, she cast a bright, Miss Marple eye over the contemporary scene, and knew as well that things had been much nastier in the past. People took their revenge on life's cruelty by inflicting more cruelties of their own – real, on anything that was in reach, like children and animals; imagined, on those pitiful ghosts. Ironically, the worst that the working class could inflict on the dead gentry was endless labour, hence all the exorcisms that involve emptying rivers with leaking limpet shells.

A strong sense of the moral economy of society pervades *The Fate of the Dead*. Village life gave Brown her sharp awareness of the prejudice, superstition and gossip that lay behind ghost stories, but she could also see what was good in them. Her heroes are to be found amongst the exorcists, the 'sympathetic clergy occasionally to be found – at a prudent distance from the Bishop's Palace', 'mature, intelligent men who possessed the compassion to tackle these problems in terms that their people could understand, and the common sense to see the value of ritual, even if of a home-made variety'.

Amateurs, in fact, with the kind of hands-on moral awareness of human and supernatural life which Theo Brown had herself, and which, to be honest, is not so easy to come by in university halls of residence. It is ironic that Brown should have died in 1993, at a time when the Folklore Society was going through one of its fits of yearning to become an academic institution. As an attempt to write folkloristic history, *The Fate of the Dead* was a book ahead of its time – but it was also a tribute to a long, self-confident tradition of amateur research which should not be thrown away lightly.

Small Stone: Megalithic TV: 'The Changes'

Barbara O'Riley describes an overlooked classic of megalithic pop culture.

Last issue's Megalithic Movie update mentioned the 1970s BBC children's TV series *The Changes*, stating: 'A central theme of the series involves a megalith in a cave, but no-one seems to remember how or why'. So, my goggle-eyed friends, let us return to the warm-bath world of yesteryear TV...

The origins of *The Changes* television series lie in three novels by Peter Dickinson, *The Weathermonger* and *Heartsease* (both 1969) and *The Devil's Children* (1970). The novels were subsequently adapted for television, and the first episode of the ten-part series was broadcast on Monday, 6th January, 1975 at 5.20 pm. Home from school, viewers were about to see one of the strangest children's television shows ever made. *The Changes'* bizarre mix of environmental disaster, pop mysticism, examination of racial scapegoating and civil unrest caused a minor stir, and the show prompted questions about the suitability of programmes then being shown at tea-time.

Episode one introduces us to plucky teenager Nicky Gore (played by Victoria Williams), whose world is about to be shattered by the oncoming Changes. At this point in the story – and for most of the series – no-one knows why the white, adult

THE DEVIL'S CHILDREN
HEARTSEASE
Peter Dickinson
THE WEATHERMONGER
Peter Dickinson
K-5805

population of Britain has taken a sudden violent abhorrence to machinery. Nicky's father smashes up the television (possibly a good idea) while many others get to work destroying technological civilisation (possibly a bad idea). Nicky's family decide to escape to France, where the Changes and its symptoms, 'the Noise', don't seem to have taken such a hold. Along the way Nicky is separated from her folks, who reluctantly decide to carry on without her.

Nicky leaves the city, which by now is a sparsely-populated dystopia. An early episode has Nicky teaming up with a group of Sikhs who are unaffected by the Noise. They travel into the countryside, finally making their home in a disused farm outside a village. In one of *The Changes*' most memorable scenes, Nicky experiences the Noise while passing under electricity pylons. The people of the nearby village are afraid of the pylons as well, and refer to Nicky and the Sikhs as 'Devil's Children' for living so close to the evil pylons. A skirmish takes place between the Sikhs and West Country bandits, who have kidnapped all the villagers' children. The Sikhs are victorious, the children are freed, and Nicky moves on.

By now Britain is in the throes of a fully-fledged beards'n'breeches technology-hating Medieval revival. Nicky finds herself being tried as a witch by an oafish 'Witchfinder General' figure because she isn't afraid of machinery, but manages to escape with the help of new pals Jonathan and Margaret. Nicky and Jonathan avoid capture by sailing away on a canal barge, but soon after the barge is struck by freak lightning.

Towards the end of the series we finally get to see some megalithic action. Nicky and Jonathan encounter Mr Furbelow, a nutty hermit who lives in a caravan in a disused quarry. The children venture into a mine working or cave in the quarry where they discover a standing stone. The source of the Changes is about to be revealed after Nicky learns that the megalith is the vessel for a sentient being which is able to communicate telepathically. The stone, possibly the angriest megalith in the world, tells Nicky that it caused the Changes to teach mankind a lesson about the environmental damage it has been doing to the world. Mr Megalith indicates that he has taken the form of various historical figures in the past, including Merlin. Nicky explains to the stone that although he is right about the damage being done to the modern world, the Changes have in fact made the world a worse, not a better place. Eventually the stone yields to Nicky's humanist appeal and decrees to end the Changes. The cave collapses, sealing the stone safely below ground for all eternity, and the children leave the quarry and head for the city. Finally, they see a road full of cars off in the distance and realise that the Changes have come to an end.

Although a bit slow moving by modern TV standards, the series works because, like *The Children of the Stones*, which followed a couple of years later, it tapped into a number of then (and still) current issues of popular interest and concern, and gave them a supernatural spin. The familiar settings (the series was shot around Gloucester and Bristol; the megalith scenes were shot in Clearwell Caves in the Forest of Dean) give the programmes an air of 'how much of this could be true?' vibe. Also, the show made a generation of Chopper bike-riding herberts suspicious of those menacing electricity pylons. Slight though its stone content may be, *The Changes* more than deserves its place in any pop-megalithic library.

The Changes has been shown three times; the original screening in 1975, then again 18 months later, and in the mid-1990s on UK Gold, the British satellite channel. Unfortunately, *The Changes* is currently unavailable on video[1], although bootleg copies of the complete series (taken from the UK Gold screening) are in circulation among cult television aficionados. The novels *The Weathermonger*, *Heartsease* and *The Devil's Children* are currently out of print, but due to be republished in 2003.

1 Inevitably, *The Changes*, like most other obscure shows, is so much easier to obtain in 2024 than it was 20 years ago, and the series can be streamed online. Only the first of the three novels on which the series was based seems to be currently in print, but the originals are easy to find. Paddy Kingsland's fantastic soundtrack is available through Silva Screen Records. Incidentally, Barbara O'Riley, the article's writer, was a pseudonym for *3rd Stone* editor Neil Mortimer, a name which was subsequently recycled as a member of festival 'acid wonk' act Rainbow Unit.

Letters

From its earliest issues *3rd Stone* always had a lively letters section. Readers and contributors would write in sharing local knowledge, adding to or challenging articles, or recounting site visits where they'd heard interesting folklore or occasionally had strange experiences. The Letters section gave the mag a sense that it was a 'clearing house' for ideas about the past, where people from different perspectives could have a voice. Sometimes writers would give an update on their previous articles as new information came to light – see for example Bill Clark's letter regarding Wandlebury published in issue 32 – and some letters started to become so long that they were short articles in their own right. To address this, a new section, 'Small Stone', began with issue 41. In the following selection of correspondence, the authors of the letters have been anonymised unless it's obvious who the letter writer was, or if the sense of it would be lost if the author was not known. The number in brackets is the issue in which the letter appeared.

Space Invaders (28)

I have recently received the latest copy of *3rd Stone* and am ever more impressed with it. The new issue is filled with good things and what with the previous pieces on stone circles, including Langdean Bottom, the magazine is becoming favourite reading for me.

I was also amused by the article about Lethbridge, a character high on my list of cheerful reading what with swinging a pendulum at the Merry

Maidens and fantasising about Beaker space invaders at Callanish. Archaeology could do with more like him.

I shall happily pay the increased subscription.

Aubrey Burl, Birmingham

Gogmagog Update (32)

In an update to my article 'Dowsing Gogmagog' (issue 27), the Cambridge University Archaeology Unit carried out their final investigations of the current series at Wandlebury in June '97. At two more sites very similar configurations to the Tom Lethbridge diggings turned up. The opportunity was taken to look around the hill-figure area for, as you will remember, Tom surveyed the surroundings and predicted that two more figures would also be found if he had been allowed to dig, and in fact gave very accurate drawings to back up his theory.

Ten pits were dug, some had features such as rubbish pits, all much disturbed and with distinct plough marks through most of them. But for me, the final nail in the Goddess' coffin was the sight of two rubbish pits in close proximity to her and both within the predicted other figures. One showed bare exposed chalk and the other gravel and stone deposits a metre or so thick. You may remember that Tom Lethbridge was scathing of the Cambridge Society's experts regarding his sling shots in the figure outline. Did the Society think the stones were sucked off a Suffolk beach in an Ice Age storm? Well no, they only had to roll downhill for 20 metres!

Bill Clark, Wandlebury

Continuity? (32)

In Phil Quinn's article 'The Folklore of Modern Sites' (issue 29) he quotes several examples of standing stones with associated legends regarding them moving, often to water. He used this as a basis for discussing examples of modern 'moving' monuments.

On Bredon Hill, within the ramparts of Kemerton Camp Iron Age hillfort, we have the Banbury/Elephant stone. A car-sized lump of conglomerate limestone split through the centre, and looking, not unsurprisingly, like an elephant from certain quarters. It is said that on a clear night it will move down to the River Avon to drink if it hears the bells of Pershore Abbey, a feat I am still waiting to witness!

To explain this belief we might either presume the tale was invented to warn people away from a 'supernatural' site or was sheer fancy. But could it possibly be a confused folk memory? As stones do not move, perhaps it would be sensible to presume that people moved towards it? If standing stones were erected in the Bronze Age at a time when a water cult was in full bloom, is it unreasonable to suggest that libations could have been duly delivered to the stone? Unfortunately this does not help make sense of my example, as it is a natural outcrop!

If such long-term memories were possible, we are being asked to believe that oral traditions can traverse millennia although they might of course get distorted along the way. Whilst researching the coffin paths of the North York Moors that make up the Lyke Wake Walk, I found a reference by local author John Hillaby who suggested these straight 'sacred' paths may in fact be a continuation of practices stemming from the cursus monument. A great deal of time separates the two and it seems very unlikely, but it is not impossible.

Perhaps other readers have come across similar echoes in their research?

WP, Evesham

The Ghost of a Cat (32)

My grandfather had a very old farmhouse in Hornsey Lane, London where I often stayed. I have an excellent visual memory and can picture the layout of the house and rooms, including one where I spent a sleepless and terrified night in 1923 when I was 18.

The inhabitants of the house had lived there so long that they were not annoyed by the many ghosts that also occupied the house. Aunts Lilian and Evelyn had two dogs which would be terrified at certain times – Lilian's was a well-behaved poodle and Evelyn's a nasty little dog that chased any cat it could. Lilian, being the youngest and competent aunt, went to the kitchen each morning to give orders to the cook, who had a happy black cat. One morning Evelyn's dog got out of the bedroom and chased a cat upstairs – Lilian rushed to the kitchen where Cook's cat was sat purring happily in front of the fire!

I myself once saw the ghost cat appear from behind a screen – used to keep out draughts near the dining room door – and go up the stairs.

I like to think that he or she was so happy in the place that it had remembered the house and its owners.

JER, Ross-on-Wye

Perspectives on the World (33)

I found the conclusions on medieval art in issue 31 interesting ('Stretching Credibility: A perspective on the Long Man of Wilmington' by Rodney Castleden). I think it is right to say that perspective was known in Classical art, but what is strange is that the concept seems to have been lost and then rediscovered at a later stage, probably as a result of Byzantine influence, in the 14th century. I wonder if it may have something to do with the medieval attitude to 'reality'. For many the spiritual world seems to have been more real than the world of the flesh, and perhaps portraying the world as flat is a statement of the world's ultimate unimportance in the face of the greater world of God. What we refer to as perspective becomes not a statement of relative distance, but of relative importance in the overall scheme of the world. Perhaps perspective could not be rediscovered in art until this didactic element was superseded.

DG, London

Blue is the Colour (34)

As a new subscriber to *3rd Stone* I am writing a letter to introduce myself on the subject of Stonehenge, a monument long dear to my heart. Many years ago, before the days of Heritage Management, Stonehenge was looked after by the Office of Works. One very wet summer the shoes of visitors took away the damp grass between the stones and then the earth below them so that, as Robert Newall [1884–1978, Stonehenge excavator 1919–1926] told me, they looked like the teeth of an old horse. The Office of Works took alarm and liberally sprinkled gravel in place of the grass. Then these sharp fragments were carried on the soles of the visitors' footwear, who as usual walked carelessly over the prostrate stones and wore away their protective weathering. I went to see this, and passing by a prostrate bluestone noticed with interest its exposed natural colour of blue-grey with white spots. So I do not call these particular stones just 'dolerite', but more correctly 'spotted dolerite'.

In the Middle East I remember seeing worked pieces of precious lapis lazuli, brought all the way from what is now Afghanistan. The very best of the matt blue stone is speckled with acicular rutile, and I was told that in ancient days it was sacred to the night sky. So there at Stonehenge I pondered that surely the spotted dolerite stones were brought all the way from Wales to assist in the worship of the stars in the night sky here in Wiltshire.

SB, Warminster

Stone Circle at Churchill (34)

Long-time readers of *3rd Stone* may remember that back in 1994 (issue 19) I relayed a story about a possible lost stone circle near the village of Churchill in Oxfordshire. Standing in a row at the side of the church steps are several weathered old stones, very Rollrightish in appearance. There are a few more stones about 30 yards down the road at the entrance to the rectory. We were told by an old villager that the stones were brought from a stone circle in Sarsgrove Wood about a mile away when the new church was built in 1827 (the abandoned church can be found at the other side of the village). We couldn't gain access to the wood so could not confirm if there were any remains of the fabled circle.

In February 1998 I was sifting through the archive of Alfred Watkins' Straight Track Postal Portfolio Club in Hereford Library when I came across a couple of papers about Churchill. In July 1936 the annual club gathering was being held in Cheltenham and on Monday 20th July three of the club members took a trip out to Churchill as they had been told about some interesting old stones in the village. Major Tyler writes: 'At the other end of the village, forming a boundary across the raised footpath, and at the southern limit of the church enclosure wall, is a line of about six ancient stones forming a fence. These might very well have come from any stone circle; they are just the shape one is accustomed to see in circles'.

Major Tyler goes on to say that the oldest inhabitant of the village told them that the stones were brought from Sarsgrove Wood and that they could find others like them still lying in the wood. Tyler and his two companions went up to the wood and 'without any difficulty found about half a dozen of the stones'.

The story related by Major Tyler is strikingly similar to the one I was told in 1994, even down to the old boy telling the tale. Recently I paid a return visit to Churchill and noticed that two of the stones at the rectory had been pulled down to allow access to a field, but on a happier note, at last I found the elusive Churchill Stone. Major Tyler and friends located it in 1936 as did O.G.S. Crawford 11 years earlier, but when I scrubbed around for it five years ago I drew a blank. In fact the stone is still *in situ* on the side of the road from Churchill to Chipping Norton. It was buried in dense hedgerow but this has now been cut right back revealing the stone.

The other paper in the archive was written by W.W. Tyrell in 1947. Mr Tyrrell, inspired by Major Tyler's paper, paid a visit to Churchill to collect some fragments of the stones in order to have them analysed to find out what kind of stone it was. The interesting part of Tyrrell's account is that when he went to the wood to find the stones they were no longer there. During the war years the stones had been removed.

So what are we to make of the fabled Sarsgrove circle? My letter to the Sites and Monuments Office in 1994 drew a lacklustre response. There was no stone circle in the woods and the Churchill Stone was not regarded as archaeologically significant. All we have is a record of enthusiastic amateurs getting excited by the same thing over several decades.

Jo-Anne Wilder, Stroud

Sacred Stonehenge (35)

I read an article in *The Daily Telegraph* of 24th April [1999] with the headline 'Welcome Aboard the Stonehenge Experience Tour', about its development so as to maximise the number of visitors to the site, who would be entertained at some distance from the monument, itself only to be approached on foot and isolated on downland well away from roads or car parks. Readers of *3rd Stone* will, I believe, approve of this idea in general because Stonehenge is not like a disused dockyard or 'stately home' for their attractions to be emphasised at all costs. No, it must have been built with great reverence and intense employment of labour, for religious purposes we can only dimly perceive. But I, and doubtless other persons, have had experience of the spiritual values imbued within Stonehenge by its construction.

SB, Warminster

April Fool? (35)

'Archaeologists found that ruts on the left-hand side of a Roman road caused by heavily-laden waggons travelling to a quarry were much deeper than the ruts on the right caused by empty waggons making the return journey' (Short Cuts, last issue). Heavily-laden waggons travelling to a quarry, empty for the return journey? Have I spotted the April Fool or was Londinium already exporting its refuse to land-fill sites in Wiltshire?

Chris Wood, *Place Magazine*

Standing Stones – A Warning (35)

Whilst doing some field-work on standing stones in Anglesey in the 1950s, I became extremely confused on finding that practically every tiny field in the area of my study contained a megalith, although the excellent Royal Commission (1937) volume only marked the odd example. When I challenged a farmer, he informed me that he and his colleagues had noticed how much their cows enjoyed rubbing themselves up on stones, and so over the years they had set one up in every field for their use. As the stones were well-weathered it was impossible for those not in the know to distinguish the ancient from the modern.

James Dyer, Luton

The Atlantic Celts (36)

I read the enthusiastic review of *The Atlantic Celts: Ancient People or Modern Invention?* in issue 35 with some amusement. It appears to be a fact that nobody asks Simon James, the author of the above book, a very relevant question, i.e. If the main body of people living in Britain at the time of the Roman invasion were not Celtic, then who were they? After all, one of the reasons given by the Romans for the invasion was that Britain was the main training ground of the druids. Were they not a Celtic priesthood as the Greeks and Romans assert? And as the British tribes had the same skull type, blood line, artistic forms and methods of war as their Continental cousins, how could such a cultural transfer come about? Traces of Celtic people exist throughout Europe, and Asia. In fact, the Caucasian burials recently discovered in a Chinese desert give every indication that these people were Celtic. So if the Celts reached China, the Atlantic coast of Europe is certainly within their scope! Of course, there were and are pseudo claims made on behalf of the Celts. But to say the Celtic tribes of Britain did not exist is like saying the Plains Indians were a myth because much of the costume and dancing etc attributed to them are Hollywood inventions. There is something very sad about this denial of Celticness by the English who are a very mixed lot anyway. Could it be because the Welsh appear more individual and talented than they are?

VG, Swansea

An Eerie Glow (36)

I picked up the snippet in Short Cuts issue 34 concerning burials accompanied by pebbles of white quartz. For the last couple of years I have pondered the question – why is quartz, be it pebbles or pieces of different descriptions, found in prehistoric locations such as pits, graves etc? Also, why were white quartz pebbles given to certain wells as votive objects? I believe rock crystal is a very different subject – the very way it develops with its pointed facets, and its clarity, make it magical alone – but quartz pebbles?

I am taking notes traditions concerning rain-making and health-giving qualities, as well as seering. However, an old chap told me of something else. He said they used to play with quartz pebbles where he lived in Gwytherin. When I asked him what he meant, he said they used to go into a cave and rub them together. I asked why. He said they shone – it was magic. I picked up two sea-washed quartz pebbles from the beach a couple of days later and tried to obtain the effect myself, and hey presto! It's not fiction. The ancient people surely would have known of this phenomenon. I believe it was this quality alone which made the stones magic and maybe alive. I would be delighted for any info concerning quartz or rock crystal being found in a prehistoric context or other traditions concerning them.

PP, Prestatyn

More Eerie Glows (37)

Regarding PP's letter in *3rd Stone* 36, the glowing quartz (formerly also called rock crystal) results from the release of electrical energy trapped in the quartz crystal-lattice structure as light when two pieces are rubbed together, and may well be the source of many 'earthlight' phenomena, as these seem to often occur preferentially near stressed crystal rocks (e.g. near a fault-line, though the rocks probably do not need to be in motion to create the light). This natural piezoelectricity is one of the characteristic attributes of quartz, and is partly why it is used so heavily in the electronics industry ('silicon chips'). Quartz as a mineral (chemically SiO2) is very common in a large variety of forms, and silicate rocks generally are the most abundant on Earth. I have a couple of small lumps of quartz here that I was sent, marketed as 'Glow-Stones', a number of years ago during the then-upsurge in gem shops on the crest of the New Age retailers. Of course, the label cunningly doesn't tell you the rocks are simply common white quartz, only that they are 'special rocks' with this almost magical property... Other 'magical' glows can be realised using reels of sticky tape (masking tape works very well) or opening the seals of self-sealing envelopes in a darkened room; breaking the adhesive bonds produces a line of light along the join, usually either yellow, yellow-green or blue-purple.

Alastair McBeath, Northumberland

Natural Light (37)

PP (letter, *3rd Stone* 36) is quite correct – I have used this dramatic triboluminescent effect in lectures and demonstrations for 10 years or so. The lecture hall or theatre needs to be totally dark. Then, with a crystal in each hand and a back and forward friction motion of one against the other, after a few seconds first a glow then a brighter light is emitted from the crystals. Listen to the intake of breath from your audience! I use a 6" long quartz crystal with a 5" long amethyst.

Anne C Arnold Silk, Buckinghamshire

For Those About to Rock (37)

I was interested to read the letter from PP in *3rd Stone 36* regarding quartz stones which glowed when rubbed together. Local (Welsh) folk in the Preseli area have claimed that certain stones around about glow at night. As quartz crystal is plentiful in these parts perhaps there is also a spontaneous reaction?

On another matter, with reference to VG's comments on the Letters page that the English are a very 'mixed lot' – presumably compared to the pure Celtic Welsh. I would like to inform your correspondent that the Welsh are a gloriously mixed lot as well. They are composed of Celtic (whatever that is),

Irish, Norse, Anglo-Norman, Flemish and Saxon blood. Also I remember reading somewhere that most English people have a strong strain of Celtic DNA. Attempting to divide the British people on racial lines is almost impossible – and can be highly dangerous.

Mike Howard, *The Cauldron* Magazine

Sar-Stans (38)

In a letter that you kindly published in *3rd Stone* 37, 27–8, I suggested that the origin of the word 'sarsen' might come from the Anglo-Saxon 'sar-stan'. During the preparation of a revised edition of *Prehistoric Avebury*, however, I was rereading *3rd Stone* 33, 11, and discovered that Ken Watts had anticipated me by several months. 'The name may however have developed from the Anglo-Saxon meaning troublesome and stan meaning stone, the sarsens having proved to be a great impediment to agriculture'. I apologise, Mr. Watts. Unacknowledged plagiarism has never been one of my many faults.

Aubrey Burl, Birmingham

An Apology (40)

As the writer of 'The Third Stone' in *3rd Stone* 40, 48-55, I have half an apology to your generally unsuspecting readership. John Michell, long-suffering friend, and author of the brilliant *Who Wrote Shakespeare?*, Thames & Hudson, 1996, now on sale in that temple of orthodoxy, the Royal Shakespeare Theatre, Stratford-upon-Avon, has kindly corrected my 'Grey ruined Choirs' on page 54. The true quotation, of course, should have been 'Bare ruined choirs, where late the sweet birds sang' of Sonnet 73.

I offer only half an apology for my carelessness because I was half right. 'Grey' was the original version of 'the man from Stratford' before Francis Bacon with the help of the Earl of Oxford, who was probably dead, and Christopher Marlowe, who certainly was, improved it to 'Bare'.

In consequence, this is something of a grey area which hardly bares altaration.

Yours rather sincerely,

Aubrey Burl, Birmingham

Don't Mention the Cats (42)

I lived in Spain for nearly a year and this story was told to me by a couple of old men, who lived in mountain villages at least forty miles apart. It does seem to be a genuine local tradition, although I've not had the chance to look further into it; it's just one of those tales which seems to be passed on by word of mouth. Apparently, during the Spanish Inquisition, when all the witches and heretics were being rounded up, all of the cats in Spain were also collected and burned as witches' familiars. However, within a few months the country experienced a dreadful epidemic of mice and rats, and in their desperation, the Spanish people were obliged to buy new cats from Rome, at an exorbitant price. So, the story claims, all cats in Spain are Roman cats; and one way to insult a Spaniard is to point to a cat and say 'Nice Roman cat'. How true it might be, I have no idea; but I'm sure there's a moral in there somewhere. Has any reader got more information?

Ian Brown, Cleveland

Merlin and Wales (44)

In his assessment of my book *Merlin and Wales* carried in *3rd Stone* 43, the reviewer complains of my use of a 19th century Welsh dictionary. As a matter of fact I relied on another, listed in my bibliography, the multi-volume *Geiriadur Prifysgol Cymru*, begun in 1950 and only now nearing completion.

However, since language, myth and bardic tradition are all living processes, continually evolving, I see no need to apologise for turning at times to Evans' Dictionary of 1852. Rather, it would seem as perverse to cut his layer of understanding from the organic whole as to remove his enthusiasm of 18th century eisteddfod revivalists, upon which the modern eisteddfod partly relies.

Similarly, instead of a pedantic search, doomed to fail, for the mirage of 'scientific' absolutism, I have followed a lyrical impulse towards inclusiveness, as demonstrated in the medieval *Mabinogion*'s attitude towards place-names.

There, as in my book, place-names are regarded as encapsulating repeatable mythic events, so that the landscape can be animated from within by the re-emergence of divine characters-in-action. Then, for example, through a resanctified mundane shell, Dinas Emrys may utter its latent sacred word again, piercing the dead skin of abstraction.

That is the magician's landscape which I have tried to explore, and the poetic synthesis which the reviewer both thanks and blames me for.

Michael Dames, Worcester

Smoky, No! (46)

Your magazine continues to publish a wide variety of interesting and thought-provoking articles. Sadly, this high standard of content is let down by the rather out-dated mega-mythic images of smoking being 'mellow', cool and attractive. Specifically, I refer to the *3rd Stone* t-shirt, and many of Ian Brown's otherwise entertaining cartoons. 75 percent of adults do not smoke and I suspect a similar number of megalithomaniacs do not smoke. 70% of smokers say they want to quit. 100 percent of our prehistoric ancestors did not smoke. In this respect, our ancestors may be seen as positive role-models for modern people, young and old. The earlier that smoking dies out as an image of 'cool', the better, because smokers are, literally, dying earlier than non-smokers. Therefore, I challenge Ian to create more positive images of 'mellow' and 'cool' without displaying smoking. Or why not just leave the smoking images out of the cartoons? It'll save you time and ink, and could save lives.

For further information on the huge negative impact of tobacco and smoking on health, wealth and the environment, have a look at the extensive website of 'Action on Smoking and Health' at www.ash.org.uk.

BP, Lincolnshire

Just Say Maybe

I cannot surely be the only readers to raise a quizzical eyebrow at BP's letter on smoking (Letters, *3rd Stone* 46)? The sentiments he expresses are not only more suited to an American publication, but are based on at least two misconceptions. Firstly, a t-shirt bearing the image of a personage of the Georgian era engaging in a pursuit (*id est*, pipe-smoking) which was undoubtedly popular during the era, can only be described as historically accurate. BP would no doubt have complained of anachronism had the t-shirt shown Dr Stukeley relaxing with a 'Game Boy' or a 3rd generation mobile phone!

And secondly, BP informs us that 75% of adults do not smoke, 70% of smokers want to abandon the habit, and '100 percent of our prehistoric ancestors did not smoke'. He should explore the work of A.G. Sherratt (for example in *Consuming Habits: Drugs in History and Anthropology*, Routledge, 1995), or he could look at page 113 of Ann Woodward's *British Barrows: A Matter of Life and Death* (Tempus, 2000). Shocking to tell, our prehistoric predecessors did not spend their time sipping sparkling mineral water, breathing fresh air and eating low-calorie salads. No, indeed not, until the puritans of the early Bronze Age weaned them off the habit by introducing alcohol ('Strange mixtures of mead and mixed fruit wines, laced with opiates' says Woodward), the folk were busy smoking, not tobacco but opium and cannabis. Perhaps BP would argue that all of our prehistoric ancestors are now dead, thus proving the ill-advised nature of their habits, but take note that they were careful to bury the pottery braziers and pouches of hemp seeds with their dead, in case such pleasures were needed in the afterlife...

Personally, the strongest thing I inhale is Friar's Balsam, but I wish BP would get his facts right, and more seriously, lay off the anti-smoking hysteria. Your illustrations are wonderful: keep them as smoky as possible!

PK, East Sussex

Graffiti (47)

I recently read your news article regarding graffiti painted on the stones of Avebury in an old issue of *3rd Stone* (no. 24, Autumn 1997). I live in southern California, and have been working on pictographs of the local Native Americans (the San Luis Rey Band of the Luiseno Indians) through my university. We are studying a large hilltop boulder which carries figures made in the course of girls' puberty ceremonies hundreds of years ago. The rock receives new graffiti every time the site is publicised. Presently there are large white and blue markings on the rock, put there less than a year ago. It's a sorry sight. However, members of the Luiseno and local rock art authorities maintain that such modern paint weathers off the rock within a few years, and the ancient pigments persist. I hope the stones of Avebury are as resilient.

ER, California

River of Stones (47)

Having lived within sight of the Preseli Hills for many years, and for the past three at the bottom of Carn Meini itself, I thought that readers concerned with the Stonehenge transportation issue may be interested to know about the 'river of stones'.

From up close, the full face of Carn Meini looks as if it has been blasted by a major earth upheaval, with stones scattered over a wide area. Perhaps it was the work of Merlin! I think it would have taken all of the 14,000 Irish navvies mentioned by Geoffrey of Monmouth to choose and dress, as well as transport the sixty-odd bluestones from here. And probably at that period the slopes would have been heavily wooded.

An easier and more accessible site of the bluestone's origins could be from Rhestr Gerrig, a 'line or way of stones', that curves southwards for roughly 2 km between Carn Meini and Carn Arthur. A periglacial feature formed prior to ten millennia ago under very cold conditions, now it is roughly five metres wide and strewn with boulders. The sound of the stream below is audible, and water is quite evident in places. The River of Stones appears to begin in a gully just below a ruined circular cairn (OS 14043262). The capstone is off and reveals the interior chamber in the centre of the ring of boulders that formed the cairn. A triangular passage stone is upright and gives quite a ringing tone when struck.

At the end of the stream, closest to Mynachlogddu village, there is a large quantity of dolerite stones of all shapes and sizes, many of them over 3 m in length. The first time I passed this stretch of the stream, the fact that there were so many bluestones readily available in one place immediately answered one conundrum I always had in relation to the massive disturbance of Carn Meini, and the difficulty of gathering dolerites from there. It could also answer the question posed by David Kaiser in *3rd Stone* 46 as to why the stones from here may have been particularly venerated and therefore seen as being worth moving to Stonehenge. Not only would it have appeared that the stones themselves would have been mysteriously moved from the hill face, but in winter they would have been continuously washed smooth by running water. A cosmic marriage of sky god and earth goddess. In fact, when I went there to check it out before writing this, a two-foot long adder was basking on a white quartzite boulder by the side of the stream!

JS, Pembrokeshire

Contributor Biographies

Dr Jenny Blain had her PhD from Dalhousie University, and taught there and elsewhere, most recently as a Senior Lecturer in Sociology at Sheffield Hallam University where she led the MRes in Social Sciences. Her research interests have included family structures; culture and gendered identities; heritage policy and 'sacred site' user practices; shamanism and paganisms; and constructions of history, archaeology and 'the past in the imagination of the present'. Her books include *Nine Worlds of Seid-Magic: Ecstasy and Neo-shamanism in North European Paganism* (Routledge 2002), the co-authored *Think Twice! Sociology looks at Current Issues* (Simon and Schuster/Prentice Hall 2005, 1998), co-edited *Researching Paganisms* (Altamira 2004) and with Robert J. Wallis, *Sacred Sites, Contested Rites/Rights* (Sussex Academic Press, 2007). Dr Blain is now happily retired, back home in Dundee where she is involved with local history and genealogy, being currently chairperson of a regional Family History society, with interest in how people relate pasts and presents and how landscape, heritage and folklore stories form part of their imaginings of 'who they are'.

Aubrey Burl (1926 – 2020) was a teacher and scholar of history and archaeology. His international reputation was based upon his work on neolithic stone circles in Britain and Europe. He also published more widely, on poets and their poetry including Catullus, Shakespeare and Villon, and on subjects as diverse as the Albigensian Crusade and pirates. He was elected a Fellow of the Society of Antiquaries of London in 1981 and an Honorary Fellow of the Society of Antiquaries of Scotland in 2000. In 1974 he received a letter from Professor G. Evelyn Hutchinson, advisor to Yale University Press. As Aubrey had written papers for various American journals, Professor Hutchinson wondered whether Aubrey might like to write a book about stone circles for Yale. *The Stone Circles of the British Isles* was published in 1976. As a result of its success, Yale re-issued it seven times. The University of Leicester awarded Aubrey a DLitt and the University of Sheffield awarded him an Honorary PhD. Perhaps the honour which most surprised and touched him was the writing of a Festschrift: *Prehistoric Ritual and Religion* (Sutton Publishing, 1998) by archaeological colleagues. The book was instigated and edited by his friends and colleagues, Dr Alex Gibson, formerly of the University of Bradford, and the late Professor Derek Simpson, Queen's University, Belfast. Aubrey died in 2020 at the age of 93. He never lost his courtesy, his sense of humour, or his love of words.

Paul Devereux is the co-founding managing editor of the academic Routledge publication, *Time & Mind – The Journal of Archaeology, Consciousness and Culture* (www.tandfonline.com/rtam). Earlier, in the 1990s, he was a Senior Research Scholar with the International Consciousness Research Laboratories (ICRL) group (www.icrl.org), then at Princeton University, and he was the former founder/director of the Dragon Project Trust, and also a Research Affiliate with the Royal College of Art. His main research interests include archaeoacoustics (sound at archaeological sites), the ancient mind (including shamanism), ancient sites and landscapes, geophysical anomalies. He has written academic papers, many articles in major and minor journals, and is a prolific book author: https://www.amazon.com/PaulDevereux/e/B001HD1M42. Devereux has lectured in the UK, North America, Russia, Germany, Portugal, Holland, Scandinavia, and elsewhere.

Brian Edwards is a Visiting Research Fellow at the Regional History Centre, UWE Bristol. His research surrounds past and present public engagement with heritage.

Pete Glastonbury is an independent researcher with particular interests in megaliths, prehistoric Wessex, archaeoastronomy and astrophotography.

Jeremy Harte roams the green lanes of England looking for legendary beings and the people whose lives have been changed by them. Old yew trees, changelings, patches of dragon skin and devils' footprints obscure his view of the real world. A Council member of the Folklore Society, he is also curator of the Surrey Gypsy Archive and knows more about Dorset watermills than is strictly necessary in a pre-apocalyptic world. His book Explore Fairy Traditions won the Briggs award of the FLS for 2005, and other publications include The Green Man,

Fairy Encounters in Medieval England and Cloven Country: Legends of the Devil. He is curator of Bourne Hall Museum in Surrey, for which he puts things in cases and then, later on, takes them out again. He lives with a small population of ladybirds in a converted butler's lodge, where his children have stopped worrying about him.

Leslie Ellen Jones received a doctorate in Folklore and Mythology Studies at UCLA, concentrating in comparative and Celtic, especially Welsh, mythology, and published 5 books and several dozen articles on these subjects. Somehow this led her to spend the last 20 years as the executive editor of the journal *African Arts*. She is currently working on her own contribution to *Bad Anthropology*, a novel rife with druids, airships, bellydancers, and the Thirteen Treasures of the Isle of Britain.

Alastair McBeath was for over two decades the Vice-President of the International Meteor Organization during the 1990s and 2000s, and ran the Meteor Observing Section for the UK's Society for Popular Astronomy for nearly thirty years from 1983. He has also written extensively on aspects of visual astronomy, mythology, folklore and ancient history since the early 1980s. Although largely retired now, he still maintains active interests in all these spheres.

John Michell (1933 – 2009) was one of the founders of the Earth Mysteries movement. He authored over 40 books including *The Flying Saucer Vision: the Holy Grail Restored* (1967), *The View Over Atlantis* (1969), *City of Revelation* (1972), *The Old Stones of Land's End* (1974), *A Little History of Astro-Archaeology: Stages in the Transformation of a Heresy* (1977), *Megalithomania: Artists, Antiquarians & Archaeologists at the Old Stone Monuments* (1982) and *Who Wrote Shakespeare?* (1996). He was a founder and editor of *The Cereologist* magazine, and was instrumental in the 1960s rediscovery of Alfred Watkins and leys.

Neil Mortimer was the editor of *3rd Stone* from 1996 to 2003. His previous jobs have included a lithographic printer, a publishing assistant, a local council traffic information collector, a cleaner of redundant industrial cooling towers and the archaeology columnist for *Fortean Times* magazine. He is the only person to have had two books published about the 18th century antiquarian William Stukeley, one of which was co-authored with his archaeological hero Aubrey Burl. Neil is, with Paul Devereux, a founding editor of the peer-reviewed journal *Time and Mind: the Journal of Archaeology, Consciousness and Culture*. Nowadays he runs a microscopic record label, Heavy Rural, where he is the only permanent member of the psych rock band Urthona and one half of the cosmic synth duo Luminous Foundation. He is still bothering stones.

Dr George Nash is an Associate Professor at the Geosciences Centre, University of Coimbra, and an Honorary Research Fellow within the Department of Archaeology, Classics, and Egyptology, University of Liverpool. A leading expert in prehistoric rock art, Dr Nash currently oversees several fieldwork projects in Jordan and South Wales. In addition, he is an active member of the First Art Team, based in Portugal and Spain, which focuses on identifying early prehistoric rock art in some of the world's most elusive cave systems, including Rising Star Cave in South Africa and, more recently, Altamira in northern Spain. Regarding Neolithic research, Dr Nash has led excavations at Arthur's Stone in Herefordshire and La Hougue Bie in Jersey.

Paul Newman (1945 – 2013) was the editor of *Abraxas* magazine: 'Colin Wilson, Literature, Philosophy, Ideas, Poetry & Fiction', which incorporated the Colin Wilson Newsletter. He was the author of more than ten fiction and non-fiction books, including the instant classic *Lost Gods of Albion: The Chalk Hill-Figures of Britain* (1999).

Hilary Schrafft-Mortimer is a former journalist and co-editor of *3rd Stone* magazine. For the last 18 years she has worked in education, at a school for pupils with learning disabilities.

Alby Stone was born and grew up in Southend-on-Sea in Essex, but has lived and worked in London for many years. He is the author of several books dealing with myth, shamanism, Arthurian legend and traditional cosmology, and has published various novels and short stories.

Adam Stout specialises in the straight history of Wyrd. He's long been interested in alternative ideas of Englishness, and in particular Glastonbury. He is fascinated by the way in which this small west country town came to be seen as the place where England kept its soul, and has spent years trying to tease out the historical complexities. *Glastonbury Holy Thorn: Story of a Legend*, published in 2020, charts the history of this remarkable shrub, whose legend is at the heart of the Glastonbury mythos. *When the King's Road went to Glastonbury and the Skies were Full of Saucers*, was published in 2025, looks at the impact that Glastonbury and the Sixties had on each other.

Cheryl Straffon is one of the 'boom baby' generation, and a graduate of London and Cambridge universities. She returned to her native Cornwall in 1986, where she worked as Library Manager of her local community library. She was co-founder of the Cornish Earth Mysteries Group, and subsequently chair of CASPN

(Cornish Ancient Sites Protection Network) for 15 years. She has produced and edited the magazine *Meyn Mamvro* since 1986, and is also author of a number of books, including *Pagan Cornwall: Land of the Goddess; The Earth Mysteries Guide to Ancient Sites in West Penwith; The Earth Goddess: Celtic and Pagan Legacy of the Landscape; Megalithic Mysteries of Cornwall; Daughters of the Earth;* and *Between the Realms: Cornish Myth and Magic*. She lives in West Cornwall (and Crete) with her partner and their cat.

Danny Sullivan took over editorship of *The Ley Hunter* in the 1990s, where he continued to promote the less sensational aspects of 'Earth Mysteries' generally, and ley hunting, in particular. The expansion of theoretical archaeology in the 1990s began to overshadow the once derided notions of alternative archaeology and this was a major factor in Sullivan's decision to close down *The Ley Hunter* after twenty-odd years and to attempt to reignite popular interest in Watkinsian ley hunting and the love of the British landscape. His *Ley Lines* was published in the late 1990s followed rapidly by *Leys* and both are still in print today. He co-founded The Society of Ley Hunters with Lionel Stanbrook in the mid-1990s and invited John Michell to be its honorary president. The Society still exists today, though Sullivan has moved on, preferring to keep a low profile on the subject these days and to concern himself more with the noble art of architecture.

Dr Robert J. Wallis is a Senior Lecturer and Staff Tutor in the Department of Art History at the Open University. He is interested in the archaeology and anthropology of art and religion, human-raptor sociality and the re-presentation of the past in the present. His books include *Shamans/neo-Shamans* (Routledge, 2003), *Sacred Sites, Contested Rites/Rights* (with Jenny Blain, Sussex Academic Press, 2007), *Historical Dictionary of Shamanism* (with Graham Harvey, Rowman and Littlefield, 2016) and most recently *The Art and Archaeology of Human Engagements with Birds of Prey* (Bloomsbury, 2023). His co-authored book (with Dominic Alessio) on racist and anti-racist Heathenry, *Faith, Folk and the Far Right*, is in press with Manchester University Press. His Heathen manual, *Galdrbok*, written with Nathan Johnson, was published in paperback in 2022. He is currently working on a monograph on *The Art and Archaeology of Falconry*. He is a Fellow of the Society of Antiquaries, a Fellow of the Royal Anthropological Institute and a Senior Fellow of the Higher Education Academy.

Jennifer Westwood (1940 – 2008) Born in 1940 in Norton Subcourse on the edge of the Norfolk marshes, Jennifer's 'rootedness' in her village nurtured her sense of place and tradition. Despite time away at university in Oxford and Cambridge, research in Scandinavia and Iceland, living in America, Iran and

London, and fieldwork in the Camargue, Norton Subcourse remained her world. That she was able later to live in the 300-year-old house in which she had been born, and reside in the village of her grandparents, gave Jen more than an abstract understanding of continuity and change. The little girl who cycled home on winter evenings pedalling fast and singing hymns to ward off 'Shuck', the black ghost dog of East Anglia, eventually became the author of 20 bestsellers such as *Albion: A Guide to Legendary Britain* (1985) and twenty years later *The Lore of the Land* (with Jacqueline Simpson, 2005). Jen's aim was to make folklore accessible to the public, without compromising accuracy. The tenacity with which she would track references to their earliest source revealed the way the tales we tell today were formed – and reformed.

Dr Juliette Wood is an American folklore historian who has written extensively on mythology, magic, medieval and Celtic folklore, and medievalist revivals. She is a member of The Folklore Society and is a past president of that organisation, who has been a frequent presenter for television and radio. She has published on a wide range of subjects and is the author of several books, *Eternal Chalice: The Enduring Legend of the Holy Grail* (London: Bloomsbury, 2008) and *Fantastic Creatures in Mythology and Folklore* (London: Bloomsbury, 2018) and is currently a Tutor at Cardiff University.

Andy Worthington is the author of three books, *Stonehenge: Celebration and Subversion, The Battle of the Beanfield* and *The Guantanamo Files*. Since 2007, he has secured a reputation as the world's foremost independent expert on Guantanamo via his website www.andyworthington.co.uk and since 2012 has run the Close Guantanamo campaign and website: www.closeguantanamo.org. He has worked with the United Nations and Wikileaks, and is also the lead singer and main songwriter of The Four Fathers, playing contemporary protest music: thefourfathers.bandcamp.com.

Acknowledgements

Thank you to all the former ***3rd Stone*** contributors – writers and artists – who generously agreed to their work being republished in this anthology. I'd like to offer special thanks to Judith Burl for permission to republish Aubrey Burl's articles, and to Brian Chandler for Jennifer Westwood's. Thanks also to Brian Edwards, Pete Glastonbury, Jeremy Harte and Danny Sullivan, all of whom helped out in various ways, and John Billingsley, Laura Cannell and Mark McIntyre, who helped with contact details for contributors I was trying to get in touch with.

Finally, thank you to all the people who made the original ***3rd Stone*** happen, including of course the mag's lovely subscribers – some of whom I hope will enjoy this trip down Earth Mysteries memory lane as much as I did putting it together.

Index

Strange Attractor Press 2026